LOW TECH

LOW TECH

FAST FURNITURE FOR NEXT TO NOTHING

BY RICK BALL
AND PAUL COX

Edited, with an introduction, by Mary Smith

The Dial Press
Doubleday & Company, Inc.
Garden City, New York
1984

The authors would like to thank Mike Hill for his important contribution in the early stages of this book.

Text design: Levavi & Levavi

Library of Congress Cataloging in Publication Data
Ball, Richard, 1919–
  Low tech.
  1. House furnishings. 2. Furniture. 3. Waste
products. 4. Salvage (Waste, etc.) I. Cox, Paul,
1957–   . II. Smith, Mary, 1941–   . III. Title.
TX315.B27 1983 645   83-2105
ISBN 0-385-27905-1

CONTENTS

LOW TECH

INTRODUCTION

If it serves a purpose, anything goes ...and so low tech is born. A major tenet of decorating in the last twenty years is that there are no longer objects inappropriate for home use. Elegant materials and finishes are nice but not required. It has become amusing to combine materials and objects from the street and commerce with our own possessions. A garden table made from a discarded telephone company wire spool has become a classic of this genre.

Low Tech is a play upon high tech, the style of the seventies and eighties that brought commercial and industrial equipment into the home and office. *Low Tech* advocates thinking creatively, recycling objects that have outlived their original use. Low tech is an attitude; high tech is a style. *Low Tech* makes us aware, often with style and ingenuity, of the possibilities of objects that have served a purpose and have been cast off, usually with life left in them. To see the potential of the cast-off object and found object takes cleverness, resourcefulness, and imagination. To some it is a game to see a different and useful purpose for a cast-off. Whether inspired by thriftiness, a love of improvisation, or a need for temporary furnishings, *Low Tech* enables you to make your own design choices without the dictates of tradition.

We have recognized, in the last twenty-five years, how limited the earth's resources are, and how prolific waste is in our culture. With this awareness has come a more careful attitude toward materials. A vocabulary has evolved that describes our new attitude. *Found object, recycling, do-it-yourself* are recent additions to the English language. *Salvage* and *scavenge, junk* and *second-hand* no longer have negative connotations. They are the words of the shrewd and resourceful.

The town dump has always been a treasure trove; now people also scavenge at construction and demolition sites, on city streets and behind stores of every description. Cardboard and wood packaging material, pvc pipe, rubber tires, old wood are often there for the taking, or at least for the asking.

As we were recognizing the possibility of a second life for old doors, crates, and railroad ties, a new aesthetic was creeping into our lives. The form-follows-function notion made headway. We got used to seeing buildings and furniture reduced to simple shapes; our eyes became accustomed to steel, rubber, cement, the materials of construction. It no longer seems absurd to juxtapose domestic and commercial materials.

In New York a design team called SITE (Sculpture In The Environment) designed a clothing showroom on Seventh Avenue for Williwear that embodies *Low Tech* principles. It incorporates urban elements that could have come off the street. Clothes hang on window gates and grills adorn the walls, floors are cement, a police barricade is a visual divider, a wire mesh street-style trash barrel is on hand, and desks are slick glass tops supported by gray concrete blocks. Gray paint unifies everything.

Grills, gates, and such become abstract elements when they are put in a new setting. This is an important point about found objects and recycled materials—cleaned up and placed in a new setting, they take on a new life.

There is a highly practical side to this reuse of materials. Found objects and recycled components are usually free; if they are secondhand, they are cheap. People who don't want to commit a large part of their resources to possessions are given a chance to make choices without making a financial investment. They can also enjoy the satisfaction of having created something. And when they move, the table made of a door can be left behind—possibly for another recycler to use.

Using objects in new ways—turning a garbage can upside down to make a table base, for instance —becomes a game, the object of the game being to create furniture with as little effort and money as possible.

Low Tech starts us in the game by showing where to find and how to use discarded materials. Specific projects are described and illustrated, with instructions on how to achieve the best results. Pitfalls are pointed out: warping doors, sharp metal edges, bug infestations, the dangers of electricity. There are suggestions for using space where you thought space didn't exist: the area under stairs can be fitted with shelves; the floor of a small bathroom can be built up with a lift-off panel for a bathtub underneath.

Imaginative awareness of the home, street, neighborhood, and city will turn you into an explorer and treasure hunter. Seeing new uses for objects will make you a creator and inventor.

Mary Smith
New York City

INTRODUCING LOW TECH

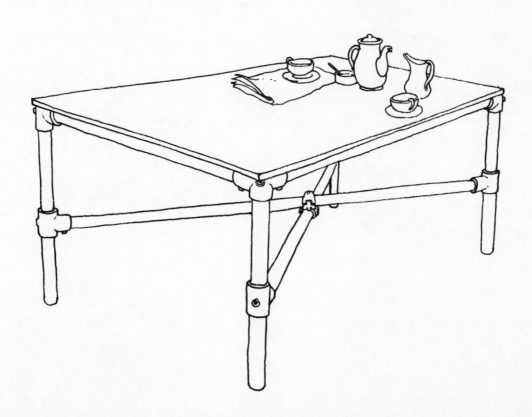

This book is about the art of improvisation applied to making simple and functional furniture. It shows how ingenuity can turn free or cheap materials into original and useful beds, chairs, tables, and storage systems. Fast furnishing is a way of exploiting industry's ready-made products as a short cut to do-it-yourself construction.

Safe short cuts are at the heart of fast furnishing. We assume that the low-tech furnisher is not an accomplished craftsman. Time-consuming craftsmanship, however admirable, is beyond the scope of low tech. The projects systematically avoid difficult woodworking joints. Experience suggests that precision joinery, however simple in theory, is in practice beyond the reach and patience of the average person in need of a piece of furniture. Low tech demands imagination rather than skill from the maker. The purist might shudder at our joints, but the joints will stand firm.

"Dirty" carpentry saves construction time and is therefore to be applauded. Joining two pieces of lumber by hammering in a row of nails is a lot simpler than linking them with interlocking dovetail joints. The nailed joint may lack elegance but it will hold, at least for a while. On occasion fast furniture will be undeniably temporary, but this is a very real virtue in many people's view. As long as the construction cost is low, the piece does not need to be durable. Cardboard furniture is a case in point. Sturdy furniture can be made from free cardboard found in the street. It would be unrealistic to expect cardboard desks and chairs to be passed down the generations as family heirlooms, but they are eminently suitable for a growing child whose demands are likely to change.

Unwanted objects have often been used to make things for children. Toys are traditionally made from discarded household articles. An empty spool, a pencil, and a rubber band, for instance, will trundle around the floor as a miniature tank (Fig. 1). Almost anything can be turned into a drum by a child with energy and a stick.

More sophisticated instruments can also be improvised. In the 1920s the jug was the poor man's bass fiddle, at the heart of the jug bands of

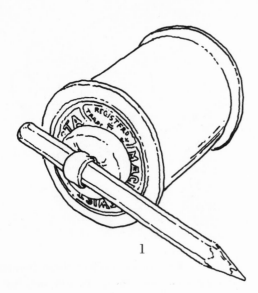

1

2

the period. One step up the musical ladder from the jug came the washtub bass (Fig. 2), made from a metal washtub and a broom handle. A washboard provided a band's rhythm section. A musical saw and a kazoo could be introduced for variety.

Such awareness of the unexpected qualities and possibilities of the materials lying around you can take you a long way—in fact it took one of the *Low Tech* authors three hundred miles across Eastern Europe, when a Bulgarian peasant introduced him to the happy art of low technology. The occasion was a breakdown on the road, when the bottom dropped out of the sophisticated truck's oil reservoir and rolled into an impenetrable pine forest. As there was no chance of a spare before Istanbul the future looked grim. Then along came the Bulgarian. Unalarmed he selected a short piece of pine, whittled it quickly to shape, pushed it firmly up the reservoir and informed the awestruck driver he could now pour in fresh oil and drive on. The repair held firm across Bulgaria and into Turkey.

The fast furnisher has a lot to learn from the third world's unprejudiced evaluation of materials. Objects discarded as rubbish without value in the western world are often put to new use in the third

world, where resources are too scarce to waste. Even the universal Coca-Cola can is beaten flat and incorporated in a long- wearing all-metal suitcase.

When a spare part fails to arrive from the European supplier, a Pakistani mechanic will cheerfully fashion a serviceable exhaust system from empty cans. When a car's days on the road are truly over, parts can still be salvaged and put to further use. In Tanzania carpenters fashion steel shafts and blades for their tools from old car springs. In Morocco shoemakers convert blown-out tires into high-mileage sandals. Windows, seats, lights, and hood are all worth saving. Western furnishers can locate old car parts in the wrecking yard.

The art of improvisation was last seen on a significant scale in the West during the war years of the

1940s. One stubborn and heroic Berliner emerged from the rubble and began reconstructing his garden fence in a most elaborate way, inch by inch, day by day. He used short lengths of wire which he found on his wanderings around the bombed-out city. Each one was added to the fence, which grew with the disjointed look of the famous webs of the 1960s spun by a spider dosed with LSD. The Berlin fence stood, and the garden was soon sprouting plants in the rubble.

The squatter housing now surrounding some of the world's mushrooming major cities displays a stunningly inventive and often very personal attitude to materials. No one would want to romanticize the life lived within these houses, yet the structures themselves remain an inspiration to the western fast furnisher. The buildings are bizarre assemblies incorporating anything from cardboard to cans.

Bottles are commonly used in wall construction all over the world. Large numbers are needed, but there is little risk of turning into an alcoholic in the attempt to drink your way through a wall full of wine bottles. A British bottle recovery company was collecting six million wine bottles a year from hotels and restaurants in central London before the market collapsed in the late 1970s. Restaurants are normally overjoyed to find a taker for their empty nonreturnable bottles, as bottles present a sizable disposal problem. If you need bottles and are too

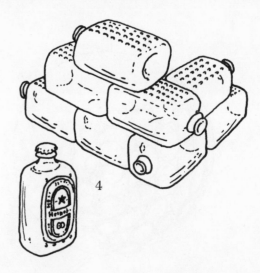

4

3

shy to ask the restaurateur, collect them from outside the restaurant when they are put out for the sanitation men.

In the 1960s the Dutch brewer of Heineken made their boldest attempt to get to the parts other beers can't reach. They designed a beer bottle which could be used as a building brick. It was brewery boss Alfred Heineken's idea. He was horrified at the housing conditions of the poor in Caribbean shanty towns and equally horrified at the vast number of empty Heineken bottles littering the world. He employed Dutch architect John Habraken to design a bottle-brick which would be known as the WOBO, or World Bottle. Plans for a simple house made of interlocking empties were to be given on a label stuck to each bottle. Having rejected such unfortunate if practical shapes as the prototype in Figure 3, a design was finalized (Fig. 4). Fifty thousand green WOBOs were manufactured with gripping pimples on the side and a dent in the base. Mr. Heineken built a WOBO summer house at his villa near Amsterdam, but the people of the Caribbean were unenthusiastic about the idea of living in glass houses. The WOBO project was abandoned.

Western office life produces its own particular supply of useful drink containers, in the form of the fast-food cup. In Indian railroad stations, tea is

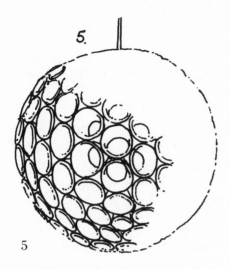

5

sold in elegant earthenware throwaway cups; the subcontinent's railroad tracks are littered with the smashed empties. The energy-intensive western equivalent is the insulated Styrofoam cup. An average office quickly generates the 250 or so cups needed to make the spherical lampshade in Figure 5, which has been a student favorite for years. To make it, start with one cup, stick another flat against it using latex adhesive, and keep adding cups until the sphere is complete. Clip the cups together while the adhesive dries.

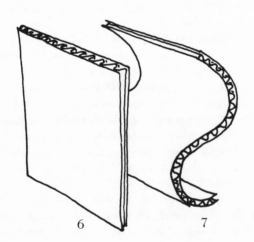

6   7

Packaging is a prime source of materials for fast furnishing. Shops are constantly in danger of disappearing under a mountain of tough packaging materials for which they have no use once the goods are unwrapped and which the manufacturer does not want back. You can help them solve their disposal problem.

Discarded packaging is the main source of cardboard for furniture construction. Corrugated cardboard boxes can be converted into strong furniture if used correctly. The basic principle for a load-bearing structure made of cardboard is to place the cardboard so that the corrugations run vertically as in Figure 6; if they are laid as in Figure 7 the structure could soon collapse.

Supermarkets are throwing away cardboard boxes all day long. Large cardboard cartons also litter city shopping streets on an average evening. Extra large sizes can be found in areas where fabric is unpacked and made up into clothing. Clothing manufacturers throw out useful bale-long boxes. Scraps of fabric often join the boxes in the street. These can be used to stuff cushions, and very patient people can defy the fast-furnishing ethic and laboriously turn them into patchwork.

Look out for extra-strong boxes which have carried heavy appliances—these often have a double, even triple, layer of corrugations. Don't forget to look inside the boxes. The Styrofoam blocks and chips used as inner packaging can be reused in low-tech seating systems.

Cable reels, fire extinguishers, cupboards, display fittings, wicker baskets, plastic crates, and wooden boxes all appear regularly in the street. The legality of walking away with this stuff should be considered. In Britain the law allows you to take away anything you find in a dumpster if you sincerely and reasonably believe that the person who put it there would not object. The best way to find out is to ask. In practice this means that it is risky to take objects with a high scrap value, as they are probably being gathered in the dumpster to be sold to a scrap dealer. Removing objects from trash bins is a more unsavory but thoroughly legal occupation.

Laws vary from country to country. Check out the local law before risking a humiliating and costly court appearance.

Dutch and German scavengers have a fine time. Every few weeks citizens are encouraged to put their unwanted furniture in the street. Throughout the night people trundle around the town collecting any pieces they fancy. In the morning the sanitation department collects the truly unwanted remains.

The demolition site is another magnet for the fast furnisher in search of materials. The normal choice of materials is vast, from the site itself or from a demolition yard. Most yards have scores of doors which are cheap and serviceable, and these are often the most economical way of creating a strong flat surface. Check any door for warping before you buy it: to do this simply lay it on edge and look along the line.

Demolitions produce huge numbers of bricks. Demand for these in rehabilitation work has increased, but they can still be bought more cheaply than new bricks. Choose nineteenth-century bricks if possible. This is not for purely aesthetic reasons: modern mortars are much tougher to remove from the brick without smashing it.

Buying certain items almost certainly involves going to the site before demolition work begins, to save them from the sledgehammer. Tell the foreman what you want, check out its condition, and ask him to save it for you. Find out when the thing is likely to be taken out of the building. Keep checking every few days, as schedules are notoriously unreliable and useful things can vanish fast from contruction sites. This is true of banisters, bathtubs, sinks, and other fittings. All are routinely ruined during demolitions, as smashing them is the fastest way of tearing them out.

Look in the dumpster outside the demolition site or where renovation work is being carried out. Useful handles are often left on doors and are well worth saving. If you don't need them, sell them to an antique dealer.

Lumber is one of the best secondhand buys for the fast furnisher. Buying large quantities of new lumber is a luxury few fast furnishers can afford. Locating inexpensive and reliable alternative sources is therefore a key money saver.

Secondhand lumber is often of higher quality than the new equivalent. Lumber is usually well seasoned before use and both shrinkage and warping are therefore comparatively uncommon.

Most building demolition jobs generate large numbers of floorboards and joists. These will be sold either directly from the site or from the yards listed in the *Yellow Pages* under "Demolition Contractors." The price will regularly undercut the price of new lumber by at least 50 percent. It is wise always to check the latest price of new lumber—and other items in the construction trade—before you buy secondhand. Otherwise you are inviting high prices.

Check every individual piece of secondhand lumber before you buy it, and reject any length showing signs of woodworm attack. The flight holes are only the final exit point after the grub has been actively eating away the inside of the plank for two or three years. Dry rot is an even stronger reason to reject lumber. The signs of this are dry and crumbling wood, cracking in a characteristically cubic pattern. It also has an unmistakable musty smell.

Good-quality secondhand planks and joists can be used for many of the projects in *Low Tech*. Rough and dirty boards are quickly cleaned up with a rented belt sander. A sanding disk fitted on an electric drill leaves ugly score marks across the wood grain which are extremely hard to remove. Used floorboards generally have holes roughly every 16 inches (400 mm) where the nails were driven through. These holes can be plugged with putty, plastic wood, papier-mâché, or a mixture of glue and sawdust from the sanding operation, which will be the right color. Rusty nails stain large

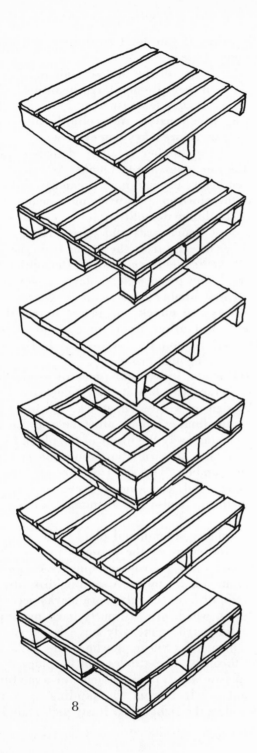

8

brown marks on the wood. This damage is best hidden under a coat of paint.

Large joists can be sawed lengthwise to create two planks of more manageable dimensions. This is an exhausting operation with only a handsaw. A lumberyard will normally be willing to push the joists through their heavy-duty saw at a low cost.

Keep an eye on dumpsters for useful wood. Builders are constantly throwing handsome lengths of valuable hardwood away as they tear a building apart at the start of a modernization program.

Scaffolding is commonly erected around buildings which are about to be gutted before modernization. Scaffolding is a very versatile component for fast furniture projects. To buy it new is expensive and well beyond the budget of the normal low technologist. However, bankruptcies are notoriously common in the construction industry, and scaffold will be auctioned off with the rest of a bankrupt builder's empire.

Scaffolding is made of rough metal, and polishing improves its looks enormously. Unfortunately, this too is an expensive operation, as it takes a long time and the charge for polishing will be based on the time it takes. Polishing every foot of a stainless steel tube will be expensive. Knuckle joints on scaffolding are unsuitable for polishing or plating. Chromium plating is of course the most dazzling treatment for scaffold. The smoother the piece you begin with, the cheaper it will be to have it plated. If the scaffolding is galvanized, this will have to be stripped off before plating can begin. There are many patent connecting systems used with scaffold. Some are comparatively unobtrusive and therefore better suited for use indoors.

You can benefit from the misfortunes of others in your hunt for furnishing materials. When an unprofitable shop closes, the old fixtures are sold off cheaply. Shop display systems make handy home storage systems. They often offer elegant solutions to storage problems. The frameworks are usually assembled quickly and easily and are equally easy to adapt to a new situation. It is worth looking closely at shopwindow displays to see the

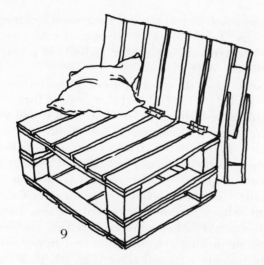

9

materials the designer used and the way the parts are fitted together. Trade magazines for display designers may contain clues to construction techniques which can be exploited for fast-furnishing projects.

Industrial equipment is available by mail order, and the intriguing illustrated catalogues and price lists are almost compulsory reading for the low-tech furnisher at the planning stage. Coldly functional laboratory equipment, such as glass and clamps, appeals to some buyers, while others prefer a more general industrial look. Many esoteric needs can be satisfied by mail order—as well as the standard ranges of filing cabinets, desks, and coffee makers without which no enterprise is complete; there are tarpaulins, partitioning screens, safety lights, storage systems, and hoisting gear.

Industrial equipment is usually far from cheap, as admirers of the high-tech style quickly found. Often this is because the equipment is designed to withstand rough treatment around the factory in the hands of people who do not love it. It is unlikely that your home will be as violently active as a factory or warehouse floor. You are therefore paying for a robustness you do not need. However desirable and potentially useful the equipment, acquiring it often makes sense only if you can find it free or buy it secondhand.

Low-tech furnishers are not so much hostile to high style as unable to afford it. Low tech is far more pragmatic than high tech. Unlike high tech, it is not an integrated style with high design principles. High tech's judgments are often strict. If an item is without the chilly appeal of stainless steel's clean lines it may be rejected on aesthetic grounds. The admirer of high tech will pay high prices in the pursuit of style. The fast furnisher cannot afford such attitudes. If an item is expensive, it is rejected. If it is free or cheap, it is examined. The exploitation of industry is an economic necessity, not a stylistic whim. Low tech is the short cut to do-it-yourself, using manufactured cast-offs to save time.

Wooden pallets are a low-grade basic element from the industrial handling catalogue. They are a splendid and versatile material for low-tech furnishing. Available in several patterns (Fig. 8), they are made to standard sizes. Wooden pallets can be used as they are (see p. 53) or quickly converted into pleasing furniture such as the seat for two shown in Figure 9. This construction simply involved sawing the pallets in half, with hinges fixed at the joints to allow for maximum versatility.

Many plastic containers match standard pallet sizes so that they can be stacked to form economical loads for transportation of the pallets. Plastic crates are expensive to buy but easy to find on dumps and in dumpsters, needing nothing more difficult than a wash. Many are stackable when loaded, nestable when empty, simply by turning them through 90° or 180°. A selection of designs is shown in Figure 10.

A supply of free crates is of little value unless you have suitable transport to take them home. Many of the materials used in low-tech furnishing are both cumbersome and heavy. Concrete drainage sections, for example, cannot be carried under the average human's arm, and a vehicle is crucial when you have to carry a load of long planks across town. Even a trio of packing crates needs careful planning, as it can be remarkably difficult to cram even one through a car door. A measuring tape is a use-

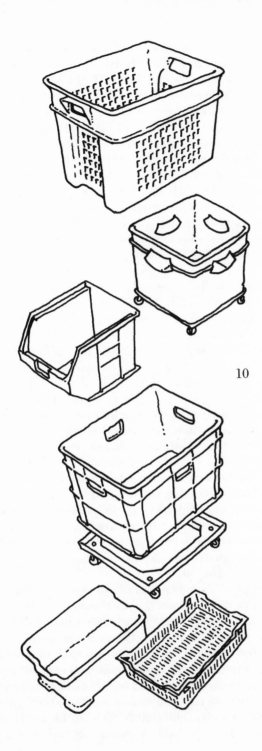

10

ful companion as you wander the streets looking for materials. Take the cost of transport into account when you are working out the viability of salvaging a particular object.

In some cases the dimensions of the materials you find will dictate the finished size of your furniture; you will have little more freedom than if you were buying from a furniture store. However, such schemes often have the virtue of extreme simplicity. On occasion the materials will be used without any adaptation whatever. The wooden fruit crate, for example, has been used for generations as an instant cabinet for book or record storage. Turned upside down it makes a low table. Other classics of instant furnishing are the cable reel tipped on its end to become a rugged table (Fig. 34, p. 37) and the hollow-core door spanning a pair of filing cabinets to make a desk (Fig. 150, p. 91). The plastic crate is also turned on its side to serve as shoe storage (Fig. 140, p. 87).

Most fast-furnishing projects allow you to design your furniture any size you choose. You can have low dining tables if you like them, high work surfaces if you are tall. Before you build, think about the way the piece will be used—it must suit your needs rather than follow the traditional sizes of furniture. For example, when designing bookshelves be guided by the size of your own books rather than the standard recommended shelf sizes. In some cases standard sizes are relevant. For example, the dimensions of standard mattresses should be taken into account in bed design. Working out the design on paper is wise. Decide how the pieces will all fit together before you cut them to size.

The main part of the book is organized in seven sections, each one devoted to a particular type of furniture. Within each section detailed step-by-step instructions describe how to construct a series of varied pieces of furniture. In order to make the construction plans easy to follow, all the drawings and instructions describing a particular piece of furniture are on the same page. In this way the whole project can be viewed at once. The text describes how to find the raw materials and how to use them.

We have simplified construction methods in the interest of ease and speed. Most of the projects should present no insuperable problems even to the novice. Making a piece of furniture usually involves attaching one element to another, and this may involve unfamiliar though simple tools, terminology, techniques, and equipment. These are explained either where they occur or in the final section of the book (pp. 195–219). In this section basic woodworking techniques are described and illustrated alongside some of the effective patent fixing devices available to the amateur. These are often found in unlikely spots, such as a mail-order catalogue for marine equipment.

Our intention is to promote the inventive use of materials. However, the art of improvisation should on no account be extended to electrical installations. We cannot overemphasize the dangers in tampering with electrical wiring if you are not utterly confident in your ability. The complexity of wiring systems in old houses, particularly when they are multioccupied, often defies understanding. Only the expert can guarantee that switching the main supply off has in fact made any particular socket safe.

Certain materials used in both amateur and professional furniture construction present a fire risk. The dangerous consequences of fires in foam furniture are well known. Once ignited, such low-density cellular plastics burn rapidly, releasing thick clouds of debilitating black smoke. A good cover reduces the danger. Slow-burning fabrics such as heavy wool are better in this respect than light cotton or polyester. A fire-retardant interliner can also be fitted to form a barrier around the foam. The foam itself is difficult to treat against fire, as the chemicals tend to make the foam turn hard. This presents no problem with the white Styrofoam slabs and pellets used in packaging. Many of these are treated by the manufacturer of the packaging material before sale.

The harsh fact remains that there is really no such thing as a fireproof cover or treatment. A smoke detector (Fig. 11) fixed to the ceiling in the right position provides an early warning system. However, it is obviously far simpler and more effective not to allow fires to start in the first place.

Old materials present their own peculiar hazards. Ferreting around dumpsters and dumps without wearing a pair of strong leather gloves is inviting trouble. There's always a risk of broken glass and sharp metal edges in such places. Poisons are another menace. It is often impossible to know what has been in bottles, cans, and drums. Oil drums may be used to transport dangerous chemicals; if there is any doubt, leave them alone.

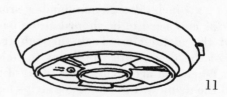

11

Bugs are not a real menace, with a couple of notable exceptions. We would not advise even the most dedicated fast furnisher to salvage mattresses and upholstered furniture from the street for use at home. There's likely to be something in there waiting to bite you.

Objects salvaged from city streets or construction sites are often battered and grubby. Clean them thoroughly before you take them into your home. A coat of paint is often all you need to rejuvenate scratched and tatty objects. Even with fast furniture it is worth wiping grease off surfaces before you try to paint over them. If you want the paint job to last, use the right primer for the particular material.

If paint will not cover the dents and ravages of time, the damaged article can be clad in an eye-pleasing cover. An ugly and creased cardboard drum, for example, can still be used to make a stylish table (Fig. 12). Cut the drum off at a suitable

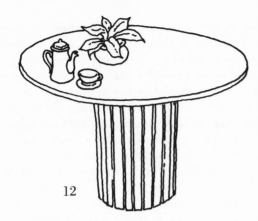

12

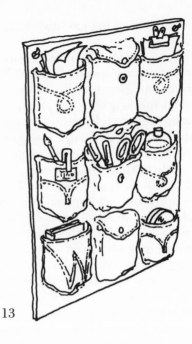

13

table height, say 28 inches (710 mm), and glue strips of 2 x 1 inch (50 x 25 mm) lumber around it. The strips may need to be shaped at the base to fit around the metal rim. Tack through from the inside of the drum into the strips to hold them firmly. When you are about three fifths of the way around the drum fit the remaining strips loosely to see if you need to plane anything off them all for an even fit. Finally add the top as in the projects described on pp. 33–34.

It is profitable to cultivate an awareness of one's own rejects. Some may be suitable cases for conversion in a low-tech plan. A selection of back pockets from old pairs of jeans can be supplemented by a few jacket breast pockets—crested for interest—and tacked onto a plywood base to form a small-scale wall-mounted storage unit (Fig. 13).

The urge to salvage need not be obsessive. It would be foolish to live amid a clutter of spare parts waiting to be turned into fast furniture. Yet it remains hard to pass by useful junk. Fast furnishers are sometimes paradoxically slow movers. Experience shows that it is easy to leave articles lying around for a year unless great self-discipline is exercised or your need for furniture is very urgent. A space to store materials is therefore a huge asset to the fast furnisher.

Our principal aim in writing the book was not to teach carpentry; many do-it-yourself manuals already do the job well. We wanted rather to celebrate applied ingenuity, to convince the reader that imaginative awareness of the immediate environment produces satisfying results. If the reader wants to make the specific pieces described in the book, the instructions given should carry him or her through the project. Beyond this we hope *Low Tech* will be used as a source book of ideas and attitudes. The projects can be adapted and attitudes applied in areas we have not explored. Industrial processes and products can be used as a constantly changing armory of available materials.

All the projects described in the book have been checked out for structural stability, safety, and efficiency. However, success will often depend on the dimensions and nature of the materials you find and on your own ingenuity. These vary so much from person to person and place to place that we cannot guarantee that any individual project will work successfully. On the other hand we most certainly guarantee that cultivating the low-tech attitude will work to the benefit of the fast furnisher.

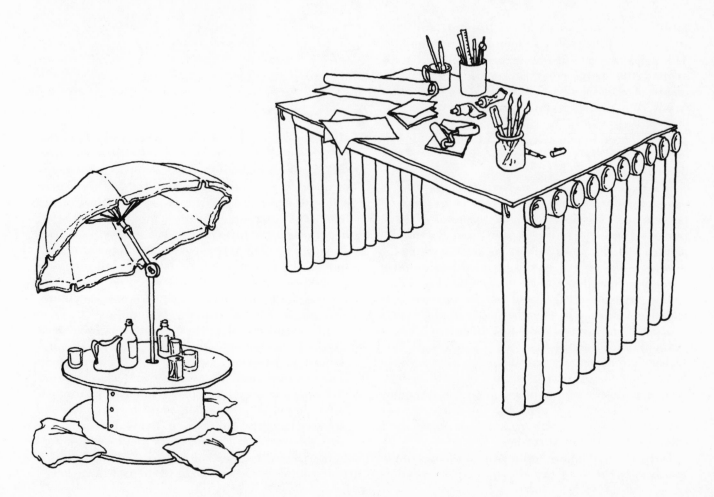

Oil drums make stable table bases, and they can look unexpectedly sophisticated when the drab metal is sprayed in a coat of silver or black enamel paint, or in a glossy primary color.

Drums come in many sizes. The forty-five-gallon drum holds the standard "barrel" of oil, and that's the size we have worked with in these table projects. Smaller sizes can be useful for making seats.

Forty-five-gallon drums are beaten and tuned in the Caribbean to make the steel band's musical instruments. The musicians value the traditional all-steel drum above some modern economy models in which steel is mixed with other metals. The drums are made in four tones, from treble to deepest bass; the bass drum uses the entire drum, but most of the rim is chopped off to build a high-pitched drum. The skilled steel-drum maker can cut around the rim in about five minutes using only a hammer and cold chisel, but the technique takes practice to master (the seam is the toughest part). An electric saw is a simpler substitute, and an electric jigsaw fitted with a high-speed metal cutting blade is an effective tool.

The drum will have to be cut down to the correct height for comfortable eating. Without the tabletop the base will need to stand 28 inches (710 mm) high. Start by marking out the cut on the less attractive end. To do this, measure the same distance up from the bottom at 6 inch (150 mm) intervals around the rim and join up the marks. If you are using snips to cut the steel, drill a hole to get started and snip along the line. However you cut the drum, smooth the rough-cut edge with a file and cover it with a strip of decorative push-on molding sold for trimming cars (Fig. 15). The chrome-finish plastic type looks good. An alternative is a length of plastic hose pipe slit along its length and pushed over the rim.

Oil drums are used in the chemical industry to store some potentially unpleasant products, though these are rarely packaged in forty-five-gallon drums. You need to know precisely what the drum contained before you can decide on a suitable cleaning method. Industrial detergent is the usual treatment for chemicals, a car engine cleanser for oil and grease. Even with simple oil or paraffin, disposing of the oil-laden residue after cleaning can

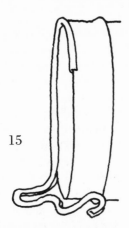

15

Locating drums can be tricky. Though they used to be discarded after a single use, recent rises in steel and energy prices mean they are now routinely reconditioned for further use until they are rusted or holed beyond repair. A reconditioned drum may contain a product different from the one marked on the drum. Paint shops and garages are good sources of empty drums.

present problems, as it is a serious pollutant of the drainage system. Some drums merely smell, but others can be a hazard: welding a dirty drum of inflammable paint solvents, for example, can cause explosions.

The project shown in Figure 16 used two drums to make a long table. The top is cut from a sheet of lumbercore or plywood 1 inch (25 mm) thick; the ends are rounded using an electric jigsaw fitted with a wood-cutting blade. The top can be fixed to the drums using short metal angle brackets—three for each drum as in Figure 17—bolted through predrilled holes to the drum and then screwed to the underside of the top. Alternatively, cut two

16

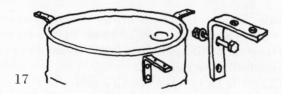

17

pairs of 2 x 1 inch (50 x 25 mm) battens, each piece the width of the drum's diameter. Round off the edges to fit snugly inside the drum lip, then cut a half-lap joint (explained on p. 200) in the center of each piece (see Fig. 18) and screw the two pieces to the top. This locates the top securely on the drums but allows the whole assembly to be dismantled instantly. If you cut off the top rather than the bottom of the drums, the drum can be used for storage space, accessible by removing the tabletop.

In Figure 19 we have used a glass top to cover the drum. This is not cheap, unless you can buy a pane of plate glass from an old shopwindow. Shopwindow insurers or replacement services can often help. You could ask a storekeeper to tell you who insures his windows, though he might then suspect you of operating a protection racket! If you are getting a piece cut you will need glass at least ½ inch (12 mm) thick for a 48 inch (1220 mm) diameter table, and the glass will need to be professionally ground and polished to remove sharp edges.

The weight of the glass will hold it in position. It is important that the drum top should be absolutely flat. Drum ends are usually recessed. You can use this feature to make a decorative detail beneath the glass. You could, for instance, house a shell collection or a display of dried flowers. Plywood or lumbercore are cheaper alternatives to glass.

Companies in the drum-reconditioning business will eventually give up on badly damaged or rusty

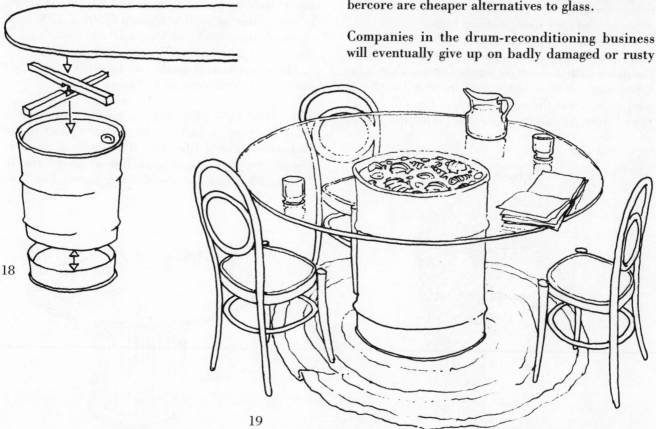

18

19

oil drums and throw them away. Cast-off drums are also commonly found on construction sites and dumps. Damaged and ugly drums can be disguised by a rope coat as in Figure 20, where the drum is used as a complete table. The rope is held in place by clear general-purpose adhesive, so the surface of the drum should be well cleaned with detergent and water to ensure proper sticking. Hold the rope in place while the adhesive dries. "Whipping" is a neat and secure alternative fixing method using no adhesive. The technique is explained on page 215.

Nylon rope can be heated at the ends with a cigarette lighter until the strands melt and fuse together; this will prevent unraveling. Start winding at the bottom of the drum and pack the rope tightly as you wind around (Fig. 21). A thinner gauge of rope is used for the top. Start the spiral at the center and work outward. When the top is covered, cut the rope using a sharp knife.

Making a removable top for the drum gives access to storage space inside. Cut out the top of the drum with an electric jigsaw fitted with a high-speed metal-cutting blade, but leave a 1 inch (25 mm) wide rim at the edge; your new top will rest on this. Cover the sharp metal edge with decorative plastic push-on trim sold in car accessory stores. The top is a circular piece of ½ inch (12 mm) lumbercore cut to fit neatly inside the drum's rim and covered with the rope.

Carpet is an inexpensive alternative to rope as a cover for damaged drums. For a self-conscious touch of style you can use a remnant of the same carpet as on the floor. This technique makes a small area feel roomier.

Mobility is the major feature of the garbage can table, with its useful handles for easy moving (Fig. 22). If the can is clean inside, you can use it for storage too. Cans can be cleaned with industrial detergent. The tabletop is a circular piece of plywood 48 inches (1200 mm) in diameter, which should comfortably seat six people. You can mark out a circle by pinning one end of a length of string to the center of a 48 x 48 inch (1200 x 1200 mm) plywood sheet and marking out the circle with a pencil held 24 inches (600 mm) along the string.

The top is located on the can by blocks glued and nailed to its underside as in Figure 18.

The barrel table (Fig. 23) has a long history. It is often featured in seventeenth-century paintings of European tavern life, and it remains a popular choice to provide a suitable atmosphere in "Smugglers' Inn" on the English coast. The beer

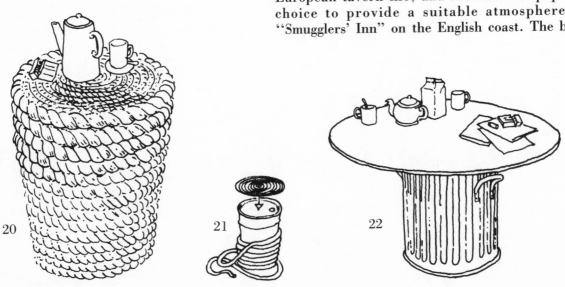

20   21   22

23

barrel or wine cask makes an excellent instant table for drinkers: the height is right and the handy lip prevents spills and falls. Traditional breweries still use wooden barrels rather than aluminum, but they are an unreliable source of old barrels. Coopers have more regular supplies and lower prices. Trace them under "Coopers—Cargo" or "Barrels and Drums" in the *Yellow Pages*.

The table base in Figure 24 can be made either from an oil drum or a heavy-duty cardboard tube such as those used by manufacturers of carpets and other sheet material which must not be rolled too tightly. Bulk dry goods are also packed in large cardboard drums which could be suitable. Choice depends on local availability and on which of your storekeepers appear cooperative. As the 144 inch (3600 mm) and 180 inch (4500 mm) tubes present carpet retailers with a disposal problem, supplies should not be hard to find. The tabletop is cut from plywood or lumbercore—½ inch (12 mm)

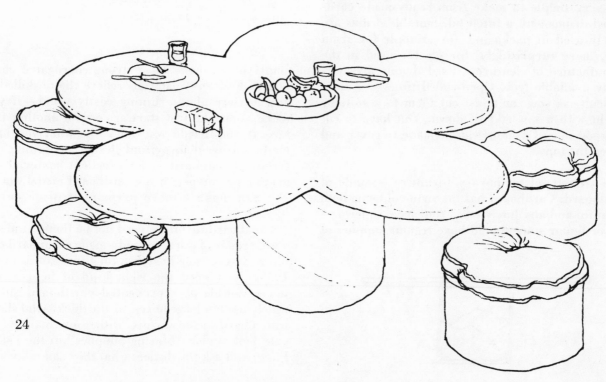

24

thick wood will do for a small table taking little weight, though the more expensive ¾ inch (20 mm) thickness would be more stable.

Cut a disk of lumber to fit tightly into the inner circumference of the tube. Glue and screw this to the underside of the tabletop. If you are using a cardboard tube, sit the top in position on the tube and then hammer panel pins into the smaller disk through the side of the tube to hold everything tight. You may find it easier with a steel oil drum to drill pilot holes through the drum to take the pins.

If you are unconvinced about the stability of your table, fill the tube to a depth of about 6 inches (150 mm) with sand or stones to lower the center of gravity (Fig. 25). If the bottom is missing, use a jig-saw to cut a disk to close the base of the tube. Pin it in place, reinforcing the joint if necessary with glass fiber tape and liquid resin, as shown in Figure 26. Auto parts stores sell this for repairs to car bodywork.

The drum seating repeats the theme. The seats are very simple to make from ready-made cardboard drums with a fitted lid. Suitable drums are widely used in packaging, for example for grain and, more surprisingly, for plaster used in the manufacture of dentures. Used drums are normally available free. Open-ended tubes are more difficult, as you can't just cut them to a suitable height with a saw and sit down. You have to cut plywood tops. Cushions can be made to cover and soften the tops.

The archetypal temporary furniture is made of cardboard. Cardboard has the virtue of being both plentiful and absolutely free. Your local supermarket or liquor store should have regular supplies of

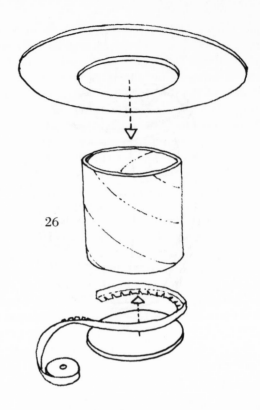

26

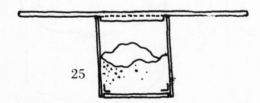

25

empty boxes made from strong corrugated cardboard. Free raw materials relieve the unskilled of any anxiety about ruining costly wood—if you make a mistake just start again with another free box. If you decide you don't like what you have made, throw it away and design something different. Cardboard is an excellent material for making prototypes: if the cardboard model works, you can make a more permanent piece out of lumber.

Cardboard furniture need not be flimsy. Indeed, a wide range of durable ready-made cardboard furniture was on sale in stylish furniture stores in the 1960s. You need the right kind of board—the tough double-ply corrugated cardboard sheets widely used in large boxes, or the thick, solid sheets with a hard waxen surface. If the supermarket fails you, look under "Moving Supplies" in the *Yellow Pages* and ask the dealers what they can sell you.

Cut cardboard with a sharp knife or scalpel, using a straight metal edge as a guide. Where the cardboard has to be folded, score it on both sides before bending. The aim is to make a groove on each side of the fold without tearing or cutting the surface. The handle of a metal spoon is a suitable tool for scoring. Any unsightly scars and rough edges can be covered with masking tape. The parts can be joined with staples or held by a system of tabs and slots. To prevent cardboard furniture from bending in use, the S-shaped corrugations in the cardboard should run vertically, not horizontally.

The table base (Fig. 27) is made from a single piece of cardboard 100 inches (2500 mm) long and 24 inches (600 mm) wide. This is scored and folded into four 24 inch (600 mm) sides, with an extra 4 inch (100 mm) fold at one end. Make two 2 inch (50 mm) deep snips, 4 inches (100 mm) apart, into the 4

inch (100 mm) strip and fold this back to make the tab seen in Figure 27. Cut out a matching hole 2 inches (50 mm) in from the end of the side facing this tab and push the tab through. The tab is secured by a piece of cardboard pushed through a slot cut in the tab. The shape of the table base is held firm by slotting together two 48 inch (1200 mm) pieces of cardboard to span from corner to corner (Fig. 28). The tabletop in Figure 27 is plate glass, which is very expensive to buy. A cheaper alternative such as lumbercore would have the advantage of hiding the cardboard base.

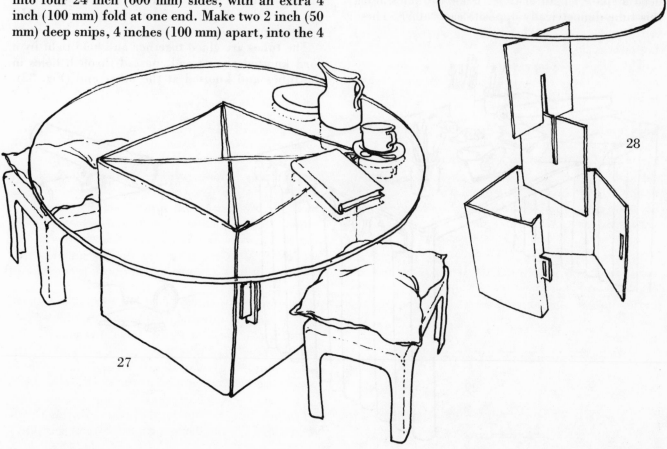

27

28

The log-cabin style table in Figure 29 is made from 32 cardboard tubes. Web printers are constantly discarding these and are often happy to give them away. A large company with its own printing department could produce several dozen rolls a day in the pressroom, and these are usually thrown away. Cloth is wrapped around similar tubes, which are extremely strong. They can often be picked up in significant numbers from clothing manufacturers.

Each side of the table is made from eleven tubes 28 inches (700 mm) long; ten 40 inch (1000 mm) tubes make up the top, which is covered by a sheet of Masonite to create a flat table surface. The main problem is to cut out the ellipse in each tube so that it sits snugly against the adjacent one. To begin you need a spare length of tube. Draw two lines along this tube diametrically opposite each other. These lines should be as long as the diameter of the tubes. Join up the two lines with another two lines at right angles to them drawn around the circumference of the tube. Now cut out this shape using a sharp knife (see lower tube in Fig. 30).

Next draw two diametrically opposed lines down the entire length of another tube and sit this tube in the notch already made in the first tube (see Fig. 31), with 2 inches (50 mm) protruding over the edge. The two lines you have drawn should touch the sides of the notch. Hold a pencil flat against the notched tube so the point touches the other tube and move the pencil around the tube, touching the uncut tube all the time. This will mark out the ellipse on the tube. Cut the ellipse out using the cutting knife and use this tube as a model to mark up the next one—you will find results improve all the time; the ellipse becomes more precise as the model improves.

The tubes are glued together and held tight by a cord knotted at one end, passed through holes in the tubes and knotted at the other end (Fig. 32).

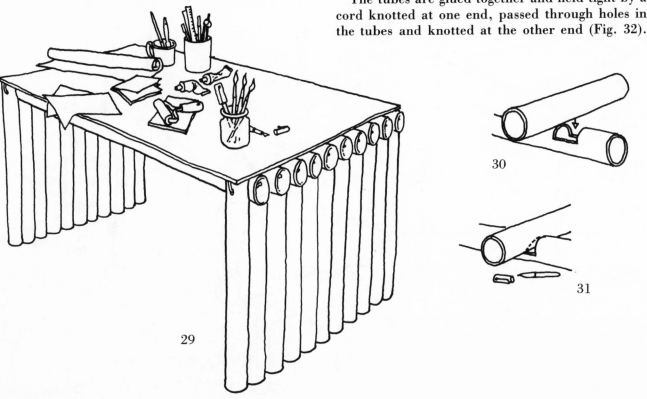

29

30

31

32

Stability is improved by adding a crossbar in the center of the table at footrest height. The design could be refined by lowering the horizontal tubes to form a shelf as in Figure 33.

Paint the cardboard tubes in a single color or, especially in a child's room, use a different color on each tube. For a more dramatic look cover them in aluminum kitchen foil.

Giant cable drums are often seen lying around construction sites, looking unwanted. They are usually just waiting for collection, as the cable manufacturers now try to recover empty reels for reuse. They are very costly to replace, and are therefore repaired in the manufacturer's workshops until they disintegrate. The moral for the fast furnisher is that reels shouldn't be taken from sites before checking with the foreman.

Nevertheless, good drums are discarded surprisingly often, and finding them presents little problem in a city. The problems begin with the journey home, for they are cumbersome and heavy. The obvious solution, if you have no truck, is to roll them home! Bear in mind the possibility of police interest in your journey.

The large drums such as in Figure 34 have a very rugged look, with rough-sawed lumber, metal straps, and stenciled lettering. These are suitable for outdoor use without alteration. You can

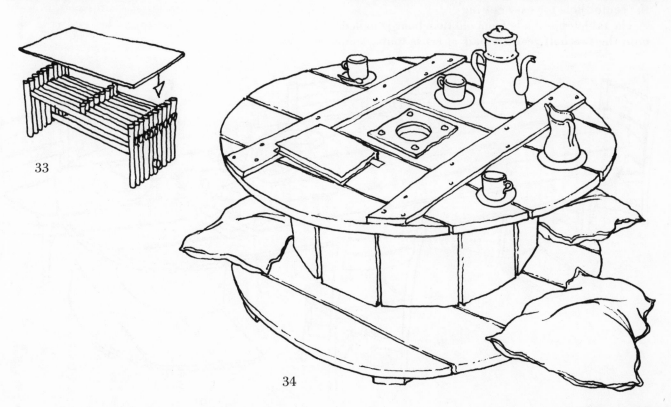

33

34

brighten up the metal using a wire brush attachment on an electric drill, and the risk of wood splinters can be reduced by smoothing the lumber with a sander or plane.

Lighter cables are wound around plywood reels, which often have a cardboard drum. They are less weather resistant, likely to delaminate and fall to pieces in the rain. However, most will happily last through a normal summer outdoors. The center hole can be fully exploited by fitting it with an umbrella (Fig. 35).

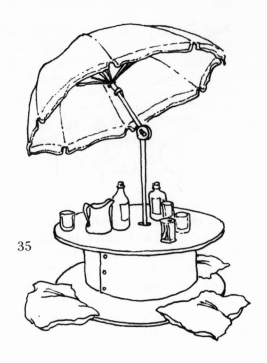

35

Large reels can be sawed in half to make a pair of bases to support a plank-top table (Fig. 36). Smaller reels will only be suitable for occasional tables. The large reels are usually held together by bolts spanning the drum. Leave the bolts in place. Before you saw, shine a flashlight inside the drum to see where the bolts are, and design your cut to avoid these. Remove the metal plate reinforcing the center hole for easy cutting.

The tabletop is made from old floorboards nailed onto the two half reels. A pair of cross timbers on

36

the reel run parallel with the tabletop boards making a gap between the reel and some boards. This gap is filled by two additional battens glued and nailed to the reel at right angles to the floorboards. The nails are then driven through the top and into these battens.

Boards can be laid with gaps to match the cable reel. The rounded ends are formed with a jigsaw. Once in place the boards can be planed to give you a flat surface, and the entire assembly can be painted.

The semicircular void in the sawed halves can be used for storage. An open shelf can be fitted and held in place by nails or dowels hammered through the drum. Simple doors are made from ½ inch (12 mm) plywood. They are hinged directly to the inner core if it is sturdy enough; weaker reels will need softwood battens screwed to the inside edges (Fig. 37). Battens ¾ x 1½ inches (20 x 40 mm) should suffice.

The alternative arrangement shown in Figure 38 could prove simpler and more convenient. There is less leg room at each end, but the cupboards are more accessible and the top is a plain rectangle requiring no shaping with the jigsaw. A door would provide an inexpensive top. If doors are too small, use ¾ inch (20 mm) plywood.

Outdoor materials, such as the pierced concrete garden blocks in Figure 39, can look good indoors. This two-person table needs the support of a solid floor, as the cement holding the blocks together would crack on a flexible floor. Loose-laid blocks are less stable. The blocks are standard 9 x 9 inch

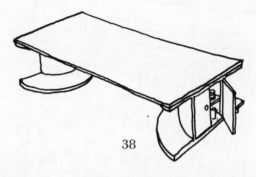

38

(225 x 225 mm), as the 12 x 12 inch (300 x 300 mm) type would give an inconvenient table height. They are sold in most garden centers.

The top is made from wooden ceiling joists salvaged from a demolition site. Pay a lumberyard to cut them in half in the direction of the wood grain and clean them up at home using a rented belt sander rather than the subtler but more laborious plane. We ended up with planks approximately 2 x 2½ inches (50 x 65 mm), and cut them into 39 inch (1000 mm) lengths.

Perfectly flat-sided battens can be bolted or glued together tightly; ours are spaced as shown in the drawing for an open-slat look which disguises the slight irregularities following sawing and sanding. The open look is particularly handy if you use such a table outdoors, as it prevents a build-up of water in rainy weather.

The project in Figure 39 called for fifteen battens 39 inches (1000 mm) long. The table can be adapted to seat more people by extending the battens over the concrete blocks on the two long sides.

Half-inch (12 mm) holes were drilled through the battens 2 inches (50 mm) from each end, using the first drilled batten as a pattern for the others. A length of ½ inch (12 mm) diameter continuously threaded metal studding, bought from a plumbing supplier or hardware store, was then passed through the battens at each side. Studding is normally available in 78 inch (2000 mm) lengths.

A waste piece of copper plumbing pipe was cut into twenty-eight ¾ inch (20 mm) lengths to use as

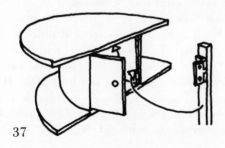

37

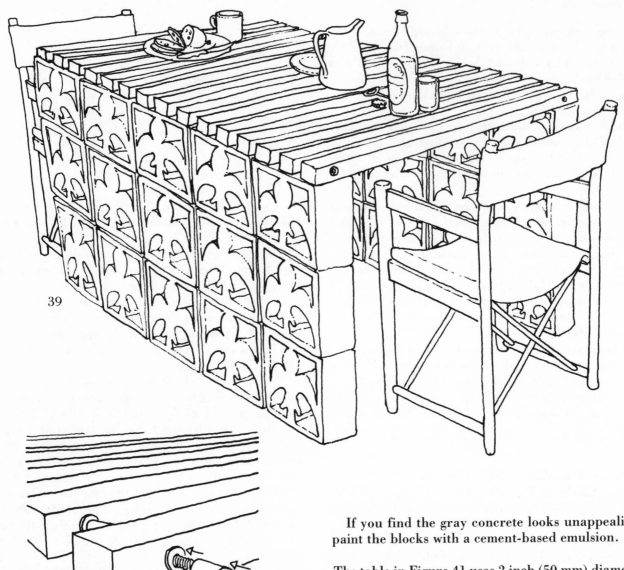

39

40

spacers between the battens. Use pairs of washers with the spacers (see Fig. 40). Retaining nuts and washers were recessed in the end battens for neatness and tightened up. Finally, the protruding parts of the threaded rod were cut off with a hacksaw.

If you find the gray concrete looks unappealing, paint the blocks with a cement-based emulsion.

The table in Figure 41 uses 2 inch (50 mm) diameter commercial scaffolding which can be adapted or dismantled whenever your needs change. If you find no local source of cheap scaffolding, a workable alternative is old gas pipe which has been removed from under the floorboards during the demolition/rehabilitation of old buildings. It is sold to scrap metal dealers, who are a reliable source.

The four legs are cut 2 inches (50 mm) shorter than the correct table height, which is 26–30 inches

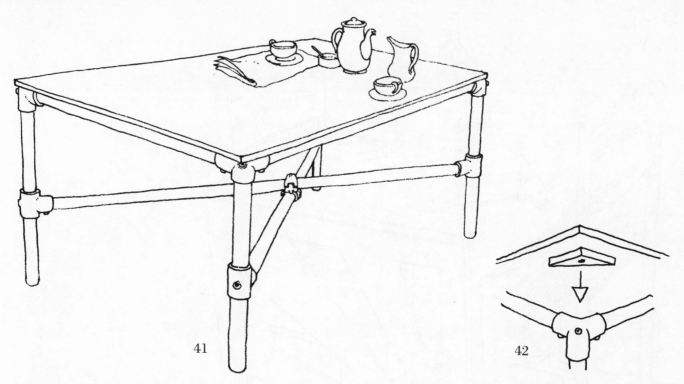

41

42

(650–750 mm) depending on your size and taste. The 2 inch (50 mm) allowance is for the tabletop and the fittings.

To make the table shown you will need four one-way connectors to join the legs to the crossbars, four two-way connectors to link legs and top bars, and a pivoted connector for the center. Caps on the feet would keep them from cutting into delicate flooring. The length of the four pieces used for the frame top and crossbars will depend on the size of your top. One of the cheapest and most satisfactory tops would be a secondhand door from a demolition site. Modern flush-faced doors are ideal if you fill in the handle holes with wooden plugs and filler. A sheet of ¾ inch (20 mm) lumbercore or laminated chipboard is a more expensive alternative. Triangular blocks of wood glued and nailed under the top in each corner hold the top in position (Fig. 42).

For information on scaffolding finishes see page 22.

Fold-away tables are ideal for rooms too small to take a permanent table. In Figure 43 we display the genuine "gateleg" table, built from a discarded garden gate. Hinged correctly, the component parts of this simple two-person table will fold flat to the wall, ready to lift into position in one simple movement when needed.

Remove the hinges and latch from the gate, patch up the damaged parts with plastic wood, sand smooth, and paint on a coat of wood primer. If no gate is available, an old door could be cut down to size and used instead. The top section of a shop or house entrance door incorporating stained glass would create a dazzling effect if it could be lit from behind.

The table must be 26–30 inches (650–750 mm) high for comfortable eating, and this height is therefore the maximum length of the tabletop from the wall. The top is a piece of ¾ inch (20 mm) plywood sawed to size. A 3 inch (75 mm) wide strip of the same board provides the batten which is

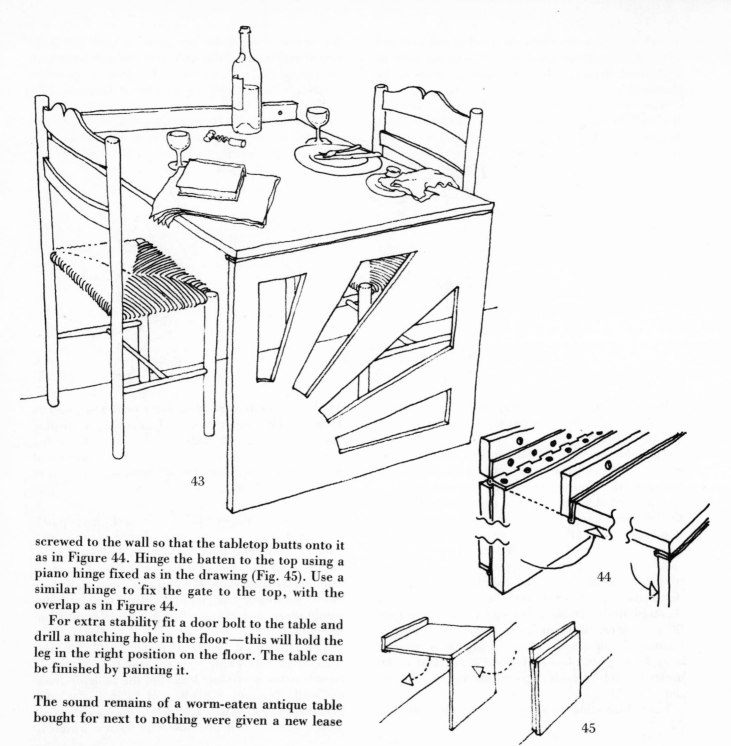

43

44

45

screwed to the wall so that the tabletop butts onto it as in Figure 44. Hinge the batten to the top using a piano hinge fixed as in the drawing (Fig. 45). Use a similar hinge to fix the gate to the top, with the overlap as in Figure 44.

For extra stability fit a door bolt to the table and drill a matching hole in the floor—this will hold the leg in the right position on the floor. The table can be finished by painting it.

The sound remains of a worm-eaten antique table bought for next to nothing were given a new lease on life in Figure 46. Only the gateleg and side rail, with its excellent traditional hinging system, remained intact. The rest was good only for firewood.

The rail is screwed against a batten mounted on the wall ¾ inch (20 mm) below the desired table height; this allows for the ¾ inch (20 mm) thick lumbercore tabletop. A batten as long as the table-top width is cut from the same ¾ inch (20 mm) board and screwed flat on top of the wall batten; it overhangs the wall batten at the front to provide room for the leg when the tabletop is dropped. The top is shaped at the corners with a jigsaw and sander and finally hinged to the batten. Most old gatelegs are made of pine or mahogany, and may look strange against the new top. The solution lies

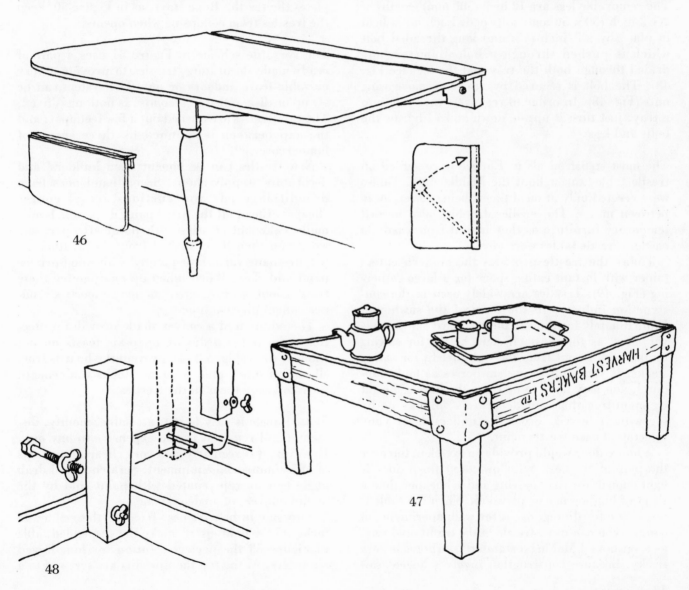

46

47

48

in a can of paint, which is the fast furnisher's standby in helping to hide the clashes and flaws in materials.

The low-level coffee table in Figure 47 is made from a wooden bakery tray with reinforced metal corners. These can be salvaged in large numbers when bakeries go broke or change to plastic trays. The removable legs are 12 inch (300 mm) lengths of 2 x 2 inch (50 x 50 mm) softwood. Each leg is held in place by a 3 inch (75 mm) long threaded bolt which is pushed through a bolt-diameter hole drilled through both the tray and the leg (see Fig. 48). The bolt is secured by easy-to-remove wing nuts (Fig. 48). In order to reconvert the table into a tray, just turn it upside down and withdraw the bolts and legs.

The most stylish meals in Europe were served on trestle tables throughout the Middle Ages. Tables were erected only at meal times, being stored away between meals. The medieval nobles also needed temporary furniture as they moved from castle to castle. Trestle tables were ideal.

Today the trestle provides the modern entertainer with instant eating space for a large gathering (Fig. 49). Trestles are widely used in the construction industry in the form of the sawhorse. Unfortunately for diners, the standard sawhorse is very low, as the most efficient height for sawing timber is different from the right height for eating steaks. If you want to use sawhorses as table supports, you may have to increase the horses' height by mounting them on decorators' planks or by screwing a board across the underside of your tabletop at each trestle point.

A house door would provide an excellent top over the pair of trestles. A hollow-cored flush door is light enough for easy moving and is cheaper than a sheet of lumbercore or plywood. When the table is not in use for dining, use it for wallpapering or, of course, you can use a trestle in the traditional way, as a sawhorse! Making a standard sawhorse is very tricky, because construction involves angled saw cuts, but trestle clamps can now be bought to make trestle construction extremely quick and easy. The system shown in Figure 50 is a simple alternative to making a sawhorse. The hinges are screwed in the exact center of the 60 inch (1500 mm) long 2 x 1 inch (50 x 25 mm) battens, then the battens are simply sawed in half. The 24 x 24 inch (600 x 600 mm) sheet of hardboard pinned to both battens completes the trestle. Rope stays, as in Figure 50, keep the trestles from collapsing when opened.

The versatile scheme in Figure 51 uses a pair of ready-made decorators' trestles to provide a very movable feast, indoors or out. The system can be set up or dismantled in seconds, as nothing is fixed. The two trestles are opened out a few feet apart and the gap between is spanned by three sheets of lumbercore.

New trestles can be bought from builders' and decorators' supply shops. Secondhand ones from demolition yards and auctions are of course cheaper. Clean off the dried paint drips which normally cake old trestles with paint stripper; the wood can then be protected from the weather by polyurethane varnish or painted with wood primer paint and gloss. When tidied up and painted these trestles look sophisticated enough to merit a semipermanent place at home.

The addition of a canvas shade provides protection from the sun during open-air feasts on hot summer days (Fig. 52). To prevent the boards from sliding around, glue wooden blocks underneath them to locate them on the trestles.

Slotted angle is easy to cut, assemble, modify, dismantle and reuse. It is also expensive to buy new. However, it is regularly sold very cheap at auctions of office/industrial equipment. Scratched and drab angle can be rejuvenated with paint sold by the manufacturers of angle systems.

Two simple box frames, fixed to the ceiling 48 inches (1200 mm) apart, make the suspended table in Figure 53 the perfect solution for long-legged sprawlers. At the top the uprights are screwed to a

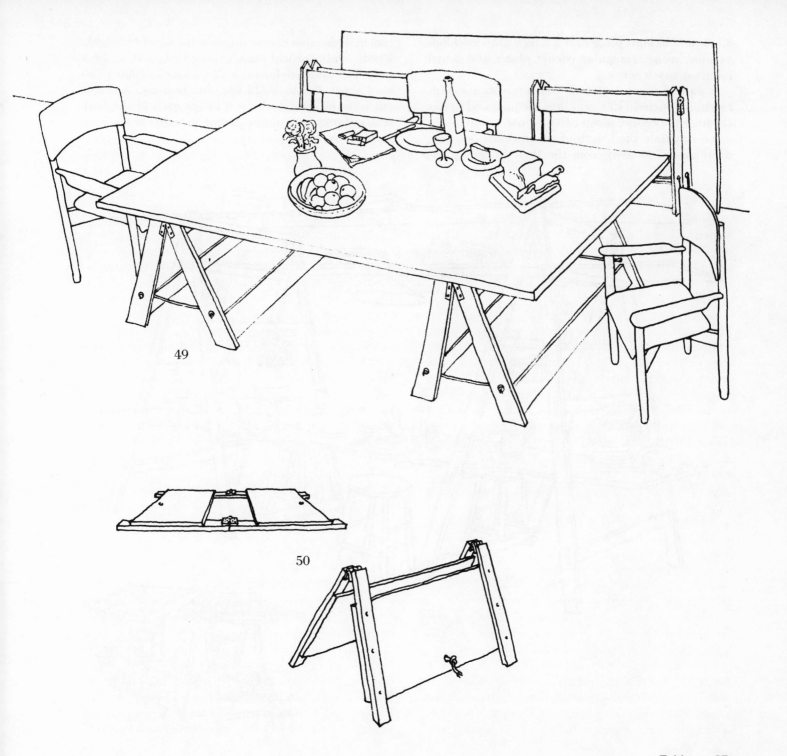

49

50

30 inch (750 mm) piece of 6 x 2 inch (150 x 50 mm) lumber, using triangular corner plates and 2 inch (50 mm) coach screws.

A pair of 4 inch (100 mm) coach screws are countersunk 4 inches (100 mm) into the joist and driven through the ceiling plaster firmly into a joist.

To calculate the length of the uprights, subtract 27 inches (700 mm) from the floor-to-ceiling dis-

tance. This allows some adjustment of table height. Plastic end caps will blunt exposed edges at the bottom. The table surface is a 72 x 30 inch (1800 x 750 mm) sheet of 1 inch (25 mm) lumbercore. A slot is cut into the board where it meets each of the four triangular corner plates joining uprights to the horizontal supports.

51

52

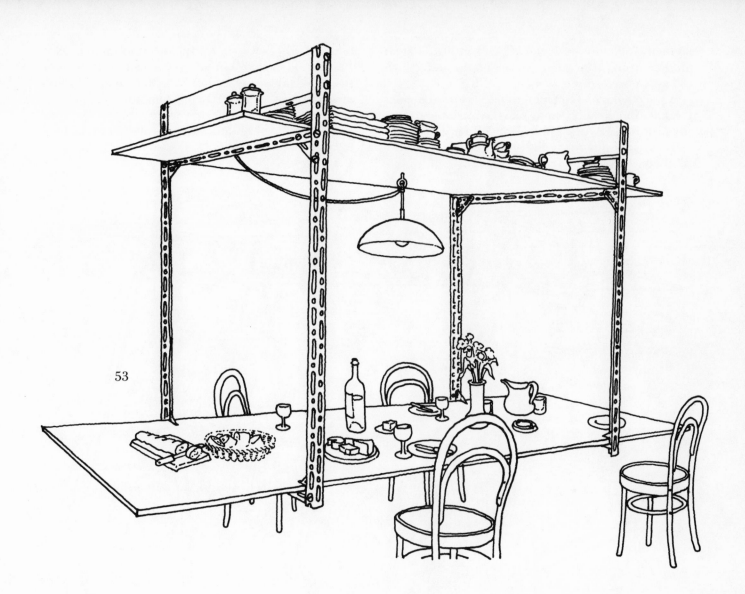

53

SEATING

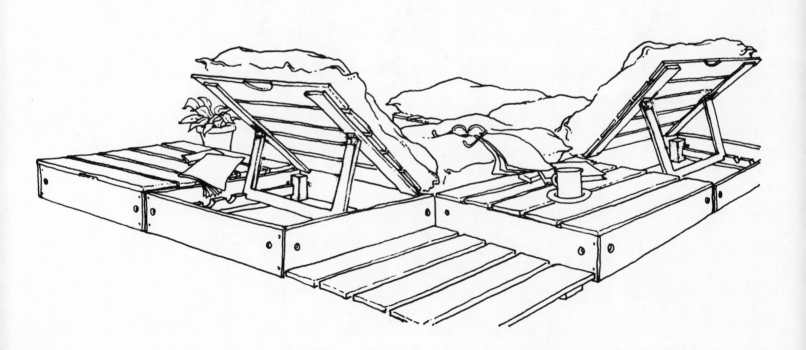

The adaptable seating scheme shown in Figure 54 brings a new dimension to sitting on the floor—it is made from 7 inch (175 mm) floorboards bought from a demolition yard. The platforms provide a combination of sitting, lounging, sleeping, storage, and low display units with slatted tops to give a lighter, slightly oriental look. The design can be as simple or elaborate as you want to make it, and when you need a change, the units are unbolted in seconds and ready for instant reassembly. The size of the platforms is variable; 36 inches (1000 mm) square would suit most rooms.

The basic platform, with unhinged drop-in top, needs eleven 36 inch (1000 mm) lengths of lumber. The rough side of the floorboards is of course used on the inside of the platform.

Inside each corner of the box put a glued block of 2 x 2 inch (50 x 50 mm) lumber; hold the joint together by driving 2 inch (50 mm) screws through the box sides into this block (Figs. 55 and 56). The top of each block should be at least 1 inch (25 mm) below the surface.

The tops are made from the same 7 inch (175 mm) boards, spaced with ½ inch (10 mm) gaps if you want the slatted look. Cut lengths to the exact width of the box (check the measurement before you cut), then screw these to two supporting battens of the same lumber. These need to fit snugly inside the box, so for a box made of 1 inch (25 mm) lumber they will be 2 inches (50 mm) shorter than the box and fixed 1 inch (25 mm) inside the outer line of the lid (Fig. 57).

You can make spare lids to sit on the floor between the boxes, as in Figure 54. You could also screw a base onto the boxes and use them for storage space.

An additional refinement in Figure 54 is the adjustable prop-up lid. To make the prop, cut a three-sided frame from 1 inch (25 mm) plywood, with sides 4 inches (100 mm) wide. Dimensions will vary with box size, but the two free ends should align exactly with the top's two support battens. The two open sides should be half as long as the inside of the box. They are fixed onto the top's battens at the halfway point with hinges (Fig. 58)

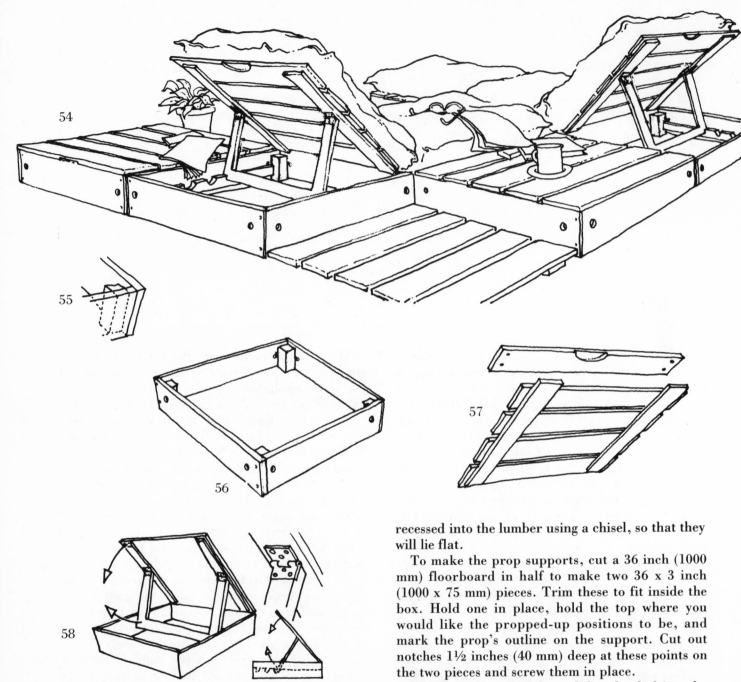

54

55

56

57

58

recessed into the lumber using a chisel, so that they will lie flat.

To make the prop supports, cut a 36 inch (1000 mm) floorboard in half to make two 36 x 3 inch (1000 x 75 mm) pieces. Trim these to fit inside the box. Hold one in place, hold the top where you would like the propped-up positions to be, and mark the prop's outline on the support. Cut out notches 1½ inches (40 mm) deep at these points on the two pieces and screw them in place.

Increase the system's stability by bolting the boxes together (see Fig. 59) using ½ inch (12 mm) drilled holes and ½ inch (12 mm) steel bolts. Measure the positions of the holes exactly—if they are not in the same place on each box they will not bolt in alignment (Fig. 60).

Wooden pallets (Fig. 61) are a rugged, ready-made alternative to building your own boxes. These portable platforms are designed for industrial work when loads are moved by forklift truck. Normal dimensions are approximately 48 x 40 x 4½ inches (1200 x 1000 x 100 mm). Used pallets are found where heavy goods are moved. Building blocks and bricks may be stored on site on pallets, and once used these are often discarded in dumpsters or left on site. Ask the foreman before you take them and arrange suitable transport for the journey home.

It is hard to adapt a pallet to take a prop-up top without dismantling it completely. However, they can be usefully incorporated in a larger scheme. Before you use pallets remove or hammer in any nails that may be sticking out.

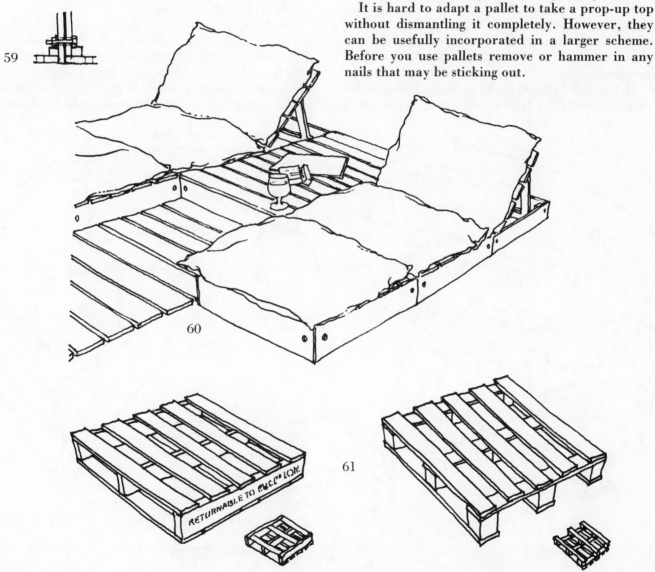

59

60

61

RETURNABLE TO M.C.C° LON.

Admirers of high-tech looks will welcome a semi-industrial sofa in the living room. The one shown in Figure 62 is built from corrugated iron—heavy, uncompromising, and usually zinc-plated against corrosion. The curved shape has long been in use for tunnel construction, subways, and sewers. It has been featured in such temporary structures as barracks and air-raid shelters. If you fail to find corrugated iron on sale cheap, you can order it through a builders' supplier. Buy the right curved shape ready-formed, as corrugated metal is too tough to bend at home. Even cutting it can be exhausting.

In Figure 62 the curves have been filled in with 1 inch (25 mm) thick lumbercore cut to shape with a powered jigsaw (Fig. 63). Mark the cutting line on the board by putting the corrugated iron on top and tracing its shape.

The corrugated iron is held by 1½ inch (40 mm) screws driven through the valleys of the corrugations at 9 inch (225 mm) intervals around the base. Drill holes for these using a high-speed metal-cutting bit. If there is any tendency for the drill to overheat, lubricate the tip.

The base is covered with a block of 8 inch (200 mm) thick foam cut to shape and tucked inside a loose cotton cover. The top edge of the corrugated iron is made more comfortable by a soft foam lip. This can be simply a length of plumbing pipe insulation foam glued in its groove and pushed over the

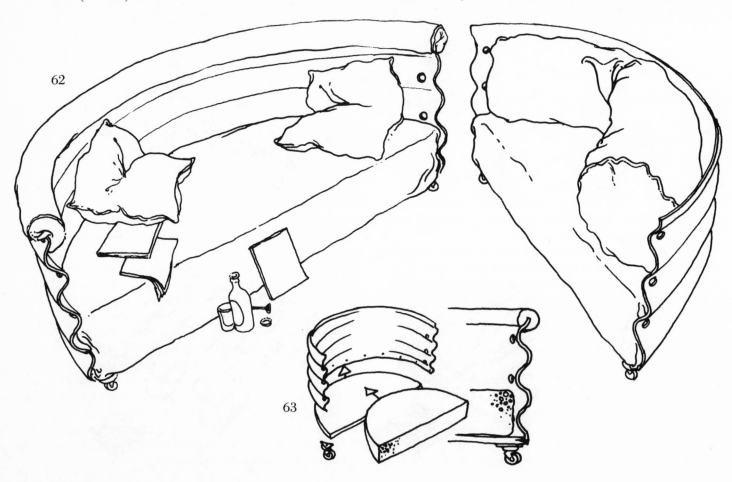

62

63

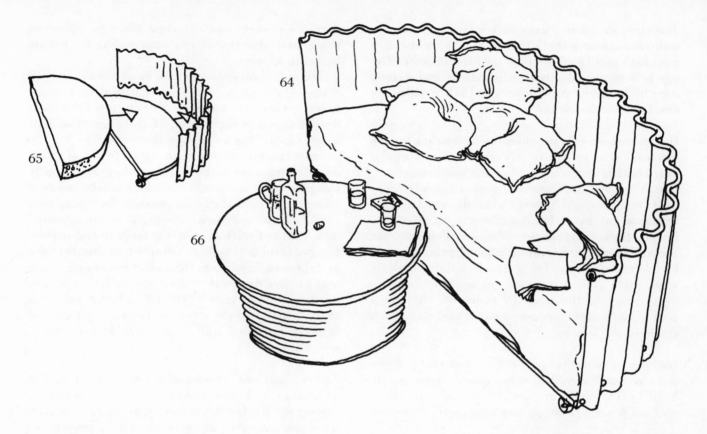

rim. For a more durable alternative, push on a length of black or green plastic hose pipe slit open with a knife. If you want to paint galvanized iron use a calcium chromate primer.

The whole construction is heavy. Make it more mobile by screwing heavy-duty castors to the base-board. When the high-tech appeal fades, dismantle the seat and use the corrugated iron outdoors for a compost heap enclosure.

Right-hand plan (Fig. 64) used the flexibility of transparent plastic sheets to produce a sofa lighter in both weight and looks. Construction method is similar to Figure 62, with 1½ inch (40 mm) screws driven through the plastic into a 1 inch (25 mm) lumbercore base. Don't try to drive screws directly through the plastic without first drilling holes wide enough to take the screws; use large curved plastic

washers to spread the load and so prevent cracks in the plastic. Screws are driven through at points where the corrugations and lumbercore meet.

The curve in the plastic is not preformed in this case, so you can design your own. We found a 24 inch (600 mm) depth at the center gave a comfortable seating depth all around the arc. The seat is not a complete semicircle, but a 24 inch (600 mm) deep segment of a circle 36 inches (900 mm) in radius, drawn on a 72 x 24 inch (1800 x 600 mm) sheet of lumbercore. The center of the circle is 12 inches (300 mm) outside the edge of the board. For a complete semicircle you will need about 114 inches (2800 mm) of plastic. Our plan used only 96 inches (2500 mm) of sheet, 30 inches (750 mm) wide. If you need to use several overlapping sheets, they should overlap by one and a half complete corrugations for adequate strength (Fig. 65).

The table shown in Figure 66 is a standard galvanized corrugated animal feed pan, 8¼ inches (210 mm) high and 18 inches (450 mm) in diameter. The top is a loose-laid circular board, 24 inches (600 mm) in diameter. Newspapers and other oddments can be stored inside the feed pan.

Old iron once again provides the framework for the low-level seat in Figure 67. The iron castings of long benches in parks and bus stations can be very fine. The park, bus, and rail authorities often renovate their best old benches when the wooden seats break or rot away. However, castings can still be bought from scrap dealers and occasionally from the authorities. Be cautious about buying cracked bench ends—repairing a crack satisfactorily is work for a skilled welder, and welds often leave nasty scars on the iron. In Figure 67 the rotten part of the boards was sawed out to make a curious single-seater bench.

Italian designers brought the tractor seat indoors decades ago. Since then it has become increasingly hard to find one. Farmers are obsessive recyclers and never seem to throw anything away. Moreover

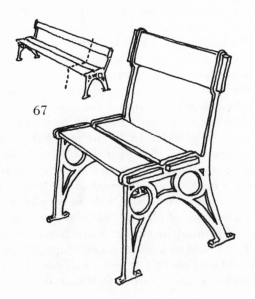

67

they often react evasively when asked to sell something, assuming that if you want to buy it, it must be worth keeping.

The older seats are cast iron or pressed steel with a marvelous shape dotted by patterns of pierced holes. Seats are attached to tractors by a bolt driven through the center of the seat. The bolt head is located in a recess in the casting.

Since tractor seats were designed to be sat on all day driving over bumpy fields, they are usually exceptionally comfortable and look good indoors if painted in bright glossy car enamel. In Figure 68 a row of them is used in an alcove. They are mounted on a length of scaffold pole which sits in end sockets bought from a plumbers' supplier or lumberyard and screwed firmly into the wall at either end. Each seat's bolt is driven through a hole drilled in a standard scaffolding clamp (Fig. 69). The advantage is that with the single screw clamp the seat can be quickly loosened and swung out of the way if necessary.

The crashed and abandoned motor vehicle found in wrecking yards everywhere is a great source of seating for the fast furnisher. When a car's traveling days are over, its seats are rarely preserved. They are almost given away at junkyards, where car seats are easily ripped out for indoor use.

Custom-made leather upholstery is a rare and valuable find. Among the standard seats Alfa Romeo (Fig. 70) has an excellent reputation for style and comfort. At the other extreme is the rear seat from the humble Citroën 2CV (Fig. 71), which brings a touch of primitivism to home furnishing. The Citroën seats are designed for instant removal from the car, which suggests the possibility of using them in both car and home.

Remember that the driver's seat has the hardest life; back seats tend to be little used except in taxis and chauffeur-driven limousines.

The standard lamp lighting up the scene in Figure 70 adds to the car-conscious decor. It is made from a scrapped car's steering column, salvaged from the

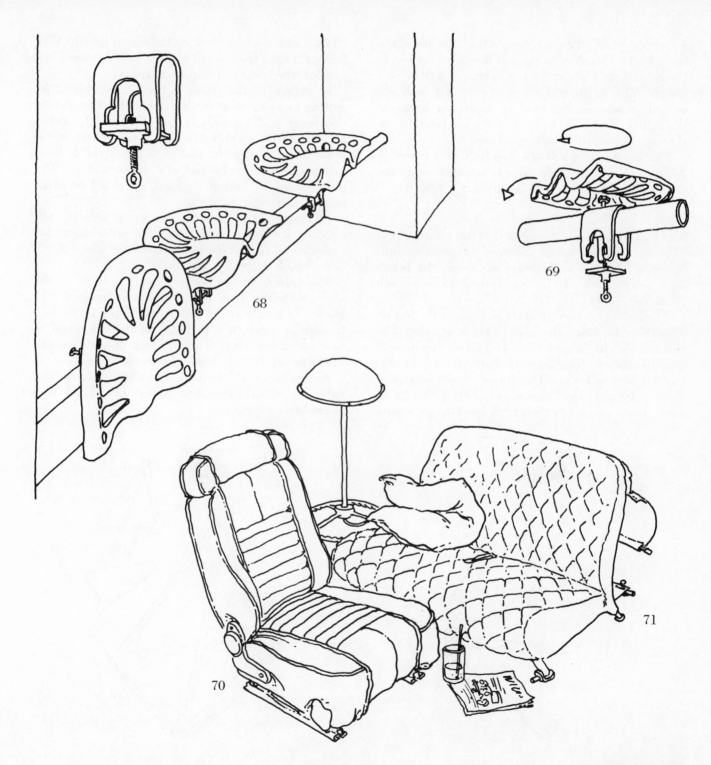

68

69

70

71

wrecking yard. The steering wheel becomes the lamp base. The electric cord is threaded up inside the column and out at the top, where it is fixed to a socket. This in turn is screwed onto a 1 inch (25 mm) thick wooden disk cut to fit tightly in the top of the column and held in place by three screws driven through holes drilled in the column.

The shade shown is the top half of an orange pedestrian-crossing light. It was salvaged when the other half was smashed by a runaway truck.

The bicycle is widely recognized as the most energy-efficient and versatile form of transportation. When a bicycle's useful days are over, the frame and seat can still be exploited as low-tech furniture.

The height of bicycle seats is easily adjusted by raising or lowering the seat in the seat tube. The two schemes in Figures 72 and 73 take advantage of this flexibility. The base in both cases is a discarded bicycle frame. The frame's front section—down tube and crossbar—is sawed off with a hacksaw; sharp edges are then filed smooth. In Figure

73 the small crossbar joining the seat stays (the twin forks running from seat to wheel hub) is sawed out to allow the forks to be splayed apart.

In Figure 72 the frame is further weakened by cutting away the seat stays completely. This makes the design suitable only for a child's weight unless the structure is reinforced by a triangular metal plate fixed across the inside angle at the bottom bracket, where forks and seat column meet. The plate could be bolted, welded, or glued in place using epoxy resin adhesive.

In Figure 72 the bottom bracket is merely softened by a rubber collar which protects the floor. Collars are also pushed onto the rear wheel dropouts, which normally grip the wheel.

The twin forks are splayed apart to improve the seat's stability. The splayed shape is preserved in Figure 73 by clamping and screwing the forms to a triangular piece of 1 inch (25 mm) thick wood to prevent movement. The corners of the wooden base are cut away to allow the frame to lie flat.

Revitalize rusty frames by sanding down and spraying with automobile paint, available from automotive suppliers.

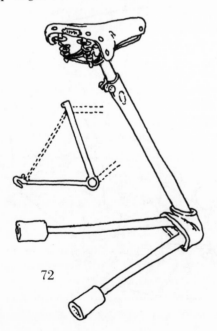

72

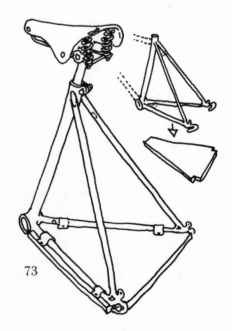

73

74

75

Classic chair construction can be depressingly tough and unsuccessful for the inexperienced maker. Success is faster and easier to achieve with soft and relatively formless seating.

Inflated car or truck inner tubes are stacked inside a tough fabric cover in Figure 74. The tubes were obtained free from a garage as they were badly punctured. A tube repair kit from an auto supply shop repaired them well enough for domestic purposes.

The cover is simple to make since accuracy is not vital. The fabric is long enough to wrap around the pile's circumference with a 2 inch (50 mm) overlap. Fabric width is total height of the stacked tubes plus one tube's diameter plus 2 inches (50 mm) for seams.

Fold the fabric in half lengthwise, with right sides together, and sew the ends together. Turn over ¾ inch (20 mm) seams on both open edges and sew ½ inch (10 mm) pockets where the tie-cords will be threaded. Turn the fabric right side out. Push the cords through—a safety pin on the leading end

helps—at both ends, put the inflated tubes inside and draw the cords tight.

The seat's profile is improved by tying cords around the tubes where they meet (Fig. 76).

The bulky Styrofoam-stuffed sag bag (Fig. 75) is 108 inches (2750 mm) long. It is extremely simple to cut out and sew together from a single 128 x 45 inch (3250 x 1100 mm) length of tough fabric. The cutting pattern is shown in Figure 77; the two 18 inch (450 mm) diameter disks are for the ends of the bag.

With the fabric folded in half lengthwise (right sides together), the long edges are sewn together using strong thread and a double row of stitches. Double stitch one of the circular ends to the tube with a 1 inch (25 mm) seam. Turn the fabric right side out, stuff the bag with Styrofoam pellets and sew in the open end.

The scheme will use about 10 cubic feet (1 m³) of pellets, which can take time to assemble. It is easy

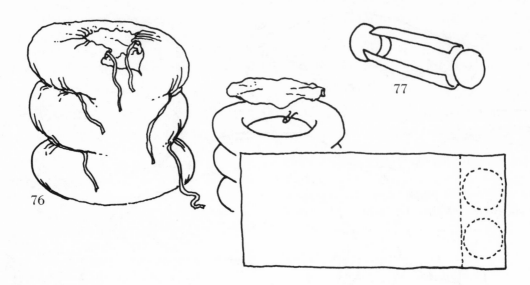

76

77

enough to find free pellets, as they are widely used in packaging and are often left outside stereo and electrical appliance stores in the evening ready for the garbage collectors. Take the pellets home in their box if possible—they can be dreadful to move. They blow around in the vaguest wind and stick everywhere, as they are loaded with static electricity. For a simple life, stuff your cushion outdoors on a windless day, pouring in the pellets through a wide funnel.

Small, light, white pellets of Styrofoam are used to fill most sag bags. Shredded tights and rags make a very cheap cushion filling, but this soon feels lumpy. The feathers from old pillows are softer stuffing but need a featherproof case.

The cheap and cheerful cushions in Figure 78 have a strong visual appeal due to the texture of the sacking from which they are made and the interesting graphics stenciled on by the manufacturer whose goods they carried.

Sacks come in many shapes and sizes. Flour and grain sacks have their own identity. The British hop sack, 6 feet (2 m) long, can be very ornately stamped with the insignia and name of the grower.

Sacks bearing messages of international goodwill under the auspices of the United States aid program have for years been put to good use all around the world, whether as sheets, shirts, or cushions.

Sacks intended to carry fine products such as flour should be impervious to almost any filling. The cruder sacks for hefty contents such as potatoes may need the protection of a lining bag. To sew up the protective bag, seal the edges with a folded strip of canvas, glued inside with latex adhesive, and sew up.

The best source of sacks could be the manufacturer who uses them. Damaged sacks may be available free and can then be patched up. Otherwise use the good sections of several bad sacks for a patchwork effect. Other sources are bakeries, breweries, wholesalers, restaurants, and even importers of clothing from India and the Far East.

For a more industrial look to your cushions, use heavy-duty plastic or paper sacks designed for carrying asphalt, cement, and fertilizer.

The industrial cardboard tube is among the most useful materials for furnishing. From carpet rolls to detergent drums, they are all discarded when their work is done. Locate a retailer and you should find a willing source of free supplies.

Tubes come in many diameters, three of which are lashed together to make the temporary seat in Figure 79. The three tubes were cut to the same length—in this case 24 inches (600 mm)—using a panel saw. Measure the circumference of each tube (or calculate it using the old formula "diameter of tube × 22 ÷ 7"). Cut a 2 inch (50 mm) thick piece of foam to wrap around the tube and stitch the ends together (Fig. 80). If you are prepared to attach the foam more or less permanently to the tube, you can glue it in place using a latex-based contact adhesive.

The tubes in Figure 79 are held together by seat belts rescued from cars in a junkyard. Webbing belts and buckles or rope would be serviceable alternatives.

The lowest tube may soon sag; you can prolong its life by the insertion of two wooden disks inside the tube. The disks are cut from ½ inch (12 mm) plywood, to the internal diameter of the tube, using a jigsaw. They are pushed in position and held by six 1½ inch (40 mm) panel pins driven through the tube before the foam cover is attached. The disks also keep the belts from slipping.

A single 144 inch (4 m) carpet tube (Fig. 81) provided the cardboard core for all eight cushions used in Figure 82. The 9 inch (225 mm) diameter tube was sawed into eight 18 inch (500 mm) lengths. These were reinforced by wooden disks as in the previous project and covered in 2 inch (50 mm) thick foam topped by a fabric cover.

The cover is made from three pieces of fabric, one to wrap around the cylinder plus a circular

78

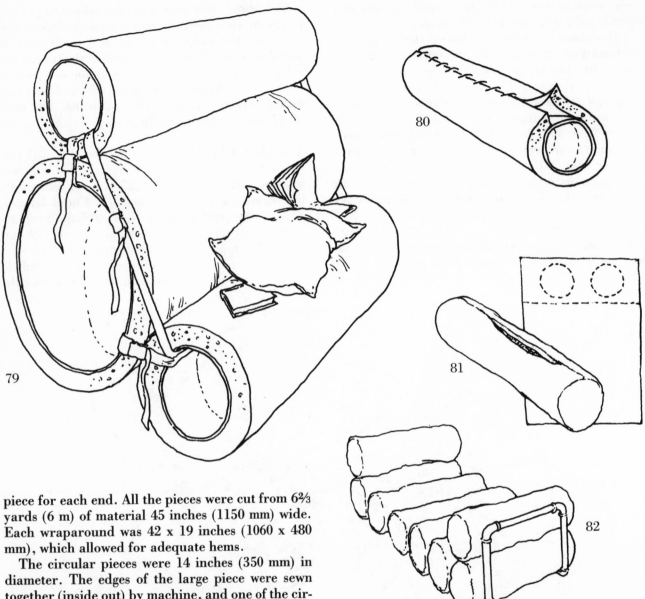

79

80

81

82

piece for each end. All the pieces were cut from 6⅔ yards (6 m) of material 45 inches (1150 mm) wide. Each wraparound was 42 x 19 inches (1060 x 480 mm), which allowed for adequate hems.

The circular pieces were 14 inches (350 mm) in diameter. The edges of the large piece were sewn together (inside out) by machine, and one of the circular ends was sewn in place. The cover was then pulled over the foam-covered tube and the other end sewn up.

The eight cushions are held in place by a lightweight frame made from plastic plumbing pipe. We used pipe with 1¾ inch (45 mm) outside section, cut to length with a fine-toothed saw. The two floor-level pieces were 78 inches (2000 mm) long, the four uprights 24 inches (600 mm) each.

For light use they can simply be glued into eight matching elbow fittings (see p. 211). To prepare them for a tougher life, stuff chicken wire into the joints so it projects about 2 inches (50 mm) into the pipes and fill the joint with concrete.

A back could be added to the seat very simply by using another 78 inch (2000 mm) length of pipe and a pair of right-angle T-fittings.

A simple cardboard tube 22 inches (600 mm) in diameter and 30 inches (750 mm) long makes the sturdy chair in Figures 83–86. The tube can be cut to shape using a hand-held saw or an electric jigsaw. Cut the tube to give an 18 inch (450 mm) height at the front. This is the seat height. It can be tricky to mark a symmetrical shape on the tube—a sheet of paper cut to shape and covering half the tube will help.

The seat is cut from lumbercore or plywood—½ inch (12 mm) is thick enough, but a thicker piece may be easier to pin in place. Cut the circle to be a tight fit inside the tube using the jigsaw, then pin it in position through the cardboard. Secure it permanently with glass fiber tape and resin (Figs. 85 and 86). This makes an immensely strong joint and is easy to use following the manufacturer's instructions. You will need 1–2 inch (25–50 mm) wide tape and the two-part pack of liquid resin. Buy these from motor repair shops, marine stores, or specialist glass fiber suppliers.

When you grow tired of opening and closing your door, sit on it! Four legs and foam transform a plain door into an attractive seat which can also double as an instant bed (Fig. 87). Flush doors are flattest, but screw-in legs can't grip a hollow-cored door. Old panel doors can be easily adapted by filling in the panel recesses with plywood.

The seat stands on four 1 inch (25 mm) diameter steel legs. Eighteen inches (450 mm) is a suitable height. Ideally, the pipes should have a screw thread on the outside at each end so they can be screwed into matching steel end sockets (Fig. 88). If your pipes lack threads, hold them in place with epoxy resin adhesive.

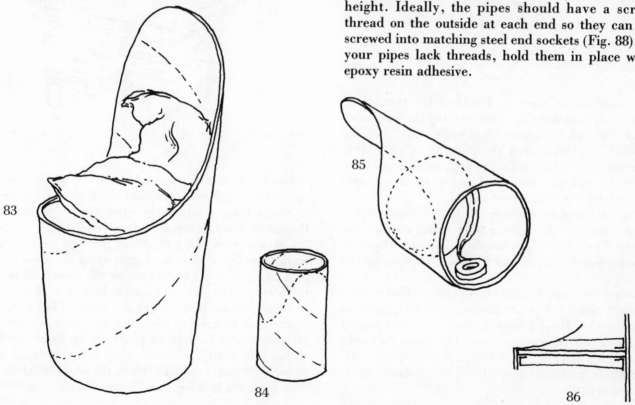

83

84

85

86

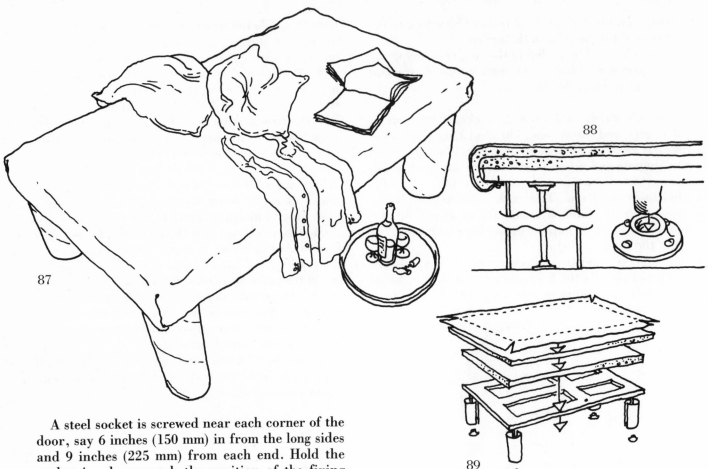

87

88

89

A steel socket is screwed near each corner of the door, say 6 inches (150 mm) in from the long sides and 9 inches (225 mm) from each end. Hold the socket in place, mark the position of the fixing screws on the door with a pencil, make small pilot holes ½ inch (10 mm) deep and screw the sockets down with 1 inch (25 mm) screws.

Screw (or glue) a length of pipe into each socket and screw (or glue) a matching socket on the pipe ends. Threaded pipes simplify fine adjustment of the leg lengths so that the table sits properly on the floor.

Steel legs can look ugly. Cover them therefore with 4 inch (100 mm) diameter plastic plumbing pipe or cardboard tubes. The plastic/cardboard can be either painted or covered by gluing on bright aluminum kitchen foil. Paint plastic with two coats of gloss paint; no primer or undercoat is necessary.

The hard door is softened for sitting on by foam upholstery. A 3 inch (75 mm) thick piece of polyurethane foam is cut to the same size as the door. Hold it in place by impact adhesive.

Cut a 1 inch (25 mm) thick piece of polyester foam 6 inches (150 mm) bigger than the door all around. Fold the overlap under the door and use tacks every 4 inches (100 mm) to hold it in place.

A cast-off curtain covers the foam. This is cut down so as to overlap the foam by 1 inch (25 mm) all around. It is held in place by tacks every 4 inches (100 mm), the tacks being driven through a ½ inch (10 mm) fold made along the edges of fabric. This prevents fraying. See Figure 89.

Prolong the useful life of a clean old mattress by converting it into an adjustable chair (Fig. 90). The simple wooden base (Fig. 91) gives it structural rigidity and allows the angle of the back to be changed simply by shortening or lengthening the side ties.

Make the base from two pieces of ¾ inch (20 mm) plywood or lumbercore, cut as wide as your mattress. Fold the mattress up as shown, then measure the lengths of wood you will need. The two baseboards could be hinged together, but two wire rings passed through small holes drilled near both edges (as in Fig. 91) would do.

Each side tie passes through a sturdy screw eye driven into the panels at least ½ inch (10 mm) from the edge and about 4 inches (100 mm) from front and top ends (see Fig. 90). The ties could be sisal or

nylon rope, which undoes easily if you want to change the angle.

A triangle of heavy canvas or leather as wide as the mattress is sewn to each side of the mattress at one end (see Fig. 90). Before stitching it in place, turn the triangle back along its base and stitch a sleeve big enough to take a ½ inch (10 mm) diameter wooden dowel or steel tube. This gives something strong for the tensioning cords to pull against (Fig. 92). A pair of brass eyelets is also fixed in each triangle of canvas/leather before stitching them in place. The tensioning cords pass through rings which in turn pass through these eyelets. Both the eyelets and the tool to spread them (see p. 215) can be bought from marine supply and craft shops.

At the back of the seat the cords are looped to a sling of the same depth, 4 inches (100 mm) longer than the mattress width. These are made of the same leather or canvas, again hemmed into a dowel-sized sleeve and eyeletted.

To make hand stitching easier use an awl to push holes in the leather where the needle must pass through. The tools for leather work are sold by craft shops.

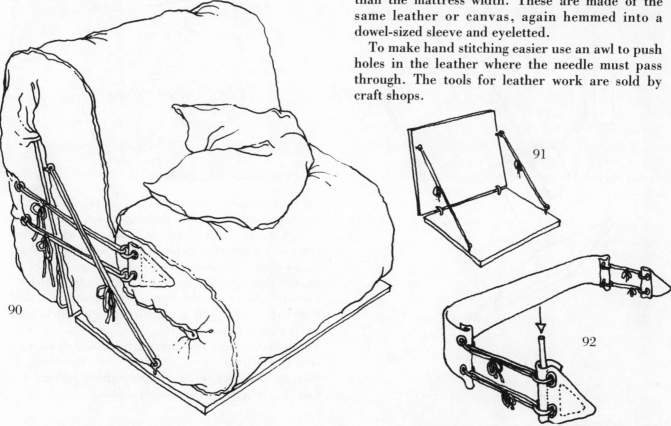

90

91

92

One of the world's simplest chairs uses the traditional African system illustrated in Figure 93. It is made from nothing but two planks, slotted together. Strong 1½ inch (40 mm) knot-free lumber is best. The planks are 15 inches (400 mm) wide, one 48 inches (1250 mm), the other 45 inches (1150 mm) long.

Cut a 30 x 3½ inch (750 x 90 mm) piece out of each side of the shorter plank. Twelve inches (300 mm) from the end of the longer piece use a jigsaw to cut a slot 8¼ inches (225 mm) wide and as thick as the planks through the center of the plank. Now just slot the two together, and there's your chair, ready to paint, use, admire.

Hanging seats rely on strong hooks driven through any ceiling plaster to bite at least 3 inches (75 mm) into solid wooden joists. Light mooring line makes good suspension rope. If your knowledge of knots or splicing (see p. 215) is limited, buy patent termi-

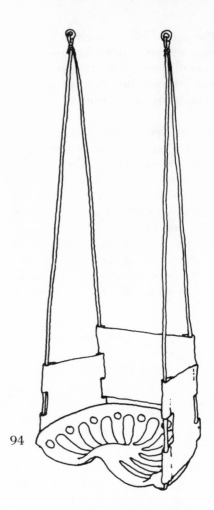

94

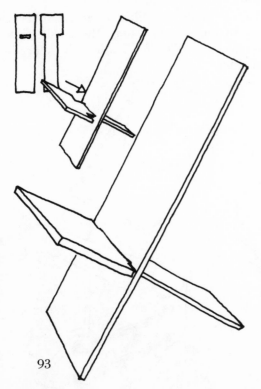

93

nal fixings from a marine supply store, designed to terminate rigging and to tie loops in cable.

The tractor seat (Fig. 96) is suspended on four pieces of no-stretch rope to make a hanging seat-cum-swing. On some seats the ropes can simply be passed through existing holes and knotted. Otherwise drill holes for the four suspension points and attach an eyelet bolt at each point. As a detail we have added heavy canvas sides and back panel. The canvas edges are turned back and sewn into sleeves through which the ropes are threaded. It may be easier to work out the cutting pattern for canvas when the seat is suspended.

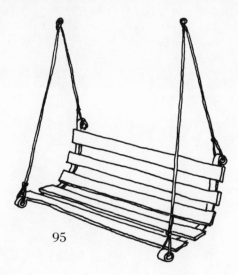

95

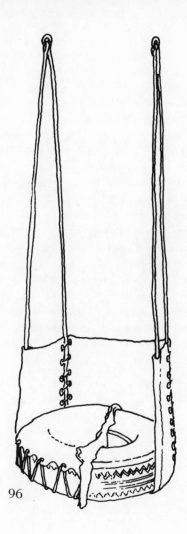

96

The hanging slat seat (Fig. 95) uses two metal end supports salvaged from a broken park bench. The original scrolled ends provided ideal suspension points. Damaged legs were sawed off and the rough metal filed smooth.

Figure 96 shows the last resting place of a flat tire. It hangs in a canvas sling threaded to the suspension ropes. Use two loops of rope of equal length, one across the front, the other across the rear. Hold them under the tire with staples. The ends of the loops are themselves looped through rings hung from the ceiling hooks and spliced.

Put the tire in the loops so it hangs level. Measure for a canvas panel to extend down one side between the ropes, underneath and then up the other side. Sew sleeves in the front edges for the front loop. Insert eyelets every 2 inches (50 mm) along the rear edges where they meet the vertical ropes. To the rear edge under the tire sew the canvas panel for the back. The two sides of this panel are also eyeletted and the side and back panels laced together.

The alert low technologist can give society's cast-offs a new life as stylish and functional furniture. A batch of salvaged bakery delivery trays inspired the schemes illustrated in Figures 97–105, but a good alternative would be wooden flats from a nursery.

The traditional shallow bread trays and flats are made of pine and reinforced with metal corners—they are strong and neat. Both the traditional and the modern plastic trays—generally designed for stacking—make serviceable drawers.

Constructing sturdy drawers can be a nightmare for the inexperienced handyman. It is far simpler to build ready-made trays or flats into a suitable frame. The precise design of the frame will depend on the boxes you find.

Trays are often left outside hotels at night, but taking them could be an offense. If you fail to discover any discarded trays, your local bakery may sell you some. Nurseries will sometimes give old flats to steady customers. Always be on the lookout for a bakery—or any other type of store—closing down. The equipment is normally sold off or even given away.

The "chest of trays" in Figure 97 uses three trays. Measure the sides of the trays and take note of the measurements. Cut six pieces of 4 x 1 inch (100 x 25 mm) lumber as long as the shorter sides of your trays. These will be the horizontal drawer runners, shown attached to the legs in Figure 98. The four legs are made from an old 7 x 2 inch (175 x 50 mm) wooden floor joist bought direct from a demolition site and sawed in half to create two pieces approximately 3½ x 2 inches (85 x 50 mm). Use an electric saw—it's almost a lifetime's work without one! The old wood was cleaned up with a hired electric plane. The length of the legs is three times the depth of one tray plus 12 inches (300 mm) to allow for the runners.

Lay the legs flat on your worktop and glue and nail the bottom runner piece to each pair of legs. Use woodworking adhesive and two 2 inch (50 mm) oval nails at each joint. Leaving just enough room for the drawers to slide between the runners, glue and nail the other two pairs of runners to the legs.

The top is a scrap of ¾ inch (20 mm) thick lumber-core held in place by four small angle brackets—nails or screws alone would not hold it for long.

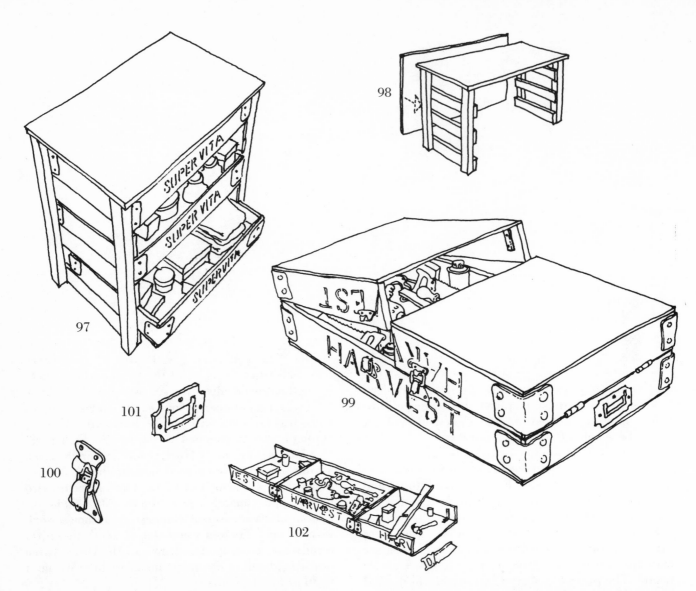

97

98

99

100

101

102

Make a supereconomy top by sawing a salvaged flush door to size. A piece of Masonite pinned to the back holds the structure rigid and keeps the drawers from sliding back too far. Drawer handles should not be necessary.

The wood can be left plain, varnished with polyurethane, or painted with a wood primer and gloss or emulsion. If the drawers stick, try rubbing the runners with a candle.

Two bakers' trays can be hinged together to form a strong chest. In Figure 99 the top tray is sawed in half, and each half is fixed to the lower box with two hinges. Any tendency for the sides of the top pair to distort can be halted by screwing metal angle brackets inside them near the opening. Two toggle catches (Fig. 100) bought from a marine supply store are screwed on at each side to hold the boxes securely closed.

103

104

105

Handles (Fig. 101) are recessed into the box at each end to lie flat (Fig. 102). The recess is marked out by penciling around the handle and chiseling out the wood to the right depth. Simple screw-on handles from an old piece of furniture are free and far easier to fit but less attractive.

Large trays can be sawed in half to make unusual lipped shelves, decorated with the bakery's stencil (Fig. 103). Sawing along the dotted line, as shown in Figure 104, makes a pair of shelves about 9 inches (225 mm) deep.

Certain stacking trays have a raised section in the center (above the dotted line in Figure 105); this can be sawed off or planed flat to improve the system's looks.

The trays can be mounted on one of the many adjustable shelving systems using a combination of slotted uprights and brackets. A cheaper alternative is to screw standard 6 inch (150 mm) metal brackets to two 2 x 1 inch (50 x 25 mm) wooden uprights fixed to the wall. Use four 2 inch (50 mm) screws in each upright, making sure that the screws bite into something solid behind the wall plaster— either the wall's wooden framework or a wall plug pushed into masonry. The uprights in Figure 103 are 36 inches (900 mm) long.

The brackets for the bottom shelf in Figure 103

are fixed at the lowest point of the uprights using ¾ inch (20 mm) screws. Nine inch (225 mm) gaps separate the shelves.

Use a spirit level to mount each pair of brackets on the same level. If you don't own one, the improvised level shown on page 208 will do the job.

Plain domestic drain and rainwater systems look good indoors. Pvc pipe is tough, light, easy to clean, and easy to cut using a hacksaw or fine-toothed saw. Rough or sharp edges can be filed and sanded smooth.

106

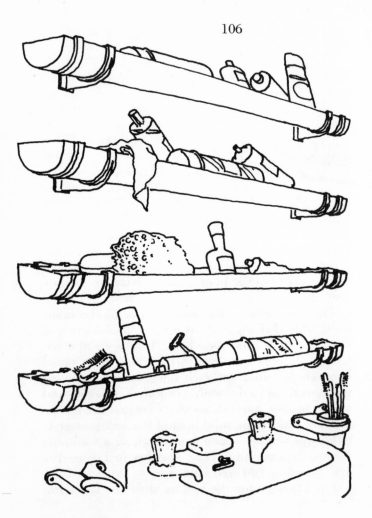

Waterproof plastic guttering is well suited to store bathroom clutter. Plants can also thrive in the damp environment of a length of bathroom guttering.

The shelves in Figure 106 are 36 inch (1000 mm) lengths of standard plastic house guttering, fitted with push-on end caps and mounted on wall brackets. The brackets are held to a brick wall by 1½ inch (40 mm) screws driven into wall plugs. If the wall is a hollow woodframe behind plaster, you will have to locate the timber uprights and screw into these.

Brackets and caps normally have to be bought from a plumbing supply shop, but ends of guttering are often left over after a building job and can be picked up—with the foreman's permission—for nothing. Note the use of the standard clamp in the drawing to make a holder for the toothbrush glass.

If standard gray or black plastic seems too drab, liven up the color by spraying with a couple of coats of vinyl paint. The manufacturer's markings can be filed or sanded off, or removed with lacquer thinner.

Cylindrical pipes come in a variety of diameters from ⅜ inch (10 mm) to 24 inch (610 mm) and are normally sold in 118 inch (3000 mm) and 236 inch (6000 mm) lengths. Different lengths grouped together make an effective hall stand for umbrellas and newspapers—even plants. The plastic system in Figure 107 can be glued together using styrene cement; the special solvent adhesive for the job is sold by the pipe suppliers.

A smaller scale version glued to a cardboard base makes a handy desk organizer like the one in Figure 108. The four lengths of piping are 9, 6, 4½, and 3 inch (180, 150, 120, and 90 mm). They are glued together with styrene cement and placed on a piece of cardboard. The outline of the organizer is traced on the cardboard and the shape cut out—a scalpel makes this job easier. The base is then glued in place and weighted down until it dries.

108

107

The most suitable pipe for making indoor furniture is also easy to find—1½ inches (38 mm) in diameter. It is used to build the sturdy shelving unit in Figure 109.

The unit illustrates a general principle of plumbing pipe furniture design—there are no open pipe ends. A plastic end cap can cover an open end, but for maximum stability always finish with a right-angled elbow fitting or a T-joint. Where pipes meet, they are pushed into one of the pvc fittings and held in place by solvent cement.

Pipes are usually pushed ¾ inches (20 mm) into a collar in the fitting: take the depth of this collar into account when you calculate the exact length to cut your pipes, and allow for the fittings themselves. To make a side of your chosen height with standard 1½ inch (38 mm) pipes, add ¾ inches (20 mm) to the height for the collar at each end of the pipe, then subtract 4 inches (100 mm) for every T-

joint you use and 3 inches (75 mm) for an angle joint.

The joints at the top corners of the structure in Figure 109 have two adjacent fittings. They are held together by a 1½ inch (35 mm) length of pipe pushed into the collar of both fittings and glued in place.

First assemble the front and back frames. Each one is made of eight 11 inch (275 mm) lengths of pipe for the sides, four 17 inch (425 mm) pieces for top and bottom, plus eight T-joints, four 90° elbow joints, and two collar joints, which are used in the center of the top and bottom rails. Assemble them on a flat surface, to keep the pipes parallel. Check to make sure it all fits without adhesive, mark the joints with a pencil so you can reassemble them precisely, sand the end of the pipes lightly where they fit in the joints, and glue together. When the sides are made, add the eight cross pieces. Now measure the space for shelves.

The shelves shown in Figure 109 are chipboard, strong enough to span 36 inches (900 mm) without sagging. The shelves are spaced 13 inches (325 mm) apart to give enough depth to store records and books.

Shelf movement can be stopped in various ways. Shelves could be clamped to the pipes at each end by a U-shaped pipe fitting, they could be shaped at the corners to fit around the upright pipes, or a 2 x 1 inch (50 x 25 mm) batten could be cut as long as

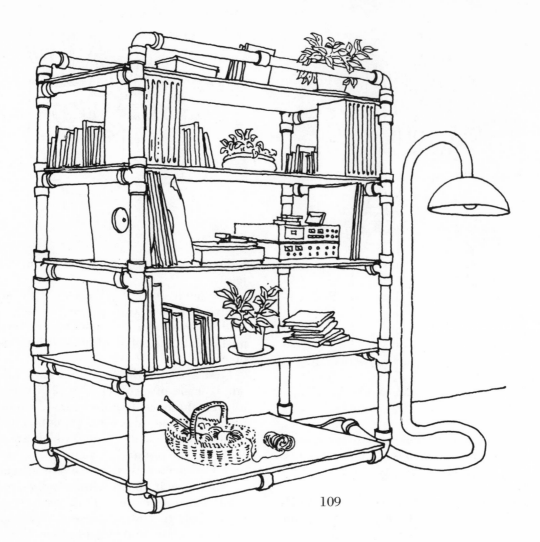

109

the space between the support pipes and glued with pva adhesive to the bottom of the shelf. This system has the advantage of reinforcing the shelf.

Boxes, cans, and other containers are at the heart of most home storage systems. Containers thrown out of factory, office, or home are a valuable resource in low-tech furnishing. In Figure 110 a selection of colorful metal and plastic containers—originally used for olive oil, syrup, candy, cookies, beer, and margarine—is mounted upright or sideways on wooden slats. Restaurants are a good source of free king-sized olive oil and coffee cans. Remove unwanted lids with a can opener, and file rough and sharp edges away.

The slats are 36 inch (1000 mm) long, 2 x 1 inch (50 x 25 mm) wide pieces of wood nailed or screwed to a pair of horizontal battens of the same wood. Leave ½ inch (10 mm) gaps between uprights. Fix the wall battens 9 inches (225 mm) from top and bottom of the uprights, using 2 inch (50 mm) screws every 12 inches (300 mm).

110

Figures 111 and 112 illustrate two ways of mounting the cans—by passing bolts through holes drilled in the slats (Fig. 111) and tightening the nut inside the can with a wrench, or by hooking the can over a screw driven part way into the slat (Fig. 112). In both cases a hole is drilled through the can just below the rim. Cans mounted on their side are fixed by a pair of screws driven through holes drilled in the base. To avoid cracking plastic containers use roundhead screws with protective washers.

Shelves are cut from ½ inch (12 mm) plywood. A shelf will sit in a circular can without support, but the square can's shelf in Figure 110 is secured by two panel pins hammered through each side of the can.

Black and yellow cardboard photographic boxes provide shallow drawer space in Figure 114. Strength is improved by sitting the box inside its top (Fig. 113). A simple box frame is screwed together using ½ inch (12 mm) laminated chipboard. The frame's sides are cut exactly to the depth of the photo boxes; they can be as tall as you like. Screw on metal drawer runners as shown in Figure 113 before you assemble the box, and make sure you fit them exactly facing each other on the two sides by careful measurement and marking.

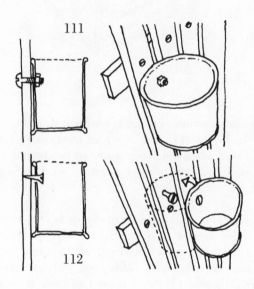

111

112

The top and bottom pieces of the frame are the width of the boxes plus 1 inch (25 mm) allowance for the chipboard sides plus another ¼ inch (5 mm) for freedom of drawer movement. Hold the box together with the special corner fittings used by kitchen furniture manufacturers and illustrated on page 205.

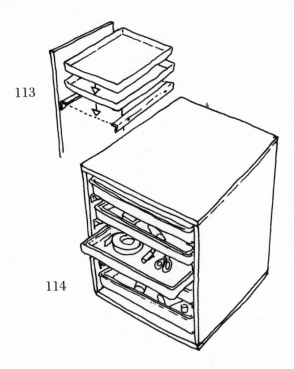

113

114

each mark cut a slot as wide as the plywood from the edge of the board to the center. A hired electric router or jigsaw will make this job easy with wood; a scalpel will cut cardboard. Using the same tool, round off the sharp corners of the strips as in the drawing, and slot the pieces together to make the box structure.

If the system wobbles or creaks, hold it rigid with copper wire ties threaded through holes drilled at the intersection points and twisted tight as in Figure 117. Pin on a Masonite base to make the structure more stable.

Change the shape whenever you like, to make, for example, a coffee table or bench seat with storage inside. The entire structure could be turned on its side and fixed to the wall.

In Figure 116 a plywood sheet has been placed on top of the boxes, drilled all over at 6 inch (150 mm) intervals for ventilation, and used with a mattress to convert the boxes into a bed. Holes drilled in the plywood boxes improve ventilation. The drawing shows a hinged top made of two boards joined by three 2 inch (50 mm) long hinges screwed to the top of both boards.

Appealing containers can transform ugly furniture fast. In Figure 115 the top pair of sliding plywood doors was removed from a cheap cupboard and a pair of handsome wicker laundry baskets pushed in.

You can slot together as many boxes as you like using the system in Figure 116. If expense is no object, you can cut a sheet of ¼ inch (6 mm) plywood into 12 inch (300 mm) wide strips—six strips 76 inches (1900 mm) long and seven strips 64 inches (1600 mm) long were used to make the construction in the drawing. You can cut costs by using tough cardboard instead, to make a less durable but cheaper and lighter structure. Long cardboard boxes are thrown out by dress manufacturers.

Mark each strip 2 inches (50 mm) in from the end, then mark off at 12 inch (300 mm) intervals, with another 2 inch (50 mm) overlap at the end. At

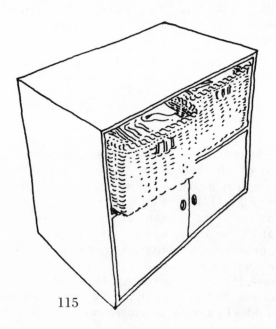

115

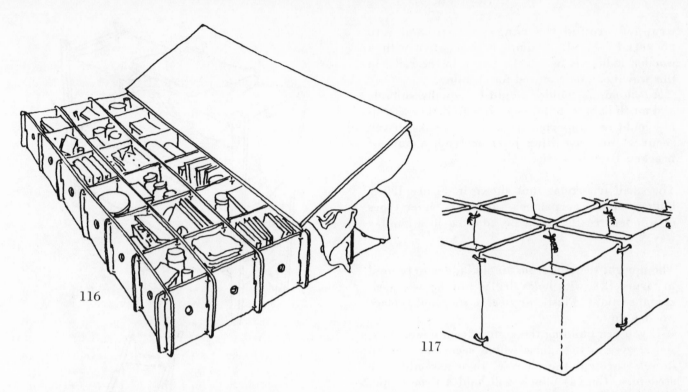

116

117

Cardboard boxes from the supermarket can be used to make a similar structure for next to nothing. They are held together with wire ties twisted together with pliers (Fig. 117). Large staples would work as well. The printing on the boxes can look very effective. If you object to it, cover the boxes in fabric, paper, or emulsion paint. If you use wine boxes and leave the cardboard dividers in, you have a very strong assembly.

The combination of doweling and fabric slings provides dozens of designs for fast and simple storage systems. All you need is a saw, a drill fitted with a drill bit of the dowel diameter, and white woodworking adhesive to fix the dowels together. Make sure that the dowel is held firmly during drilling; otherwise it is easy to drill at the wrong angle and throw the structure out of line. A drilling jig and stand to hold the drill and dowel is helpful. Most manufacturers of power tools make inexpensive stands for their drills. They can be hired by the day. A piece of colored tape stuck on the drill bit at the desired drilling depth helps to make holes of uniform depth. When designing a system, make sure the dowels are offset—two dowels fixed to an upright at the same height can weaken it.

Doweling can be expensive. Economize by setting the cylindrical dowel rods into cheaper square-section lumber uprights; these should be at least as wide as the dowel diameter. In Figure 118 the uprights are cut from a damaged and discarded wooden ladder. A 2 x 1 inch (50 x 25 mm) batten nailed diagonally across the back adds rigidity. A scruffy ladder can be sanded clean and painted.

The same wooden ladder makes a very simple and highly mobile pocket storage system to be leaned against a wall (Fig. 119). The canvas must be fixed to each rung, otherwise heavy objects will put the system out of shape. Where the mounting frame is ready made and cannot be easily dismantled, as in the case of the ladder, the fabric will have to be wrapped around the rungs and stitched into pockets by hand. A simpler alternative with a wooden ladder is to pin the fabric to the rails; in this way it can be removed for cleaning.

An aluminum ladder would be equally suitable and much lighter, but it is a rarer find. The assembly could be supported from ceiling hooks driven securely into a ceiling joist or from a pair of brackets fixed to a solid wall.

The small triangular unit shown in Figure 120 is built around a carpenter's sawhorse. Other types of wooden trestle could be adapted in a similar way.

The upright sections from an old ladder were used in Figure 121, with holes drilled to take new horizontal sections. Plastic or steel pipes could replace wooden dowels.

If you are building the system from dowel rods, sew sleeves in the fabric where necessary, thread dowels through the sleeves, then assemble the structure. Canvas panels will hold a firm shape. Netting is a less shapely but more easily fitted alternative to fabric—just slide it onto the poles and pin in place at each end (Fig. 119).

Four pieces cut from a rickety ladder provide the uprights in Figure 122. The shelves must be level, so take care to cut the ladder with rungs at the same level on all four uprights. Misalignments can be put right by sawing a bit off the longer pieces. The shelves are cut from a sheet of ¾ inch (20 mm) lumbercore and screwed down onto the rungs with two 1½ inch (40 mm) screws per rung.

The system will probably wobble too much to be left free-standing unless a batten is screwed diagonally across the back as in Figure 118.

It is safer against a wall, with a long screw securing each upright to a solid wall or studs.

The basic but extremely adaptable hanging rack in Figure 123 is extended simply by hanging on another easy-to-make loop. Each rail is an 18 inch

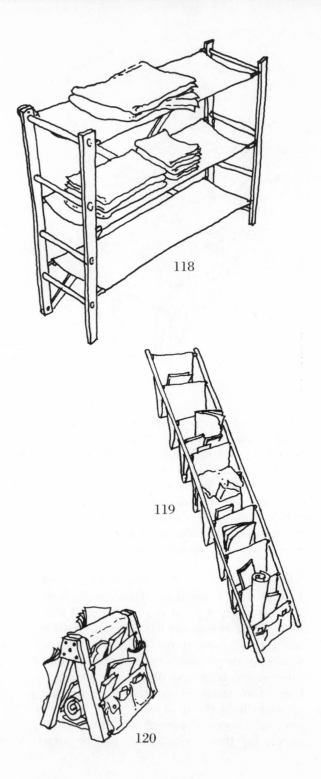

118

119

120

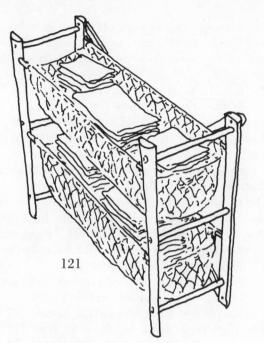

121

(500 mm) length of ¾ inch (20 mm) diameter wooden dowel. Brass curtain rail, copper plumbing pipe, or stainless steel could be used instead.

Pass nylon venetian blind cord through holes drilled through the dowel ¾ inch (20 mm) from each end. Knot the cord tightly and prevent it from fraying by heating the ends gently until the nylon strands begin to melt and fuse together. The top rail's cord hangs over a screw in the wall. Elements are added by looping each one over the one above as in Figure 124.

Various items hang from hooks over slats in the straightforward and flexible scheme illustrated in Figure 125. You could build up a storage system to cover an entire wall by linking several units similar to the one shown. Shop-bought fencing panels can save on construction time, but the lumber in most is too rough for comfort.

All lumber in the design in Figure 125 is planed 2 x 1 inch (50 x 25 mm) softwood. There are twenty

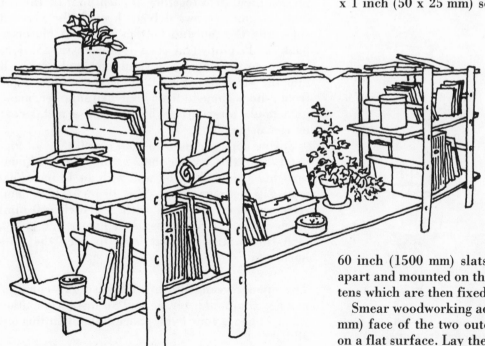

122

60 inch (1500 mm) slats spaced ¾ inch (20 mm) apart and mounted on three 54 inch (1400 mm) battens which are then fixed to the wall.

Smear woodworking adhesive over one 2 inch (50 mm) face of the two outer battens and place them on a flat surface. Lay the twenty slats on top, aligning the ends of the slats precisely with the batten edges. Fix the two outside slats in place using a 1½

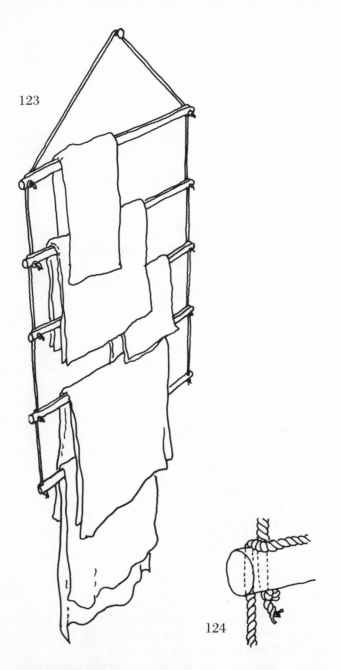

123

124

Use a damp cloth to wipe off excess glue before it dries. Sand smooth any uneven edges. Give the wood two protective coats of polyurethane varnish.

To mount the unit on the wall, drill pilot holes through the uprights between the slats at each corner. If the wall behind is brick or stone, drill and plug the wall and drive a 2 inch (50 mm) screw through each corner. If battens and lumber frame in hollow walls don't coincide, fix a pair of horizontal battens to the wall and screw onto these.

The number and length of slats can of course be varied, and the spaces between can be unequal; however, slats should all be parallel. Mixing slats of different widths—say 2, 3, 4, and 6 inches (50, 75, 100, and 150 mm)—adds variety.

Systems using slats under 48 inches (120 mm) can be made without the center verticle batten.

The simple box shelves shown in Figure 127 are 8 inches (200 mm) deep, made of ½ inch (12 mm) plywood and held together at each joint by three 1 inch (25 mm) screws driven through the vertical sides into the top and bottom pieces. A Masonite back can be pinned on as an optional extra. Shelves hook onto the slats using stout cup hooks screwed into the sides (see Fig. 126). Other objects hang from S-hooks bought from a kitchen supplier; make homemade alternatives by twisting a metal coat hanger using pliers.

Spring clips are used to hold small items in Figure 128. In this scheme the 2 x 1 inch (50 x 25 mm) uprights are fixed to the wall with an 18 inch (500 mm) gap between them. The 48 inch (1250 mm) slats are then fixed on with 1½ inch (40 mm) screws. Brass screw cups as in Figure 126 give a neat finish. Use a spirit level to keep the slats horizontal.

The open screens shown in Figure 129 combine mobile, adaptable storage and an instant partition which changes your living space without cutting out all light.

Each panel is made of two strips of 2 x 1 inch (50 x 25 mm) lumber sandwiching a sheet of plastic

inch (40 mm) screw at each joint. Leaving ¾ inch (20 mm) gaps, screw the intermediate slats in place. Finally glue and screw the central support batten in position.

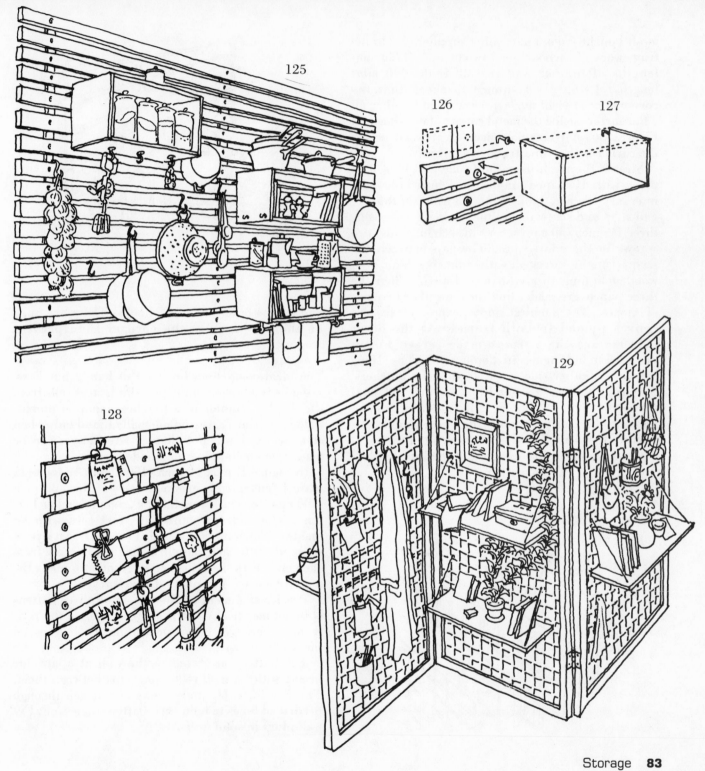

mesh bought from a gardening supplier. From the framework of each strip cut two 66 inch (1750 mm) lengths of lumber and two 28 inch (700 mm) lengths. Using a set square to check that the corners are at right angles, screw them together on a flat surface using the metal corner plates shown in Figure 130. A triangular piece of plywood across the corner makes an attractive alternative.

Stretch the mesh over the frame and hold it in place with U-shaped staples at 4 inch (100 mm) intervals (see Fig. 130). Make the frame of the second strip and screw this to the meshed frame using three 1½ inch (40 mm) screws in each long side, two screws in the short ones. The gap between the strips can be covered with adhesive tape or a wooden lipping to give a neat finish. When the three panels are made, link them together by pairs of hinges. The simplest and cheapest hinges are canvas pinned to both frames. At the other extreme are the purpose-made screen hinges designed to link panels in mobile exhibitions. Hang articles on either side of the mesh using butchers' S-hooks. Shelves are made of ½ inch (12 mm) plywood. They are clipped to the mesh by two cup hooks and a pair of nylon cords which support the front of the shelf. Tie knots at one end of the cord. Thread the cord through holes drilled in the shelf

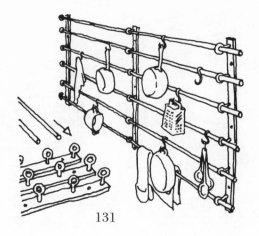

131

and tie the other ends to S-hooks. These are hung on the mesh. Singe the cord ends to prevent fraying.

The ideal companion for a set of handy butchers' S-hooks is a system of purpose-built steel rails from the display counter of a butcher's shop. Unfortunately these are rare and normally found only when shops close down, but simpler alternatives can be made from metal pipes or wooden poles.

In Figure 131 six 60 inch (1500 mm), ½ inch (12 mm) diameter rods are mounted on three 36 inch (900 mm) long, 2 x 1 inch (50 x 25 mm) lumber battens. The rods pass through steel eyes with an inside diameter of $9/16$ inch (14 mm). An eye is screwed onto each batten 3 inches (75 mm) from each end, with the others screwed on at 6 inch (150 mm) intervals. Use pliers if necessary.

Precise alignment of the eyes on all three battens is sometimes tricky—it is simpler to slide the rods through the eyes before mounting the battens on the wall.

The battens are fixed to the wall at a suitable height with 24 inch (600 mm) gaps between them. Two 2½ inch (60 mm) screws are driven through predrilled holes to hold each batten to the wall. Use wall plugs in solid walls.

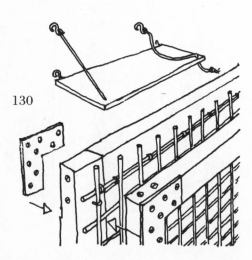

130

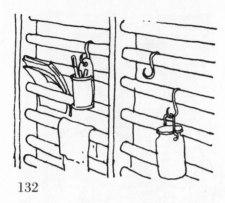

132

Horizontal bars are pushed through lumber uprights to build up the hanging rack system in Figure 132. Salvage the display rails when shops close down or modernize. The system can be constructed to any dimension; it can look very striking when it covers an entire wall, when it could also double as gym bars for the fitness fiend.

Wooden doweling 1½ inches (40 mm) in diameter makes suitable bars; old curtain rods are admirable. They are supported on 4 x 2 inch (100 x 50 mm) lumber uprights at 24 inch (600 mm) intervals. To simplify alignment of the holes, clamp all uprights together and drill through the lot with a 1½ inch (40 mm) diameter drill bit at 6 inch (150 mm) intervals. Smear woodworking adhesive inside the holes and push the rods into position. Before the glue dries use a try square to check that all the uprights are at right angles to the bars.

The frame can be mounted on the wall using 3 inch (75 mm) metal angle brackets at top and bottom of each upright.

The classic hotel message board remains an admirable and simple solution to letter litter problems. The one shown (Fig. 133) is built around a scrap of plywood 24 x 12 inches (600 x 300 mm) covered with traditional green felt.

The fabric is cut to wrap 1 inch (25 mm) around the back of the board, where it is pinned or stapled in place. The pieces of elastic which make up the trellis are also pinned behind the board and stretched a little to improve tension. Following the pattern in Figure 133, begin by running a piece from the top corner to a point 8 inches (200 mm) along the bottom edge, then fix elastic every 4 inches (100 mm) along the board's long edges. The scheme shown uses some 120 inches (3000 mm) of elastic. A rosette screw through each corner will hold the board to the wall.

Wall-mounted molded plastic storage units are widely used in bathrooms and workrooms. Alternatives which cost nothing are easy to find. All you need is a screwdriver and an abandoned refrigerator. Your target is the plastic panel inside the door (Fig. 134).

Door panels come in various sizes. Colors in old refrigerators were until recently limited to the widespread white, ice-blue, and faded green. Now dark browns and deep blues are relatively common in dead fridges.

To remove the door panel, roll back the rubber door seal to reveal the screws holding the panel in place. You will probably need a Phillips screwdriver.

Refrigerators are insulated to keep the cold in, and you should find an insulating mat behind the door panel. It is wise to wear gloves when you take the panel out, to avoid the risk of skin irritation from the fiberglass. Of course if you find a whole

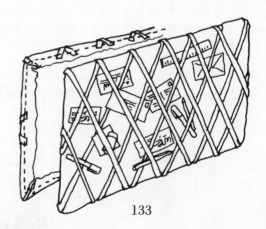

133

134

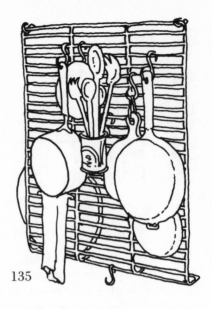

135

junkyard full of cast-off refrigerators you could collect enough free fiberglass to insulate your roof space!

After years in a chilly fridge the plastic may be brittle—care has to be taken during removal and when you screw through the panel to fix it to the wall, as there is a risk of cracking. Use the existing screw holes if possible; otherwise use a hand drill to make holes in the corners of the panel as wide as the shank of the screws you intend to use. Also put a spacer block of wood behind the panel to bridge any gap between the screwing points and the wall

behind. This prevents bending and possible cracking of the plastic.

Another cold storage item is the shop freezer shelf in Figure 135. It was discarded in good condition when the machine was replaced. It hangs on the wall from a pair of hooks.

Hooks and knobs keep clutter off the floor, a principle followed by members of the American religious community known as the Shakers. They hang even their chairs on the walls when not in use. The

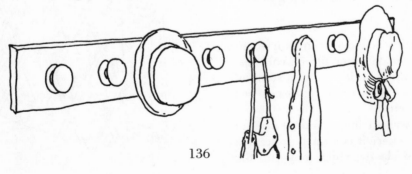

136

community's chairs—and hats—hang from knobs fixed to a wide wooden rail running around the room at picture-rail height.

You can improvise your own Shaker rail using a row of wooden or porcelain knobs salvaged from broken cupboards or discarded doors. Screw them to a 3 inch (75 mm) wide board and fix this in turn to the wall using screws every 18 inches (500 mm). The Shakers paint their rails aptly in "heavenly blue." See Figure 136.

The loops in the Figure 137 design are formed in a continuous strip of clear flexible sheet plastic. The backing board is cheap Masonite panel 12 x 40 inches (300 x 1000 mm) covered with a rectangle of canvas 2 inches (50 mm) wider all around. This is pinned to the back of the board.

Outer edges can be oversewn by machine with a fabric tape of a contrasting color. Adhesive tape is a reliable alternative. The plastic is held to the backing material by a tack at each side 4 inches (100 mm) from the top and at 12 inch (300 mm) intervals. Holes are drilled through the panel 2 inches (50 mm) from the top to take the mounting hooks. Eyelets fixed through both plastic and canvas give a neat finish.

Although wooden boxes for transporting wine are being replaced by cardboard, with some looking you still can find them. Ask for them at restaurants or in liquor stores. Lay the box on its side and use the partitions to hold shoes and shoe-cleaning brushes (Fig. 138).

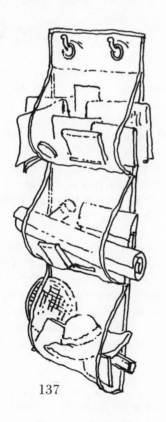

137

138

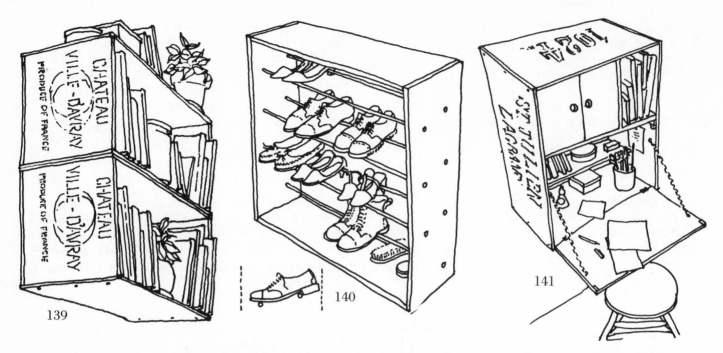

139

140

141

A wooden wine crate with its partitions removed is turned on its side and converted into a shoe holder in Figure 140 by the addition of wooden dowels. Heels hook over ¼ inch (6 mm) diameter dowels glued with woodworking adhesive into holes of the same diameter drilled 4 inches (100 mm) from the back of the case. Toes rest on similar dowels fixed 2 inches (50 mm) lower.

Wooden wine crates (Fig. 139) can be turned on their side and fixed directly to the wall using two 2½ inch (60 mm) screws driven through the strong wooden base. Drill pilot holes for the screws 1 inch (25 mm) from what will be the top of the box, and be sure that they bite into something in the wall more solid than plaster. Use wall plugs in brick or masonry. The two boxes in Figure 139 are fixed independently.

For a simpler fixing, drive two screws into the wall so that they pass between the boards in the bottom of the crate. The screws should be left protruding ½ inch (10 mm) from the wall, and the crate just hooked over them.

For maximum visual appeal choose crates and boxes with bold graphics. Shelves can be fixed inside the empty crate to make the small writing surface and directory shelf in Figure 141. The shelves use ½ inch (12 mm) thick softwood salvaged from another crate. They are sawed to fit tightly inside the crate then coated along the edges with pva adhesive and pinned in position using 1 inch (25 mm) steel panel pins driven through from the outside of the crate. Nails do not spoil the surface of the crates.

Each of the twin doors is held by a pair of small brass hinges. A magnetic catch bought from a hardware store or lumberyard is fixed in the center and holds them closed. Holes ¾ inch (20 mm) in diameter replace handles. The writing surface is hinged and also closes against a magnetic catch. Brass chain stays screwed to the flap and inside the crate hold it horizontal.

Clutter is stored neatly under the bed (Fig. 143) built around ten plastic milk cartons fitted with castors. The length of the central piece of 1 inch

(25 mm) plywood is five carton widths plus 6 inches (150 mm), the extra being allowance for the divisions plus a bit of free movement. Height is measured as carton plus castors, with an extra 1 inch (25 mm) for play. The width of the four crosspieces is two carton lengths plus 2 inches (50 mm). The ten cartons fit neatly under a bed of a suitable size for a standard single 36 x 75 inch (910 x 1900 mm) mattress.

Divide the central board into five equal sections and make four ½ inch (12 mm) wide cuts from the edge of the board to the center. An electric saw or router makes this job much lighter work. Make a corresponding cut in the center of the four ½ inch (12 mm) plywood crosspieces, but 1 inch (25 mm) wide in this case. Simply slot the framework together as in Figure 142.

This type of carton is made for stable stacking, with indentations in the bottom corners matching protrusions in the top corners. The cartons can be stacked at home to provide frame-free storage.

Alternatively slide them onto a shelving rack such as those used in swimming pools. In Figure 144 furniture castors have been screwed to the lower corners and the cartons pushed out of sight under the bed.

Free-standing shelf units are usually pushed back flat against the wall, but the useful flat top of the low-level systems shown in Figures 145, 147, 148, 149, and 150 may be better exploited when the long side projects into the room to act as a divider.

Figure 145 shows a homemade system consisting of a series of five simple boxes built of 1 inch (25 mm) thick laminated chipboard. These are housed

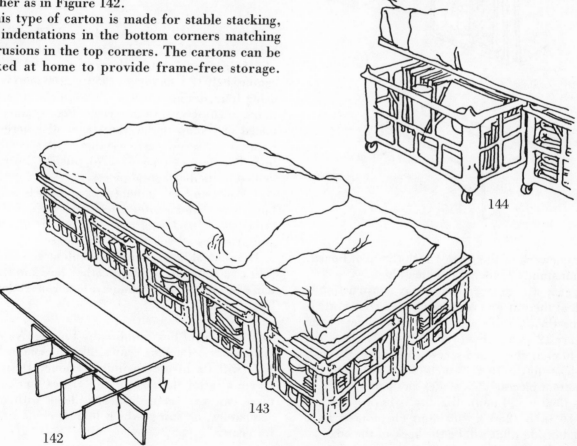

144

143

142

145

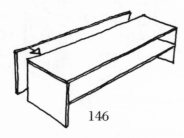

146

in a framework of the same 1 inch (25 mm) board. The unit stands 26 inches (650 mm) high.

The easy way to learn simple box construction is to look at the way an ordinary wooden wine crate is held together. In this case the vertical sides of the boxes are 12 x 18 inches (300 x 450 mm). Three 1½ inch (40 mm) chipboard screws are driven through the sides into the 16 x 18 inch (400 x 450 mm) top and bottom pieces. This makes an opening 12 x 18 inches (300 x 450 mm). Rigidity is improved by a 10 x 16 inch (250 x 400 mm) chipboard base screwed inside what will be the back of the box.

The frame's 18 x 90 inch (450 x 2250 mm) top is held to each 18 x 25 inch (450 x 625 mm) side with plastic corner joints (illustrated on p. 202). A center shelf 18 x 88 inches (450 x 2200 mm) is fixed using four similar fittings. These make a stronger fixing in chipboard than screws. Poor quality chipboard can snap under the strain of a screw. To improve the screws' grip use them with special chipboard fasteners (see p. 198) pushed into holes drilled in the horizontal pieces.

A Masonite back panel (see Fig. 146) is nailed to both frame and center shelf at 6 inch (150 mm) intervals. This keeps the structure from sagging and provides a backstop for the boxes.

The central box resting on the floor acts as a useful extra support, while the other boxes in the system can be moved or removed to accommodate different articles.

You may avoid box-building by finding five ready-made crates. Packing crates, like the one in Figure 147, will fit inside a similar frame. Design the frame around the size of the crates you find, as these can vary considerably. Check with moving companies, or stores which import china or glass, for crates.

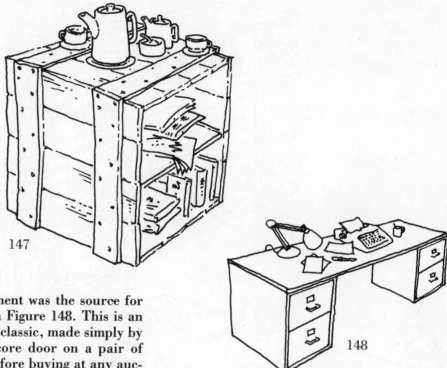

147

148

An auction of office equipment was the source for the ready-made supports in Figure 148. This is an instant-build fast-furniture classic, made simply by laying a standard hollow-core door on a pair of matching filing cabinets. Before buying at any auction check cabinets for damaged metal; open and close all drawers—they are often sold when drawers run poorly or keys are lost.

Cast concrete blocks 9 x 9 inches (225 x 225 mm) hold up the shelves in Figures 149 and 150. The garden blocks in Figure 149 are loose-laid between sheets of ¾ inch (20 mm) lumbercore 78 x 30 inches (2000 x 750 mm). The bottom shelf protects the floor from the rough surface of the blocks. Cover the standard dull gray concrete by spraying gloss paint over a stone primer. Interesting light patterns are cast by lamps mounted in batten sockets screwed to the shelves behind white blocks in Figure 149. Power comes through a wire plugged into a nearby outlet.

The system's size can be altered to fit individual schemes and spaces, and other sheet boards can substitute for lumbercore.

The holes running through hollow blocks are exploited to make a more stable structure in Figure 150. At each corner a 29 inch (725 mm) long wooden pole runs through all three blocks and holes drilled through the two lower shelves (Fig. 151).

The pole remains hidden, as the top board needs no holes.

Slotted angle constructions give homes high-tech looks in a versatile form. Assembly is fast and simple. Units can be changed instantly by bolting on more pieces. Redundant units can be dismantled and the components reused.

Units are built up from L-section lengths of steel or the more expensive aluminum alloy, joined at right angles by nuts and bolts, with triangular corner plates to improve rigidity. The multiple slots are designed to maximize possible fixing positions. Shelves or worktops can also be screwed into place through the slots or loose-laid on the angle itself.

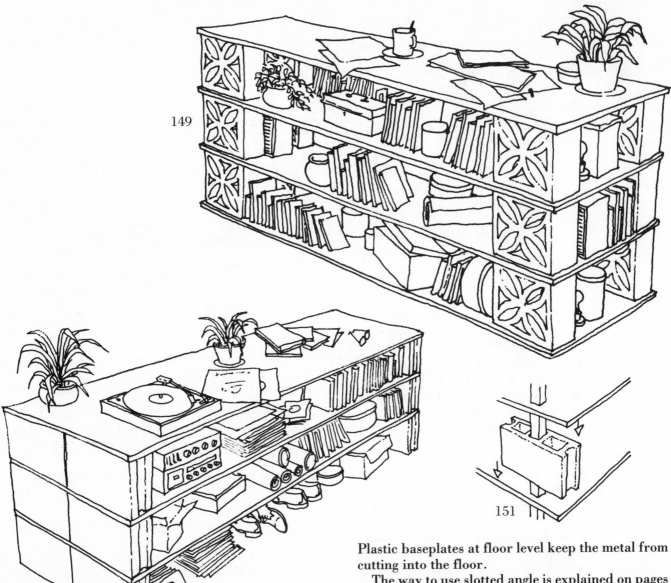

149

150

151

The most common use of slotted angle is to build racks of shelves. In each case shown here the corner uprights are fixed with the angle of the L turned outward. This is both strong and neat.

Plastic baseplates at floor level keep the metal from cutting into the floor.

The way to use slotted angle is explained on pages 216–217, where various special fittings are also shown. Basically, you start by sketching your design, calculating sizes and showing which way flanges will face. When something is to fit snugly in the frame, such as the crates in Figure 152, allow for the thickness of shelves and angle. Cut the pieces to length using a hacksaw, file rough ends smooth, and bolt the pieces together.

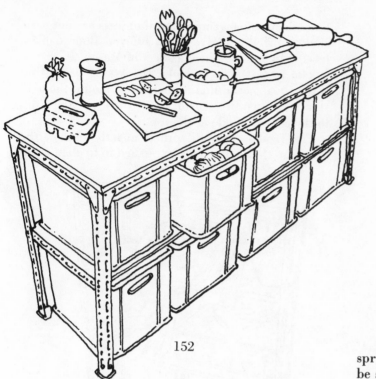

152

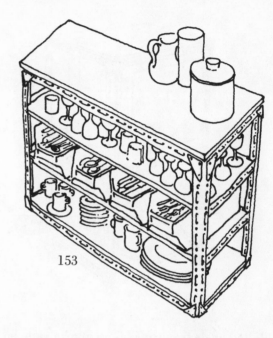

153

The shelves and tops in all schemes shown are ¾ inch (20 mm) white laminated chipboard, which looks good against the metal frames. Lumbercore and plywood are suitable substitutes. Metal shelves can be supplied by the manufacturers. Cut tops to overlap the frame by about 1 inch (25 mm) all around.

Horizontal angle beams support the shelves and are normally bolted on all four sides. Slotted angle is not cheap, so economical use is important. Horizontal beams are therefore omitted from the front in the systems illustrated, where spans are short and loads light. If shelves start to sag under their load, simply bolt on a front beam.

The manufacturers' literature gives details of acceptable loads, plus information on the fittings made to exploit the system's possibilities.

Serviceable secondhand angle can be bought cheap at auctions when shops or warehouses close down and their contents are dismantled. Touch-up spray paint in the standard light or dark gray can be supplied by the manufacturers of some systems to smarten up scratched old angle. Bright colors can enliven the system's looks. Assemble the units before you paint them. On bare metal paint on a coat of metal primer and cover this with two coats of enamel.

The worktop on the kitchen unit in Figure 152 is held to the frame on each long side by four ¾ inch (20 mm) roundhead screws driven up through the angle. Similar screws hold the tops in the other schemes.

The open shelving system in Figure 153 is also for kitchen use, with plastic trays from an industrial storage system holding cutlery and gadgets.

The television is placed on its shelf in the box (Fig. 154) before the top horizontal beams are bolted in place. In this way the frame can be made to grip it firmly enough to avoid tumbles when the mobile stand is rolled around the room on its four swivel castors, designed for the system.

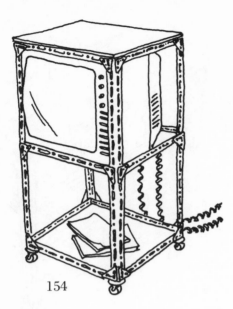

154

Smooth running is important if objects are not to be shaken off the shelves—an uneven floor can be leveled by nailing down a sheet of Masonite.

The fastest way to make the system is to find three cheap secondhand bookcases, mount them on standard furniture castors and then saw the sides to the correct angle at the top.

The front-to-back depth is exactly that of the stairs, so the shelves can be pushed in to align auto-

Slotted angle frame makes an appropriate home for hi-fi (Fig. 155). Construct the full-height rear rack first. Then either build the front section as a second, completely independent, box and bolt it to the first, or use cleats cut with a hacksaw from a length of the same angle (see p. 117) to join on the horizontals for the front extension.

The shelving system in Figure 156 is similar to the Figure 153 design, but here rectangles of chipboard are cut to fit inside the frame between the shelves at one end to act as bookends. No fixing should be needed for these. If the unit is to take very heavy loads, bolt on a diagonal cross-bracing beam across the back.

Under-stairs space is often underused space. Fit a light in a gloomy recess under the stairs and you can use the area as a small office or telephone booth with its own desk, chair, and phone. The scheme illustrated in Figure 157 uses rolling shelves to provide accessible storage space in an otherwise dead area.

The rolling shelves are shelving units on castors, built to push in flush with an under-stair surround.

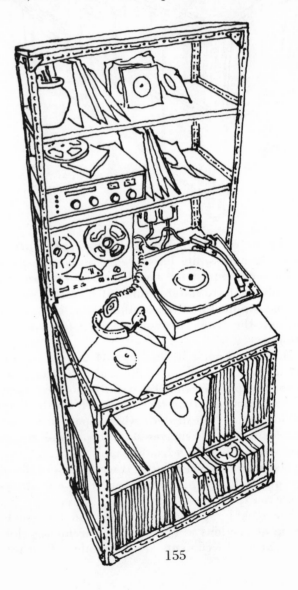

155

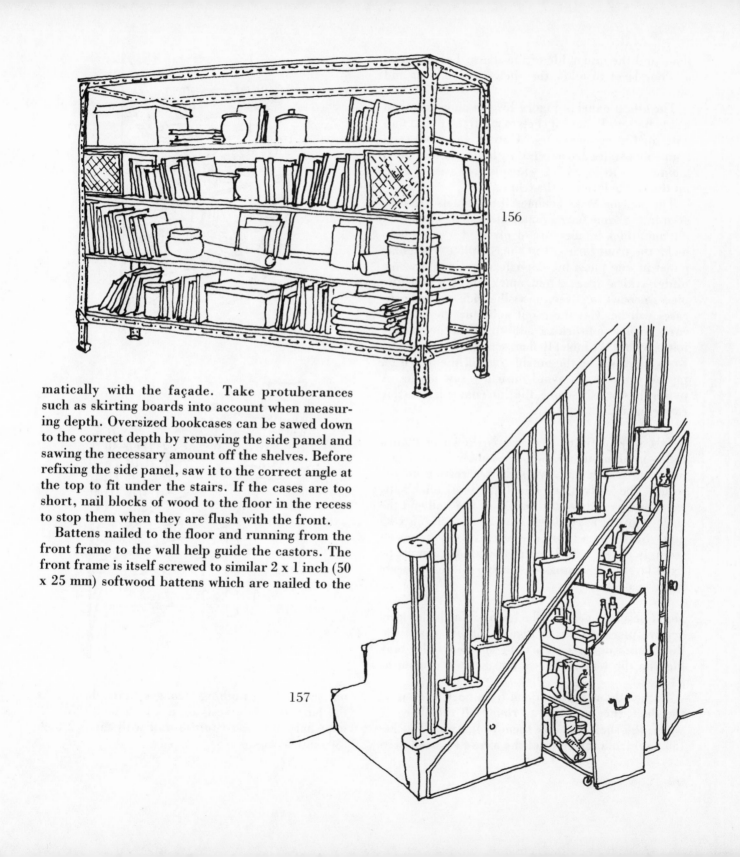

156

matically with the façade. Take protuberances
such as skirting boards into account when measuring depth. Oversized bookcases can be sawed down
to the correct depth by removing the side panel and
sawing the necessary amount off the shelves. Before
refixing the side panel, saw it to the correct angle at
the top to fit under the stairs. If the cases are too
short, nail blocks of wood to the floor in the recess
to stop them when they are flush with the front.

Battens nailed to the floor and running from the
front frame to the wall help guide the castors. The
front frame is itself screwed to similar 2 x 1 inch (50
x 25 mm) softwood battens which are nailed to the

157

floor and the underside of the stairs. Leave spaces at floor level to allow the shelves to slide in and out.

The tallest panel in Figure 157 is a door hinged to a side batten. Behind it shelves are fixed to the wall with ordinary brackets. Untidy gaps between frame and stairs are covered by half-round wooden molding (as in Fig. 157), which is also used to even up the frame levels at the front.

The scheme looks smarter if all panels are covered in the same facing material. A sheet of ¾ inch (20 mm) thick lumbercore or plywood is suitable to make the front facing. Cut the complete triangular panel in one piece big enough to cover the whole under-stairs area. Then mark on it where the pieces needed to cover the visible side of the bookcases will be. Cut these out and glue them to the cases with woodworking adhesive, reinforcing the joints with a 1½ inch (40 mm) screw in each corner. Keep what will be the outside face of the board on top as you saw, to avoid unsightly saw marks. A power jigsaw will make the internal angles a lot easier to cut.

A fast way of filling a recess is shown in Figure 158—an aluminum or wooden ladder leans diagonally across the gap, with shelves resting on the rungs. The shelves are 1 inch (25 mm) thick softwood and as wide as the rungs. At the wall end the shelves are screwed down onto 2 x 1 inch (50 x 25 mm) battens, which are themselves screwed securely to the wall. Each of these battens must be fixed level with a rung—use a spirit level to locate them accurately.

Metal brackets need not be boring. The highly decorative pierced pair in Figure 159 are cast iron; they once supported an old-fashioned toilet tank high on the wall and were bought at a demolition site.

Rather than running them from back to front of the shelf, they are used to round off the alcove in which the shelf sits. Fix them to the wall 2 inches (50 mm) from the front of the alcove to avoid driv-

158

159

ing screws into nothing stronger than plaster. At the back the shelf rests on a 1 x ½ inch (25 x 12 mm) batten screwed to the wall with three 2 inch (50 mm) screws.

Under-shelf surfaces are another underexploited storage space. Six ways of using them are shown in Figures 160–166.

Photographic baths slide on metal runners screwed under the shelf in Figure 160.

In Figure 161 jars hang from their lids, which are fixed to the shelf above by a pair of screws.

The net in Figure 162 is looped over cup hooks screwed into the shelf.

A pair of drawer handles are screwed to the front and back of the shelf in Figure 163. Leather belts run through the handles to strap blankets in position. A four-way elastic "spider" does the same job in Figure 164—it is hooked over four cup hooks screwed at least ¾ inch (20 mm) into the shelf.

Pans for baking bread are used to store odds and ends in Figure 165. They hang from runners screwed to the shelf above as in Figure 166.

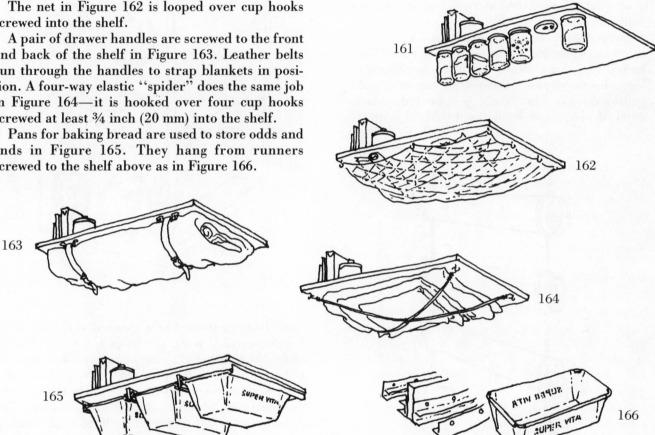

Cardboard tubes make decorative storage units. Figure 167 shows a suspended group of six 3 inch (75 mm) diameter cardboard tubes, 18 inches (450 mm) long, used to store maps, posters, and papers.

The tubes are linked simply by cord tied onto wooden or metal rings pushed over each end of the tubes. Large old-fashioned curtain rings are suitable; if no rings can be found, twist coat hangers to shape. Careful tying is needed to keep the cords at each end of a tube equal in length.

Alternatively, use double lengths of cord at each side, with the tubes set between them. Above and below each tube twist wire tight around the two cords using a pair of pliers. Two pieces of nylon cord can be joined by melting them together.

At the top the cords are tied to cup hooks screwed firmly into the ceiling—at least 1 inch (25 mm) of screw thread will normally be needed to pass through the ceiling's weak plaster and into solid lumber.

In a variation on the Figure 167 system, the tubes could be mounted between two layers of fabric to form an excellent hanging partition screen. The six tubes in Figure 167 would need a piece of fabric 15 inches (375 mm) wide and 100 inches (2500 mm) long plus the distance between the top tube and the ceiling hooks. The fabric is folded double and stitched above and below each tube. A 3 inch (75

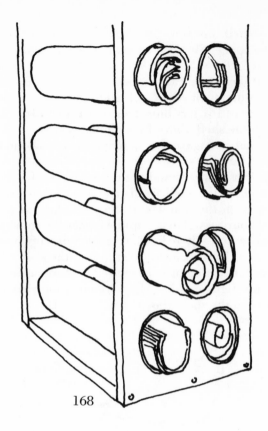

168

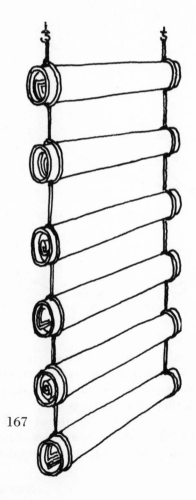

167

mm) diameter tube has a circumference of about 9½ inches (235 mm), so the twin rows of stitches should be 5 inches (125 mm) apart to allow the tube to be pushed into the gap. One inch (25 mm) from the top punch a pair of brass eyelets through the double layer of fabric to take the hooks. The punching tool and eyelets are sold by craft shops.

The tubular magazine rack in Figure 168 is made from ½ inch (12 mm) lumbercore 12 inches (300 mm) wide. Cardboard tubes 12 inches (300 mm) long and 3 inches (75 mm) in diameter are mounted in double rows with 2 inch (50 mm) gaps between rows and between the tubes in each row.

Mount as many rows as you like. For the four rows shown the sides are 22 inches (550 mm) high. They are butted to the top and bottom pieces, which are 11 inches (275 mm) long, by three 1½ inch (40 mm) screws at each joint. A smear of woodworking adhesive strengthens the joints.

Before assembling the frame, cut out the holes. To do this, mark the positions by holding a tube against one of the side pieces and penciling around it. Clamp the two side pieces together and cut through both using a power jigsaw.

Assembly can of course be completely avoided by using a ready-made wooden crate. Wine and fish travel in suitably strong containers, but the smell of fish can be even stronger than its box.

Tubes and pipes make admirable bottle storage. The seven 4 inch (100 mm) diameter cardboard tubes in Figure 169 are joined together with threaded metal rods running through them at 14 inch (350 mm) intervals, with a nut to secure the rods at each end.

Mark out the shapes with a pencil; the bottom of each cutout will be 1 inch (25 mm) above a rod, with the top 3 inches (75 mm) below the rod above (see Fig. 170). Use a sharp cutting knife or saw to cut through the cardboard.

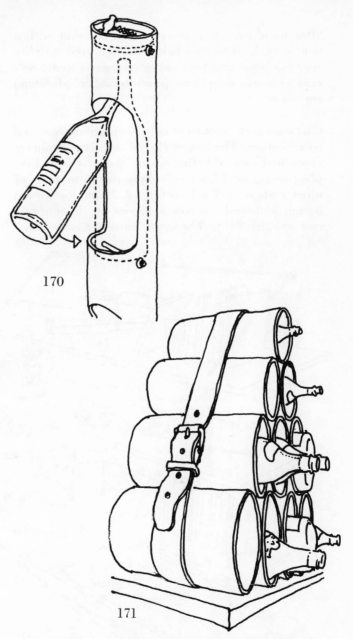

170

171

The system rests on the floor and is fixed to the wall behind by four 1½ inch (40 mm) screws driven through the back of the tubes.

The pile of 12 inch (300 mm) long plastic pipe in Figure 171 is made of scraps of drainpipe left over

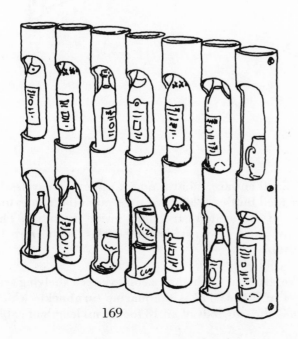

169

after building. They are strapped together with a tightly buckled leather belt. For improved stability glue the pipes together using styrene cement. Solvent adhesive for plastic pipes is sold by plumbing suppliers.

Cast iron and cardboard can be an unhappy visual combination. The baked clay of ordinary drainage pipes looks more fitting inside the cast iron fireplace in Figure 172. The front of the bottom row of pipes rests on a 2 x 1 inch (50 x 25 mm) softwood batten hollowed out with a jigsaw or shaping tool (see pp. 207–210). The upper rows are loose-laid.

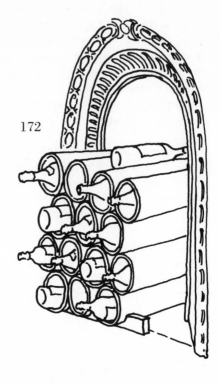

172

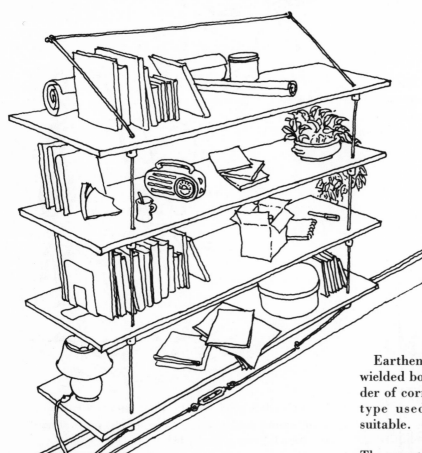

173

Earthenware is hard, and it can crack carelessly wielded bottles. For extra protection insert a cylinder of corrugated cardboard inside the tubes. The type used to wrap wine bottles is eminently suitable.

The secret of the high-tension/low-tech shelving system in Figure 173 is the marine turnbuckle which links the two ends of an 18 foot (6 m) length of cable and stretches it taut. Turnbuckles can be bought from marine suppliers.

The cable is threaded through holes drilled 6 inches (150 mm) from each end of the four 48 inch (1200 mm) long 12 x 1 inch (300 x 25 mm) planks. At each corner the cable is looped over a stout 3 inch (75 mm) hook driven into the wall.

The wall edge of each shelf is supported by three ½ inch (12 mm) diameter dowels hammered 1½ inches (40 mm) into wall plugs and into ½ inch (12 mm) diameter holes drilled in the shelf (Fig. 174).

A metal bush complete with its own turnbuckle is threaded onto the cable and tightened up to support the front edge of the shelf at each end (Fig. 175).

The free-hanging variation in Figure 176 is constructed from the same elements but without the wall fixtures. It is suspended from a joist in the ceiling by two strong hooks, with eyes at each corner screwed into the floor. The system makes a quickly mounted room divider.

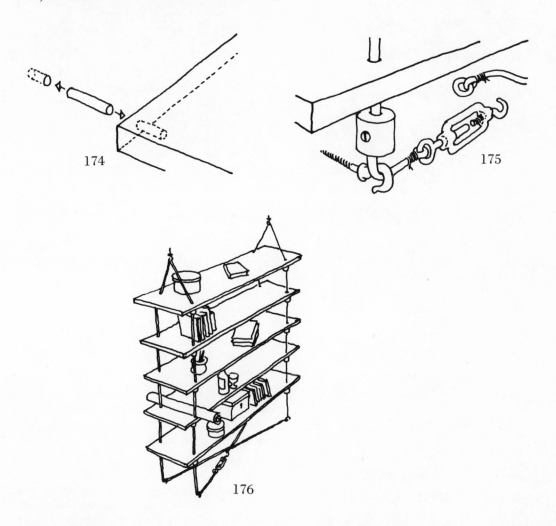

174

175

176

BEDS

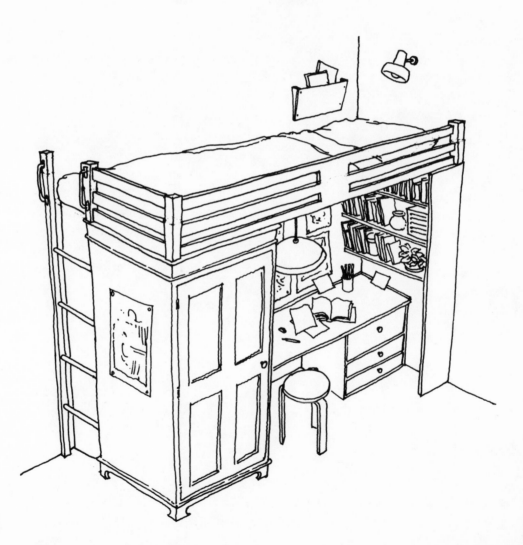

Gain floor and storage space in small rooms by raising the bed. The appeal of a raised bed increases with the height of the ceiling. If you want to avoid being one of those things that go bump in the night, make sure your bed is firmly fixed, and always fit strong safety rails around children's beds.

The bed in Figure 177 is an ordinary 39 x 79 inch (1000 x 2000 mm) base supported 60 inches (1500 mm) from the floor by battens fixed to the walls on two sides and on the third side by a shaped façade cut from two 36 x 84 inch (915 x 2135 mm) sheets of 1 inch (25 mm) lumbercore. Lumbercore is strong and it can be cut into shape for the 69 inch (1750 mm) high fascia with a power jigsaw. Use what you have cut out of the sheets when making the two halves of the fascia to cut extra shelves for the end fill-in.

Alternatively, rest the foot of the bed on a chest of drawers. The chest can be raised to the right height on a box platform underneath.

The long wall side of the bed rests on a strong piece of 4 x 2 inch (100 x 50 mm) softwood, as long as the bed. This is fixed to the wall 60 inches (1500 mm) from the floor by screws or bolts driven through predrilled holes. In a brick wall use three 4 inch (100 mm) expanding bolts. If the wall has a wooden frame, it is vital that screws be driven into the wooden uprights and not merely into plaster. Use a spirit level to avoid sleeping on a sloping bed.

A similar beam is cut to the width of the bed less 2 inches (50 mm) and fixed to the wall by two bolts (for brick) or screws (for wood) at the head of the bed.

A sound section of an old ladder provides access to the bed. Physical and psychological security is improved if the top of the ladder projects above bed level. If a child is going to sleep in the bed, the side panel should be raised, with a safety rail spanning the gap at the foot of the bed. Both the ladder's feet are held to the floor by 3 inch (75 mm) L-shaped brackets. Screws are driven through one of the ladder uprights and into the wall at 18 inch (450 mm) intervals. Another L-shaped bracket connects the ladder's other upright to a third hori-

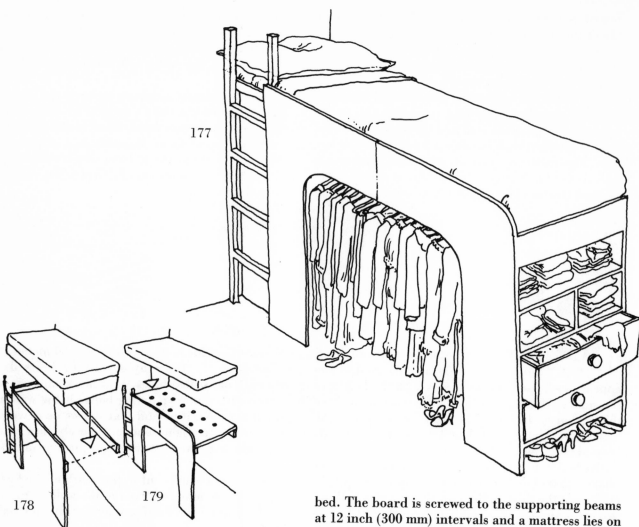

177

178

179

zontal beam of 4 x 2 inch (100 x 50 mm) lumber, which will support the long outside edge of the bed. This is also screwed to the lumbercore panels, at the same height as the other two supports. At ground level the panels are screwed to battens fixed to the floor.

An alternative to the divan base (Fig. 178) is a rigid board of 1 inch (25 mm) lumbercore, drilled with 1 inch (25 mm) diameter holes for ventilation (Fig. 179). A dozen holes should ventilate a single

bed. The board is screwed to the supporting beams at 12 inch (300 mm) intervals and a mattress lies on top.

The clothes in Figure 177 hang from a rail 54 inches (1400 mm) from the ground fixed to end sockets in the wall and the back of the chest.

In Figure 180 the bed creates a useful work space underneath. The platform rests on an old wardrobe. Beware—old cupboards are often unstable. Screwing additional shelves inside the wardrobe helps stop any wobbling, and removal of the wardrobe's plinth and decorative top improves rigidity. In similar fashion the bookshelves under the headboard provide reinforcement. If doubts remain about the stability, run a reinforcing piece of 3 x 3 inch (75 x 75 mm) lumber from floor to top inside the cupboard at the nearest corner in Figure 180, and fix this securely to the floor.

In Figure 180 horizontal beams fixed firmly to the wall support the bed on two sides. An access ladder is bolted to the wall and the back of the cupboard, and two grab handles are bolted to the ladder. The mattress rests on the same lumbercore base as used in Figure 179, but here it is screwed to an underframe of 2 x 2 inch (50 x 50 mm) softwood,

strengthened at the corners with wood blocks glued and screwed inside each corner. One corner of the underframe rests on the wardrobe, and two sides are held to the walls with expanding bolts (Fig. 181).

The addition of a canopy converts the idea into a fantasy bed for a child's room (Fig. 182). The fabric runs on curtain track fixed to the ceiling. The entrance is cut from Masonite and attached with Masonite nails to the ladder, which extends up to the ceiling. The addition of a firm safety rail is vital in a child's room.

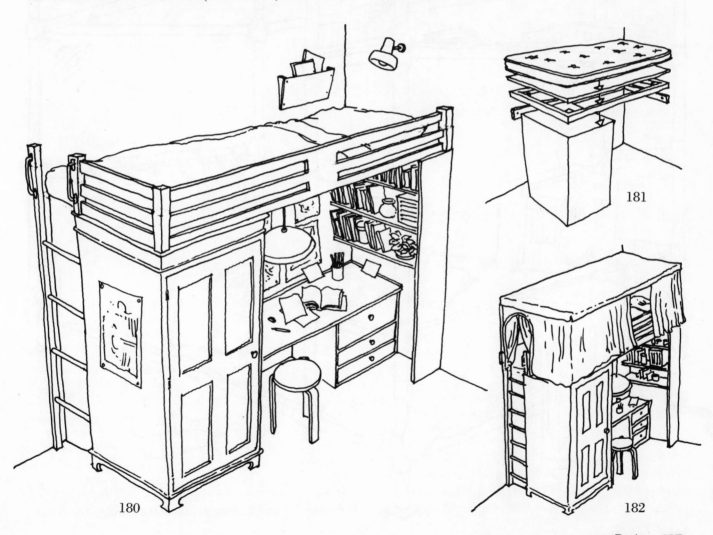

180

181

182

The versatile industrial four-poster in Figure 183 has space for both sleeping and storage. Clamp on as much or as little as you like, then change it at will, adding another bed on top or curtaining off a section as hidden storage space.

The system could be built from the construction industry's hefty scaffolding, sold in 252 inch (6400 mm) lengths, or from the scaffolding systems sold to home improvers, which may be more useful afterward. Whichever system you use, don't join the lengths with crude and sharp industrial clamps; the neat ones in Figure 183 need no bolts. New scaffold is surprisingly expensive. You can buy old lengths from a scaffolding contractor or at an auction of a bankrupt builder's stock. Paint improves dirty scaffold. On stainless steel use a zinc phosphate primer.

Some tubes come galvanized for protection. To paint over zinc galvanizing you need a calcium plumbate primer, otherwise the paint won't stick for long.

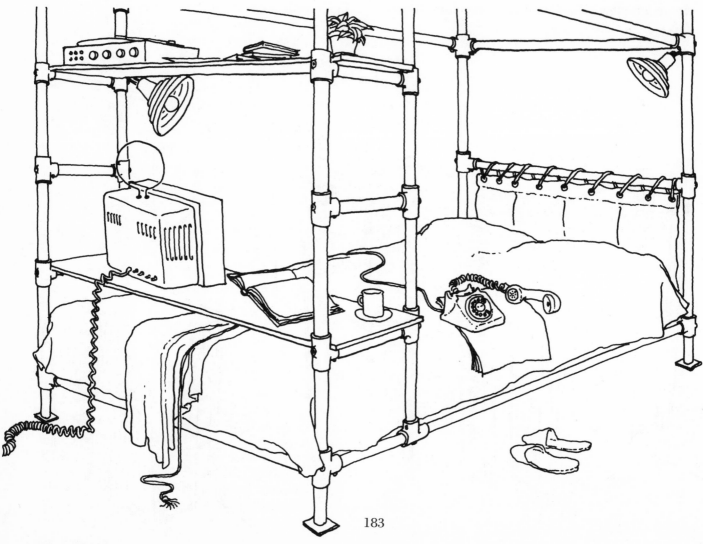

183

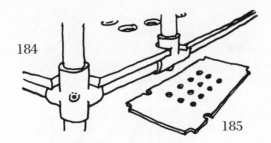

184

185

Remove any grease and rust before you start painting, and top the primer with an undercoat and gloss finish.

The corners of the structure rest on purpose-made plates with their central spike housed in the tube. The mattress rests on planks spanning the frame or on a sheet of ¾ inch (19 mm) lumbercore cut to fit around the scaffold fittings (Figs. 184 and 185). Lumbercore needs an extra central cross-piece of scaffold to support it and ventilation holes drilled at 6 inch (150 mm) centers.

In Figure 183 we show a canvas-covered padded cushion which acts as a headboard. Fold the canvas in half, turn under 2 inch (50 mm) hems at the open ends and sew seams ½ inch (10 mm) and 1½ inches (40 mm) from the edge of both the top and bottom of the cushion. Punch with eyelets bought from a marine supply store or craft shop and lace the cushion to the scaffold tubes top and bottom, using nylon cord from the same store. The hard headboard can be softened by covering it in a foam pipe-insulation collar.

Chromium-plated galvanized scaffolding looks fine but costs a lot, because the galvanizing has to be removed before plating can start. Stainless steel tube can be professionally polished. Steel scaffolding has been available throughout this century; aluminum is a more recent arrival on site. Plumbing

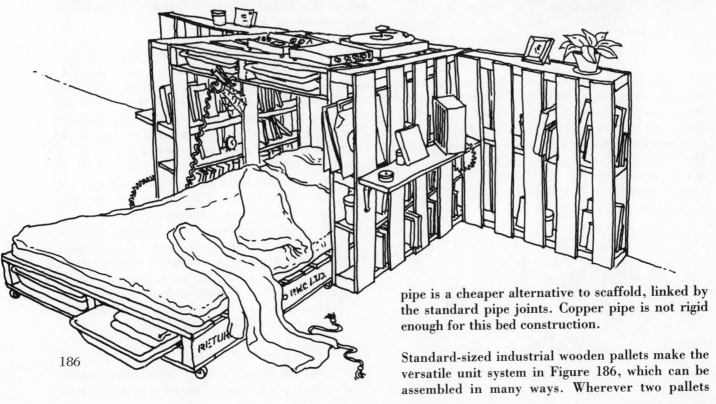

186

pipe is a cheaper alternative to scaffold, linked by the standard pipe joints. Copper pipe is not rigid enough for this bed construction.

Standard-sized industrial wooden pallets make the versatile unit system in Figure 186, which can be assembled in many ways. Wherever two pallets meet they are held together by two bolts through drilled holes. Figures 186 and 187 show some optional refinements—a shelf bracketed to one of the pallets; other shelves slipped inside the pallets and held by nails knocked through the outer planks; trays for storage; castors attached to the pallet for a roll-out bed; a lamp clamped to the overhead pallet (Fig. 188).

The pallets' rough wood can be sanded or planed smooth and stained or painted with a wood primer and gloss.

Pallets are a common street find. Firms listed in the *Yellow Pages* under "Racks—Industrial" supply new pallets. Some also sell secondhand and renovated pallets.

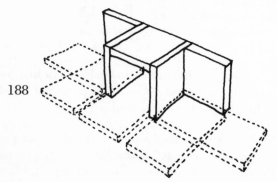

187

A length of fabric turns a tedious and exposed bed into an intimate retreat. In Figure 189 fabric creates a cozy instant guest room under the eaves. The front curtain hangs from a standard curtain pole held by center support brackets to the ceiling. The edge of the triangular curtain is held against the sloping ceiling by a ½ inch (15 mm) square wooden batten screwed into the ceiling. A cord is pinned between curtain and wall. Its two ends are

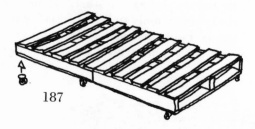

188

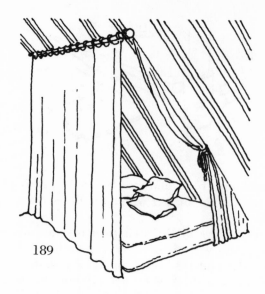

189

tied together to hold the drape back. Both the open side of the curtain and its bottom edge are hemmed to prevent fraying.

A canopy has been a high-powered status symbol for centuries, used by medieval monarchs on state occasions. It is a simple matter to boost your own status by making one for yourself. One end of the fabric for the scheme in Figure 190 is turned under 1 inch (25 mm) and stapled or pinned to the baseboard behind the bed. At the top it runs over a pole fixed to the wall by center support brackets near each end. A steel pipe or even a car bumper could replace the standard brass or wooden curtain pole on a strong wall. A second pole is fixed securely to the ceiling over the bed—make sure the screws bite into something solid behind the plaster. Two or three staples hold the fabric in position on the rail. The fabric can either hang loose or be stretched tight. For a medieval look cut the hanging end into a scalloped pattern (Fig. 191) and trim the edge with tape or use pinking shears.

Fabric dramatizes a drab bed in a dull room. In Figure 192 the three pieces of fabric are all gathered at the top into drapes, hemmed at the bottom,

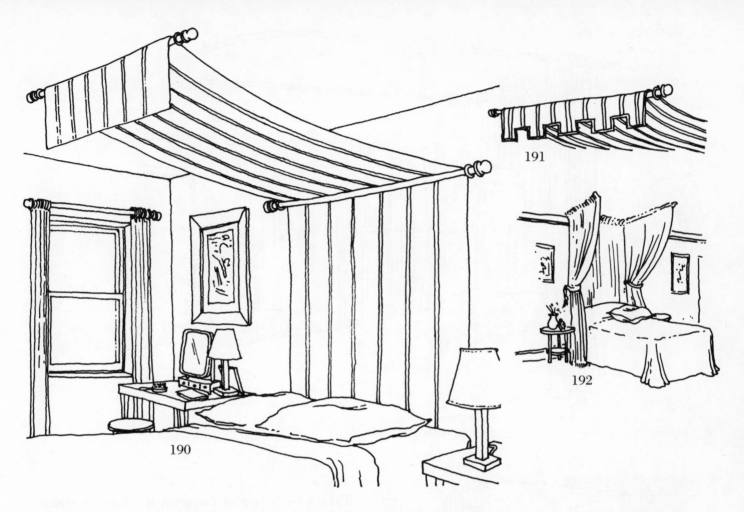

191

192

190

and hung on three separate lengths of curtain track. Make the curtains half as long again as the rail so they hang in drapes. Heavy curtains hang best. If they do not hang well, put lead shot in the hem. At the head of the bed the fabric is pinned or stapled to the baseboard. At each side of the bed the fabric is held back by a cord pinned to the wall. A strong attachment is needed to hold the fabric's weight.

In Figure 193 the curtains at each side screen the bed. Flexible plastic track bends around the foot of the bed and is fixed to the ceiling with the standard fittings. Screws should be driven into solid lumber. A ceiling track from a hospital cubicle is suitable and is being used with regularity to partition large spaces.

When drapes are drawn back they can be left hanging loose or tied back to the wall. Instead of tying them with the traditional bowed cord use a webbing belt or a studded waistband from a worn-out pair of jeans, fixed to the wall through the middle.

These schemes bring an instant improvement but they need long pieces of fabric, which can cost a lot. A cheap alternative is a roll of fire- or flood-damaged fabric. Bankruptcies are common in the rag trade, and unused rolls of material are auctioned off by the liquidators.

193

Take a fresh look at forgotten furniture—certain items make fine headboards. A kitchen wall cupboard or the top section of a cheap phony antique dresser could be suitable for conversion. A coat of black or metallic enamel paint can turn these grotesque pieces into very dramatic headboards. Do not attach the new headboard to the bed; screw it securely to the wall using mirror fittings.

Overmantel mirrors, designed to dominate the fireside in old homes, are suitable for conversion into bright headboards (Fig. 194). Many nineteenth-century models were made a suitable width to span a 39 inch (1000 mm) single bed. The buyer's choice usually lies between polished mahogany and cheaper pine covered with gilded plaster.

Paint rejuvenates tatty gilded frames; you can buy the right gilding material at an artists' supplies store. Remove badly damaged plaster and varnish the pine underframe or polish it with furniture wax. Immersion in water softens plaster, which can then be removed with fine steel wool.

When the mirror surface peels with age and damp, the glass looks dowdy and reflects poorly. Resilvering a dull mirror is usually too expensive, although it's worth considering for a mirror with nicely beveled edges. Peeling mirrors are sold cheap in junk shops and auctions. Plain replacement mirror glass can be bought, but the wisest course is simply to remove the mirror glass, which could be smashed by violent sleepers. Replace it with a polished metal sheet.

No sharp edges lurk in the soft pillows shown in Figure 195. Sewn inside fabric pockets, they hang from an old wooden curtain pole fixed to the wall by its original brackets. A long handle from a broom or hayfork would make a suitably stout substitute for the pole.

Convert pillowcases into pockets simply by unstitching 2 inches (50 mm) of the pillow's closed end to allow the pole to pass through. Oversew the opening to prevent tears. For a stronger finish sew a double row of stitches 2 inches (50 mm) from what will be the top of the case.

Pockets are also easy to make from scratch. The fabric should be long enough to fit around the pillow, with a further 5 inches (125 mm) to slide over a 1 inch (25 mm) diameter pole. A piece 27 x 40 inches (700 x 1000 mm) should suffice.

Fold over the top 2½ inches (60 mm); fold fabric double from the bottom to overlap the top fold by ½ inch (10 mm) with the end turned ½ inch (10

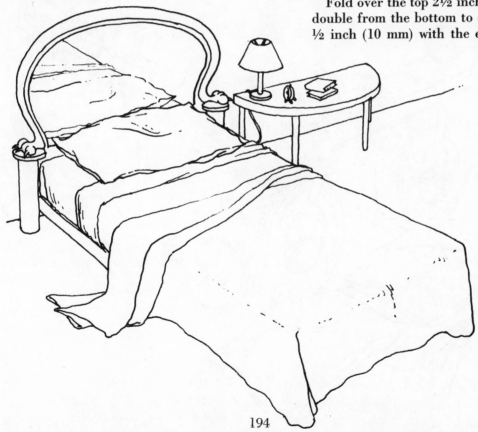

194

195

196

197

198

mm) under. Now sew two rows through all folds to create the top loop.

The scalloped edge is optional. Cut out two 3½ inch (90 mm) deep pieces from one end of the fabric; continue the cuts a further 1 inch (25 mm) into the fabric and fold the flaps created over (see Fig. 196) to prevent the cut edge from fraying. Sew up as before.

The car lover's headboard in Figure 197 combines fantasy and practicality. The twin tires are soft enough for comfort, and the inside is a handy space for bedside books. A wreckers' yard provided the tires, the seat belts which support them, and the chrome-plated bumper from which they hang. Use the brackets fitted to the bumper by the manufacturer to hold it to the wall. On most models a bolt can be passed through both the bumper bracket and a metal bracket fixed to the wall. Firm fixing is needed to hold the considerable weight. The ½ inch (10 mm) ply shelf was cut to shape and laid on the brackets.

Figure 198 shows a checkered cover made to fit around a pillow. It has a 2 inch (50 mm) wide seam through which eyelets are driven at 4 inch (100 mm) intervals. Use nylon cord to hang the pillow from the bumper.

A wooden base for a bed can be transformed with a covering of carpet or matting matching that on the floor (Fig. 199). Any legs or castors are removed to let the wooden base sit directly on the floor. Carpet is then run up the three exposed sides of the bed. It

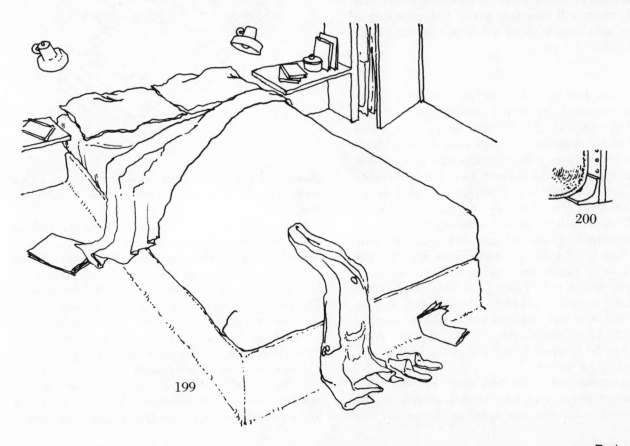

199

200

is simply tacked to the wooden frame both on the top and around the base where bed and floor meet. As such schemes reduce ventilation under the bed, the mattress should be removed for airing from time to time.

In ready-carpeted rooms, mark the base's position on the floor and use a sharp cutting knife to make two cuts in the carpet as long as the sides of the bed, allowing a 4 inch (100 mm) overlap on top. Part of the remaining central strip of carpet is cut out and used to cover the end of the base, once again overlapping by 4 inches (100 mm).

To round off the junction of floor and base, pin a strip of 2 x 2 inch (50 x 50 mm) cove wooden molding (see Fig. 200) around the frame at floor level; miter the corners at 45° for a neat appearance.

The mattress is simply placed on top to complete the structure. Loose tacks can scratch sheets and hands; many will therefore prefer to fix the carpet on top with double-sided adhesive tape or Velcro hook-and-loop tape.

Improvised bed bases benefit from similar disguise behind carpet. Wrap carpet around a base of plastic drink crates which have been strapped or bolted together. Use carpet to cover loose-laid concrete blocks topped with a sheet of Masonite or plywood. Lay carpet over old railway ties, but remember these are horribly heavy objects to move to an upstairs bedroom. Girders (Fig. 201) or bricks (Fig. 202) are other possible base materials.

The girder bed base in Figure 201 is simply a pair of 78 inch (2000 mm) long rolled steel joists bought from a scrap metal yard, laid parallel on the floor, and spanned by nine 7 inch (175 mm) floorboards. When the carpet is tacked to all the boards at both sides, the structure becomes stable without further support. As an alternative to tacks, spiked carpet grips can be screwed to the top of the boards and hooked to the carpet.

Leaving the end of the bed uncovered simplifies the carpet laying and creates storage space. The twin trays occupying this space in Figure 201 are

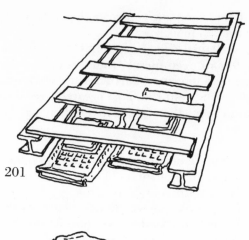

201

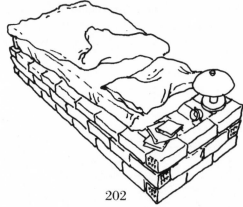

202

plastic bakery trays which come ready-fitted with a useful handle. These are merely pushed under the bed.

Figure 203 shows a further refinement, with an under-bed storage cart running on tracks. If you cannot find a suitable drawer—those from old display units in menswear stores are fine—make your own from ¾ inch (20 mm) laminated chipboard. The parts are cut to shape using a jigsaw, butted together and glued and nailed. Finally, a handle is screwed on the front. To see how a simple box is made, look at a wooden wine crate or fruit box.

The wheels could be salvaged from an abandoned toy wagon, as in the drawing. Furniture castors work just as well. If wheels are used, fix the track to the floor by screws; countersink the heads below

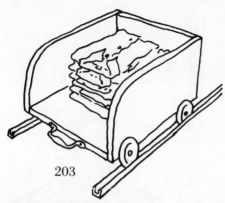

203

the surface to allow free running. The wheels can run in U-shaped aluminum, wood, or plastic track; shelf runners or double-glazing frames are suitable.

Figure 204 illustrates a grander, two-tier version of the carpeting scheme, featuring a combination of the factory-built divan base and homemade improvised framework.

Upturned wooden crates—plastic crates, concrete blocks, bricks, sleepers, or girders would also do the job—are placed under three sides of the bed, overlapping the bed on all three sides by 12 inches (300 mm). Nine floorboards 7 x 1 inch (175 x 25 mm) span the gap between the crates as in Figure 201. The divan base is placed on this framework. Carpet is then run up both plinth and divan and tacked in position on top of the divan frame, where base and plinth meet and at floor level. Cove molding is again used to soften the junctions (see Fig. 200). The carpeted step makes a useful bedside seat or shelf.

If you run out of carpet for the front piece, the front can be clad in tongue-and-groove lumber or open slats, which also improves ventilation. The inventive may like odd alternatives to a traditional

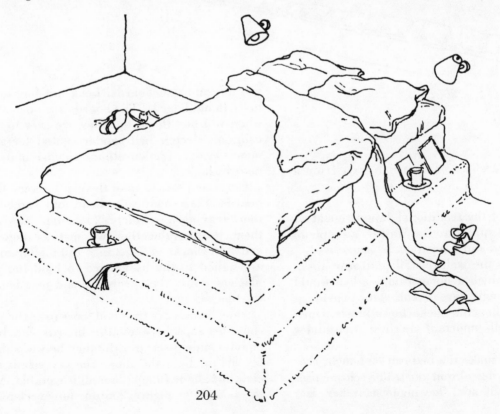

204

205

206

carpet, such as a sheet of artificial grass from a market supplier.

The popularity of the traditional Japanese slatted platform bed has spread to the West. It's simple to build, it's healthy, and it need not be expensive.

In Figure 205 the wall-to-wall platform fills a small room, in which a normal double bed would look overwhelmingly large. The slats provide a firm base which benefits backache sufferers. Open slats also allow all-important air circulation under the mattress.

The lumber to make the bed can be bought economically from a demolition yard. The scheme uses 7 x 2 inch (175 x 50 mm) flooring joists (other sizes will do) and floorboards. Look out for woodworm holes in old boards. The boards are normally filthy when you buy them, but they are easy to clean up using an electric belt sander rented for an afternoon. A coat of polyurethane varnish improves the boards' looks.

Cut four joists to span the gap between the baseboards. Place one at the head and another at the foot, leaving a 78 inch (2000 mm) gap between them. Position the other two joists as shown in Figure 206. Blocks of 2 x 2 inch (50 x 50 mm) lumber are nailed to the baseboard to hold the joists in place (see Fig. 206). Only the end joist is nailed to the blocks.

Floorboards are first laid loose over the joists, so that the gaps between the boards can be made equal—slide a scrap of lumber between the floorboards to check the gaps. The gap size is not crucial, but about 1 inch (25 mm) is suitable. Although the boards in Figure 205 do not overlap the end joist, an overhang of some 6 inches (150 mm) is a useful variation. Another alternative is to make the bed in three free-standing sections. This allows access to the space under the bed for cleaning or to rescue dropped earrings. Boards are easier to remove and replace if they are held by screws rather than nails.

The open-ended bed in Figure 207 is also built from inexpensive lumber retrieved from the floors of a demolished building. The slats for the top are 66 inch (1700 mm) lengths of floorboard. The four longer boards at the head are 96 inches (2400 mm)

long. The boards in Figure 207 are 5 x 1 inch (125 x 25 mm); other sizes are suitable, but the number needed will vary with the size of the boards.

The boards are nailed onto five 90 inch (2250 mm) flooring joists, 6 x 2 inches (150 x 50 mm). First lay the two outer joists on the floor, parallel and 54 inches (1400 mm) apart. Lay a third joist exactly in the center and position the two remaining joists in the gaps. Check that all are parallel and nail the end floorboard in place using 2 inch (50 mm) oval nails, and overlapping the end by 2 inches (50 mm). Before nailing, coat the surfaces in woodworking adhesive to strengthen the joint. Hammer two nails into each joist.

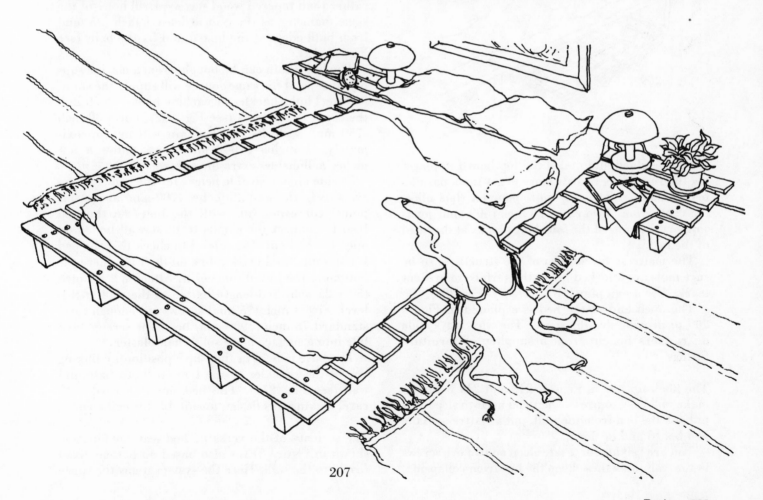

207

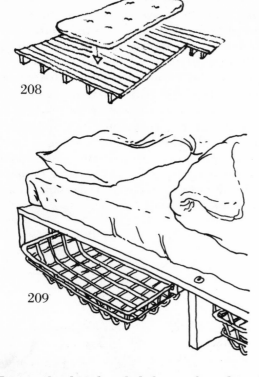

208

209

Having glued and nailed the top board in place, lay the remaining boards loose to get them parallel before nailing. The tiny gaps between slats allow for ventilation. Two extra 20 inch (500 mm) joists support the ends of the four long planks at the head of the bed.

The mattress lies on top of the structure, so be sure nails are knocked below the surface to prevent tears. Use a nail punch if necessary (Fig. 208).

The open end of the bed is exploited in Figure 209 to provide drawer space. The wire trays slide on runners bought from a supplier of furniture fittings.

The hook-up bed in Figures 210 and 211 is fast to make and easy to use—when you need to sleep just unhook the bed from the wall, put a mattress on the bed board and lie down.

You are relying for a safe sleep on two eye screws in the wall; only these keep the bed from collapsing, so the design is unsuitable in rooms without strong walls. Flimsy plasterboard partition walls are inadequate. In hollow walls the screws should be driven at least 2 inches (50 mm) into studs behind the plaster. You will therefore need 3 inch (75 mm) screws, without counting the length of the eye itself. In masonry walls drill a pilot hole and fit a wall plug for the screw to bite into.

The bed base is cut from a sheet of 1 inch (25 mm) thick plywood or lumbercore and is a maximum of 30 inches (750 mm) wide. Bolts are fitted to the two outside corners of the base to hold the two supporting chains, as in Figure 210. For security use eyebolts complete with nuts and washers, rather than tapered wood screws. Drill holes of the same diameter as the bolt at least 1 inch (25 mm) from both edges of the board and fix the bolts (see Figure 212).

The link chain can be bought from a marine supply store, and the same source will supply the stainless steel link shackles or carbine hooks which link the chain to the bolts (see Fig. 212). For a 30 inch (750 mm) wide bed each chain will be approximately 41 inches (1040 mm) long. Allow a few inches/millimeters extra for adjustment.

Decide on a desirable height for the bed. Fix two eyebolts in the wall 28 inches (700 mm) above this point, corresponding with the bolts on the bed board. Connect the chains to these wall bolts and open the bed out. Use a level to check that the bed is horizontal and mark a line on the wall where the bottom of the board touches it. Attach a 2 x 1 inch (50 x 25 mm) bed-length batten to the wall at this level. Five 3 inch (75 mm) screws are enough for a standard 75 inch (1900 mm) bed. The screws must bite into a surface more solid than plaster.

The base is held in the "up" position by linking one of the shackles to the bolts in both base and wall (see Fig. 211). The bed must be used with care, making this design unsuitable for children.

The security of the versatile bed/seat combination shown in Figure 213 is also based on battens fixed firmly to the wall. Here the system spans the space

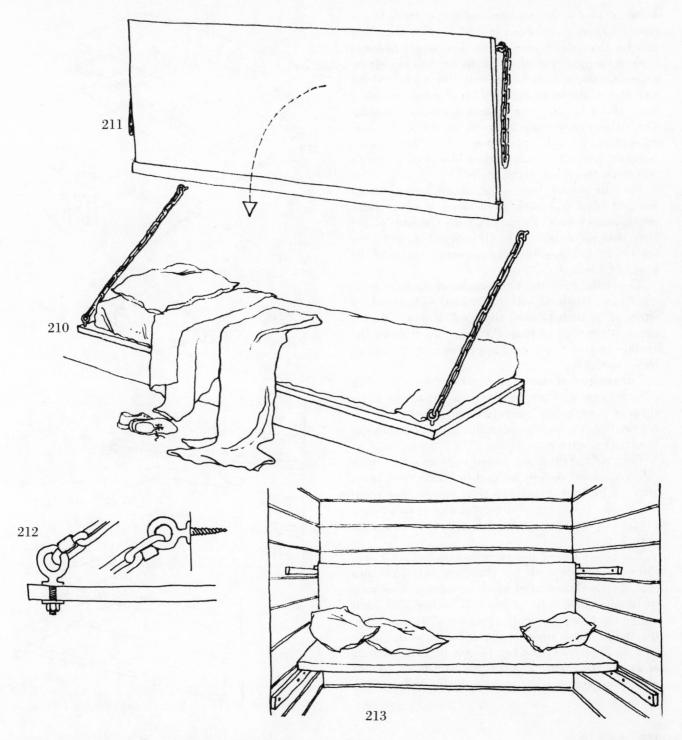

211

210

212

213

between two walls, maximizing the potential of a narrow room or a dead corridor. The structure can be changed in an instant. The single bed/seat becomes a pair of bunks or a double bed merely by moving a single board. The way the top board fits together is shown in Figure 214. The framework is built of 2 x 1 inch (50 x 25 mm) softwood. Its sides are as long as the gap between the walls, the four crosspieces 22 inches (560 mm). Avoid the need for complex joints by using corner blocks or brackets where pieces join at right angles.

For the upper board use glued and screwed wooden blocks at each joint to fix the two outer crosspieces 1 inch (25 mm) in from the ends of the long side pieces as in the drawing (Fig. 214). No such overlap is necessary in the construction of the lower bed board.

The surface for top and bottom of each frame is cut from a single 48 inch (1220 mm) wide standard sheet of ¼ inch (6 mm) plywood. Buy as short a sheet as possible to span the gap. Saw it down the middle to give two pieces approximately 24 inches (610 mm) wide.

Cut the two surfaces for the top frame 2 inches (50 mm) shorter than the gap to be spanned and fix them in place using 1 inch (25 mm) panel pins. For a neat finish a hardwood molding can be glued to the front of each board (Fig. 215).

Each side of the lower board rests on a 2 x 1 inch (50 x 25 mm) batten 48 inches (1220 mm) long, secured by four 3 inch (75 mm) screws. For security's sake take care to drive the screws into either plugged masonry or studs as in the previous design (Fig. 216).

The upper board also rests on a pair of 2 x 1 inch (50 x 25 mm) battens, but these are only 26 inches (650 mm) wide, secured by three screws. This pair of battens should be at least 27 inches (700 mm) above the other to create adequate clearance when the top board is used as a seat back, as in Figure 213. In Figure 217 the two boards lie flat as a pair of bunks. In Figure 218 the two boards are placed alongside each other to make a double bed.

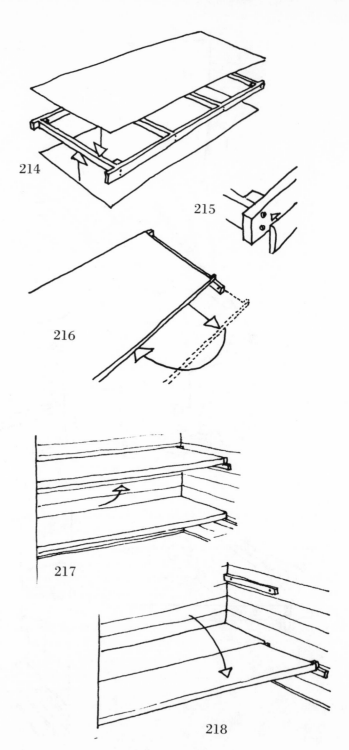

214

215

216

217

218

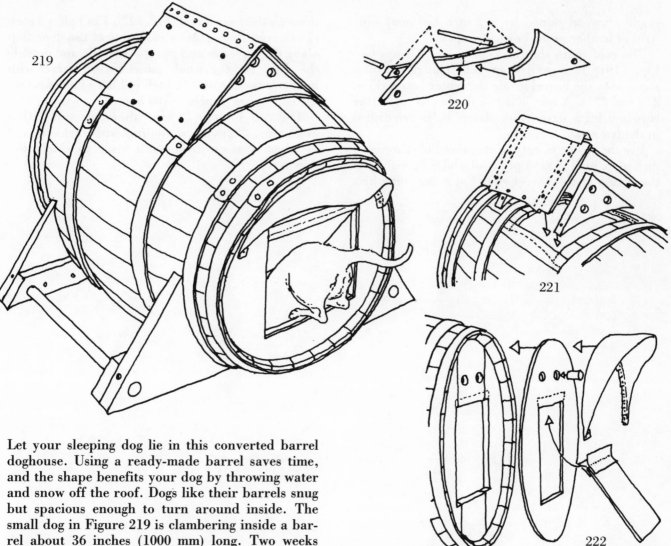

219

220

221

222

Let your sleeping dog lie in this converted barrel doghouse. Using a ready-made barrel saves time, and the shape benefits your dog by throwing water and snow off the roof. Dogs like their barrels snug but spacious enough to turn around inside. The small dog in Figure 219 is clambering inside a barrel about 36 inches (1000 mm) long. Two weeks before he moved in, the old barrel's odor was neutralized using creosote diluted with petroleum spirits.

The barrel sits in two cradles which keep it from rolling and lift it off damp ground. The curved ends (Fig. 220) are made from a piece of 9 x 1 inch (225 x 25 mm) softwood, shaped with a jigsaw or rasp. Get the right curve by tracing the shape of the barrel end and transferring this to the softwood via a sheet of carbon paper underneath the tracing paper. Use the same method later to mark out the

curves for the end pieces of the cupola on top and the door disk.

The curved pieces are glued and nailed to 3 x 1 inch (75 x 25 mm) battens. The two cradles are joined by 1 inch (25 mm) dowels glued into 1 inch (25 mm) diameter holes in the battens and secured by a nail (Figs. 219 and 220).

The cupola (Fig. 221) provides ventilation. Its roof is two pieces of ¼ inch (6 mm) thick exterior grade plywood joined by a 2 inch (50 mm) wide strip of leather pinned over the apex.

The roof spans the two central metal hoops (see Fig. 219). It is nailed to two triangular sides screwed to the barrel inside the center hoops (Figs. 219 and 221). A hole is cut in the barrel under the cupola using a jigsaw. Ventilation holes are drilled in the triangular sides.

Use the jigsaw to cut the entrance hole through a disk of ¼ inch (6 mm) plywood which fits tightly in the recess at the barrel end. Cut a matching hole through the barrel end (Fig. 222). Pin half a 3 inch (75 mm) leather strip on each side of the door flap along the top edge and pin these inside and outside the disk. Fix the whole panel to the barrel with impact adhesive and ½ inch (12 mm) nails around the edge every 4 inches (100 mm).

The two 1 inch (25 mm) diameter ventilation holes (Fig. 222) can be stopped with corks in cold weather. Pin on an asphalt visor to shield the doorway.

The traditional pendant light dangles from the ceiling in the center of the room, usually providing the only light source. Its light is often harsh and unappealing. Fortunately it is very easily converted into a truly mobile light.

The schemes sketched in Figures 223 and 225 both depend on lengthening the original wire. Electrically competent converters can switch off the electricity supply, disconnect the existing wire from the ceiling fixture and simply replace it with a much longer one. This is the neatest solution. Those who lack the confidence to tamper with house wiring can still make these mobile lights. The key is to buy a light wire extension fitting from an electrical shop. Simply take the bulb out of its socket, just as you would to exchange a bulb, and push in the extension fitting. At the other end of the extension wire fix a new socket.

The rise-and-fall light in Figure 223 needs a 72 inch (2000 mm) wire. The length of wire for the traveling light shown in Figure 225 will depend on the positioning and length of track used.

Once the wire is extended, the fastest way of changing the light's position is to screw hooks in the ceiling wherever you would like light. To change the light's position, loop the wire over a different hook.

The rise-and-fall light in Figure 223 uses two small pulleys bought from a hardware store or—more decoratively—from a marine supply store. The pulleys should be as small as possible but capable of taking the wire without sticking. One of the pulleys hangs from a ceiling hook driven securely into a solid beam near the ceiling fixture.

It is wise to check the wiring inside the fixture—with the electricity supply cut off—as the wire must be gripped so that no pulling strain is taken on the terminals. In other words there must be no risk of the weight of the light dragging the wire out of the fixture.

The weight needed for the counterbalance will depend on the shade and fitting—a plastic shade will clearly need little weight. To make a precise weight you need the shade, socket, and bulb in position. Fill a small leather bag—for example a pocket watch cover—with lead shot (sold by fishing stores), adjusting the amount until a very precise point of balance is reached. When the weight is

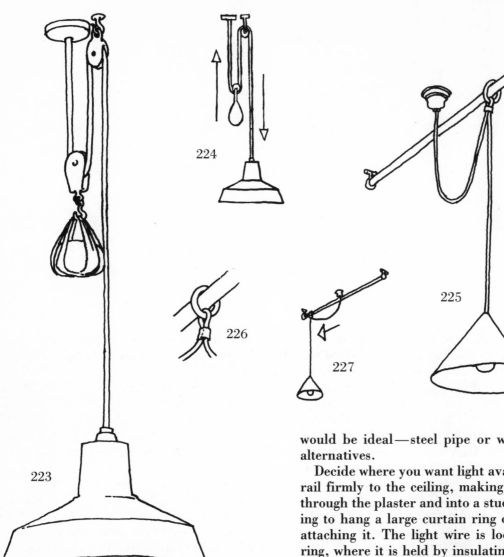

224

226

227

225

223

right the lamp should move easily up and down, and it should stay put in any position (Fig. 224).

Figure 225 shows a simplified track light system. It needs only a rail attached to the ceiling by standard end sockets. A wooden curtain pole

would be ideal—steel pipe or wardrobe rail are alternatives.

Decide where you want light available and fix the rail firmly to the ceiling, making sure screws pass through the plaster and into a stud, and remembering to hang a large curtain ring on the rail before attaching it. The light wire is looped through the ring, where it is held by insulating tape (Fig. 226). The wire must not rub against the pole. If wire is extended over a long distance use two or three loops of wire, each one taped to a ring, rather than the single loop shown here (Fig. 227).

The ingenious wall-mounted light shown in Figure 228 gives three-way movement. The light itself is not fixed in position—it stays where it's put due to a lead counterweight hung over the wire on the wall side. The wire passes over a dowel in the wall

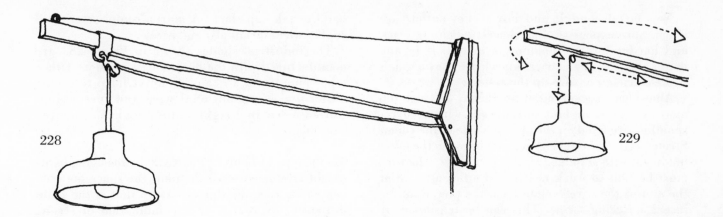

228

229

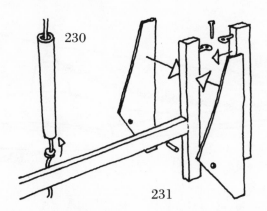

230

231

mount and through a pulley above the shade. In this way the light can be moved up and down. It also moves backward and forward simply by sliding the clamp along the horizontal bar. This 36 inch (900 mm) long bar is also movable, designed to swing freely through a 180° arc (Fig. 229).

Most of the wood is cut from a 54 inch (1500 mm) length of 2 x 1 inch (50 x 25 mm) hardwood. A 9 inch (250 mm) length is screwed firmly to the wall through its 1 inch (25 mm) side. Metal eyes are screwed to this side 1½ inches (40 mm) from top and bottom (see Fig. 231). A matching pair of eyes is screwed to a similar 9 inch (250 mm) length: the two can now be loosely joined by a couple of pins through the pairs of eyes.

The 36 inch (900 mm) bar is held to the upright by two pieces of thin ¼ inch (6 mm) plywood cut as in Figure 231 and glued and screwed to both upright and bar. The bar is under some strain and is therefore further reinforced by a length of wire twisted through two eyes (see Fig. 228).

The light wire rolls over a smart pulley bought from a marine supply store. This in turn is hooked over a metal clamp which fits closely over the bar. A leather strap is a good cheap substitute. At the wall end the wire goes over a short piece of ¼ inch (6 mm) dowel glued into both plywood sides.

Below this point is the counterweight. We used a drilled-out weight from a clock, slipped over the wire and held in place by a rubber grommet which grips the wire (see Fig. 230) below it.

Although the wire could be connected to a ceiling fixture, the system is well adapted for use with a straightforward fused plug.

The industrial look of the adjustable lighting scheme shown in Figure 232 comes from the factory-style conduit carrying the power cable along the wall near ceiling height.

The tubular metal conduit from an electrical shop is screwed together in sections, with metal-boxed socket outlets fitted in as required. The system has the advantage of rapid and flexible assembly avoiding the normal wiring labors of channeling walls and lifting floorboards.

New metal conduit and box socket outlets are much more expensive than domestic lighting track and harder for the amateur to install. If in any doubt about your electrical knowledge, pay a qualified electrician to wire up the system.

Above each socket outlet fit a heavy 2½ inch (60 mm) eye screw or bolt to the wall, with a corresponding eye fixed on the opposite side of the room. Stretch stainless steel rigging wire between the eyes, holding it with standard rigging terminals. The wire must be taut to work neatly and efficiently, so at the end of the wire remote from the power source insert a rigging screw. This can be tensioned by hand to take up slack. A marine supply store will supply wire, terminals, and screw.

The industrial shades shown in Figure 232 are manufactured with the hook for suspension. Other types hang from a chain. Connect lamp to socket outlet via a conventional wire and fused plug. Coiled wire in bright colors makes a neater coupling.

The heavy old lamp in Figure 233 runs along lightweight rigging wire which spans the space between two walls. Keeping this crosswire taut is the main difficulty, overcome by a combination of strong

232

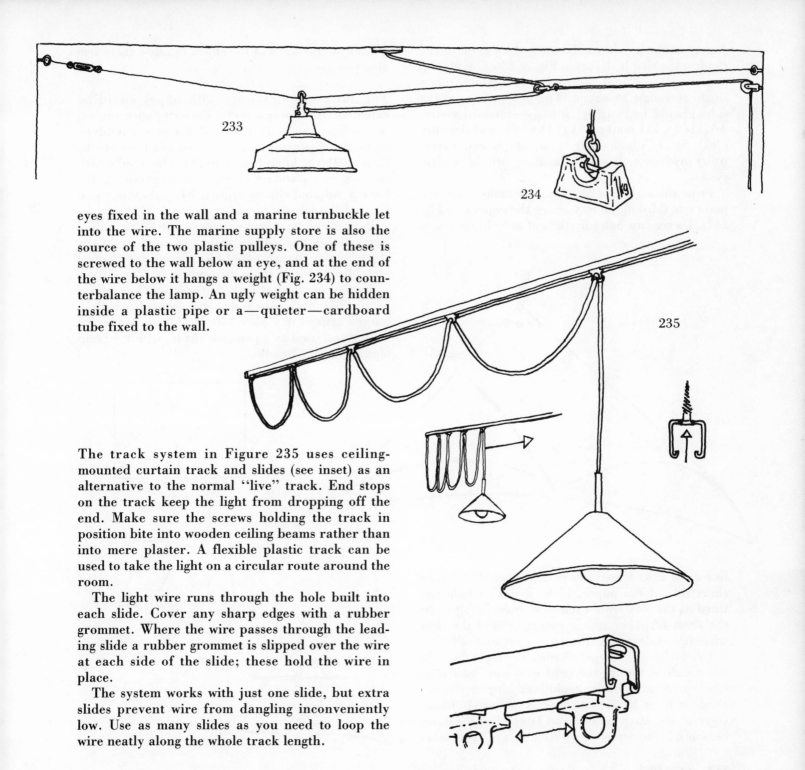

233

234

235

eyes fixed in the wall and a marine turnbuckle let into the wire. The marine supply store is also the source of the two plastic pulleys. One of these is screwed to the wall below an eye, and at the end of the wire below it hangs a weight (Fig. 234) to counterbalance the lamp. An ugly weight can be hidden inside a plastic pipe or a—quieter—cardboard tube fixed to the wall.

The track system in Figure 235 uses ceiling-mounted curtain track and slides (see inset) as an alternative to the normal "live" track. End stops on the track keep the light from dropping off the end. Make sure the screws holding the track in position bite into wooden ceiling beams rather than into mere plaster. A flexible plastic track can be used to take the light on a circular route around the room.

The light wire runs through the hole built into each slide. Cover any sharp edges with a rubber grommet. Where the wire passes through the leading slide a rubber grommet is slipped over the wire at each side of the slide; these hold the wire in place.

The system works with just one slide, but extra slides prevent wire from dangling inconveniently low. Use as many slides as you need to loop the wire neatly along the whole track length.

Japan is the traditional home of elegant paper shades; the simple design in Figure 236 provides an instant international alternative. It is made from a single rectangle of paper. The proportions of the sides should be roughly 10 to 7—standard metric A0 (1189 x 841 mm) or A1 (841 x 594 mm) sizes are ideal. Stores which cater to architects and advertising professionals will be familiar with this coding system.

From the middle of one long side make a cut to a point one third of the way across the paper (see Fig. 237). Pierce two holes by the cut near the edge, as

holes near the apex of the shade to allow the warm air to escape.

The Japanese virtuosity with paper could be exploited by turning a pretty Eastern paper parasol into a light shade. In Figure 240 a more mundane umbrella illustrates the idea. It simply rests on the floor, with the lamp holder held to the handle with the help of a standard clamp. Car inspection lights have a suitable clip-on fitting. Keep the bulb well clear of the fabric.

Part of the light glows through the fabric, while some washes against the wall. Two or three of the shade's lower panels could be covered in reflective metal foil to throw more light upward.

Antique umbrellas make interesting alternatives to the oriental sunshade. An umbrella with a curved grip as in Figure 240 can be hooked to the ceiling and used as a pendant shade, with the lamp clamped to the handle.

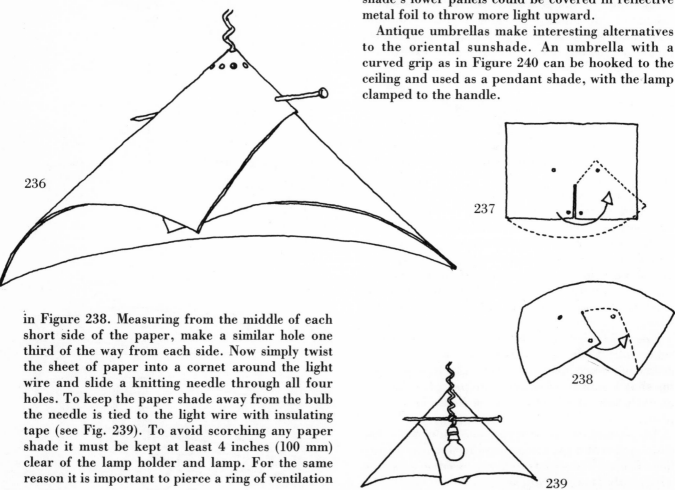

236

237

238

239

in Figure 238. Measuring from the middle of each short side of the paper, make a similar hole one third of the way from each side. Now simply twist the sheet of paper into a cornet around the light wire and slide a knitting needle through all four holes. To keep the paper shade away from the bulb the needle is tied to the light wire with insulating tape (see Fig. 239). To avoid scorching any paper shade it must be kept at least 4 inches (100 mm) clear of the lamp holder and lamp. For the same reason it is important to pierce a ring of ventilation

The bucket lamp shown in Figure 241 is crude but effective. If you find an attractive old red brass-studded bucket you are in luck. Otherwise take any bucket you like the look of and fill it with sand. The lamp itself (Fig. 242) is the relatively expensive self-sealed type for use outdoors. These have a strong glass casing and a sealed rubber connector for safety. Suitable flexible connectors are used on

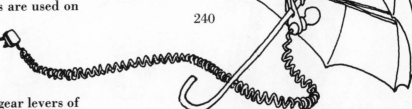

240

the front forks of motorbikes and the gear levers of cars.

Merely lodge the lamp in the sand at whatever angle you need it. If you use a properly sealed exterior fitting, the whole lamp can be buried in the sand with the top standing clear to give a hidden up-lighter.

Lighting is one area where the industrial look has been welcomed into the homes even of those who loathe the cold appeal of the full-fledged, all-metal, high-tech house. The cost of a complete industrial lighting installation can be very high, but fast and cheap variations abound.

In Figure 243 the light cable is channeled inside a hollow wall. A dull and damaged fitting has been removed and the wire extended via a junction box in the wall. Don't attempt this without electrical knowledge. A 12 inch (300 mm) length of steel pipe is screwed or glued into an end socket fixed to the wall. A standard elbow fitting at the open end is plugged with a drilled rubber bung bought from a wine supply shop or laboratory supplier. This holds the wire in place. The wire is attached to a standard socket. An aptly industrial enameled metal shade completes the fitting (Fig. 244).

A lamp clamped to a clumsy piece of pipework (Fig. 245) makes the most of its odd looks. The adjustable rubber-covered clamp comes from a laboratory equipment supplier and is designed to grip lab-

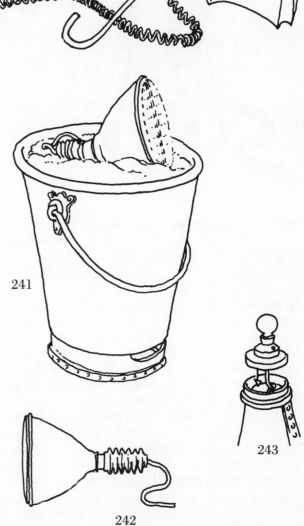

241

243

242

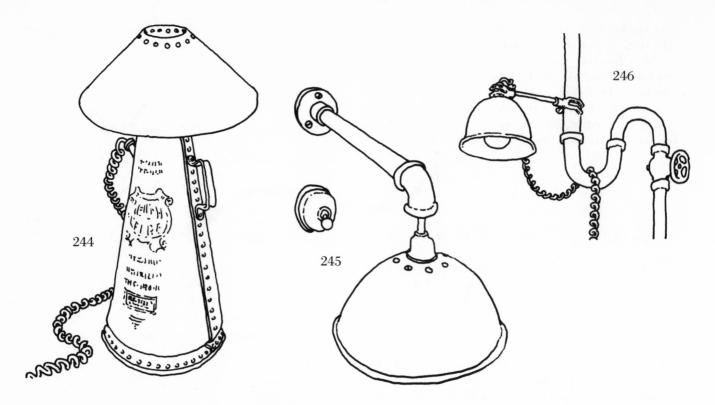

244

245

246

oratory glass during experiments. Here it holds both socket and pipe. The coiled wire is looped over the pipework and down to a fused plug.

However unlikely it looks the bizarre suspended system shown in Figure 246 really does work. It relies on a length of cable fixed firmly to both floor and ceiling, and terminated by a turnbuckle bought from a marine supply store. The double bend in the pipe provides the extra friction which keeps it in position without extra support.

The bends are formed by a plumber's pipe-bending spring. Rent this tool for an afternoon to form the regular bend. Without the spring the metal usually flattens on the bends. With the spring pushed into the pipe, you can form a neat bend in copper pipe over your knee without the strength of Tarzan. Pipe bending is easier on a long pipe, so saw the pipe to length after it is bent. Mild steel pipe is tougher to bend and will require a large saw.

Saw the finished pipe in half and fit a T-junction capillary fitting (see Fig. 246). You will need a blowtorch to melt the solder inside the fitting. This is straightforward, as the joint need not be water-tight. An 8 inch (200 mm) horizontal pipe is joined to the T-junction. An elbow fitting is attached to the open end and in this is jammed a rubber bung with a hole drilled through its center. The light wire emerges through the bung, where it is connected to a switched lamp holder. The silvered bulb shown in Figure 246 casts light upward.

The assembly will stay put in any position and can be moved up and down or swung sideways simply by hand pressure. To avoid the risk of the suspension wire cutting through the live wire, the wire should bypass the vertical pipe and be fed into the horizontal section of pipe through a drilled hole protected by a rubber grommet (Fig. 247).

Figure 248 illustrates a design which wittily exploits a spaghetti of pipework. The top section of the pipe is bent outward into the room (Fig. 249). Steel conduit pipe is clamped to the wall above a socket outlet (Fig. 250), where the lamp is plugged in. The light wire runs inside the tube and is terminated as in the previous schemes.

Smart lighting stores sell high-priced swing-out lamps. This design (Fig. 251) looks good and saves money. It consists of a 72 inch (1800 mm) length of copper tubing bent with the aid of a rented plumber's spring. The wall mounting is made of 1 x ⅛ inch (25 x 3 mm) section flat mild steel. Cut one length of steel about 10 inches (250 mm) long and round off the corners using a file. Bend each end over at right angles to give tabs about 1¼ inches (30 mm) long. To do this, clamp the steel in a vise and hammer the tab over, heating the bend with a blowtorch if necessary to soften it up. Drill one of the tabs through to take the diameter of the copper tube.

Now cut another length of the same steel an inch (25 mm) shorter. Again bend tabs over, but this time drill through both ends to take the tube. Abut the two sections of steel as shown (Fig. 252) so that the tube passes through three holes and sits on the undrilled tab. Once this is correctly aligned (adjust the alignment of the holes with a round-section file), keep the two pieces tightly together and drill two holes through the back of both. These take the screws which hold the fitting to the wall.

Drill a hole 3 inches (75 mm) from the end of the tube where the wire enters (Fig. 252). Finish this hole cleanly with a round file to smooth the edges, and protect the wire by fitting a rubber grommet. Now thread the wire through the tube and allow enough for the socket and shade to hang at the height you want. The wire exits from the tube through a drilled rubber bung which holds it in

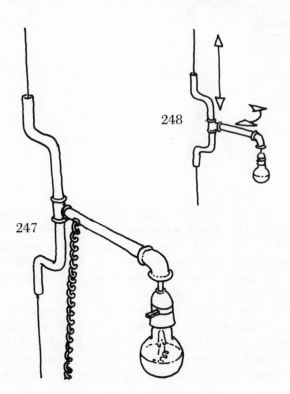

247

248

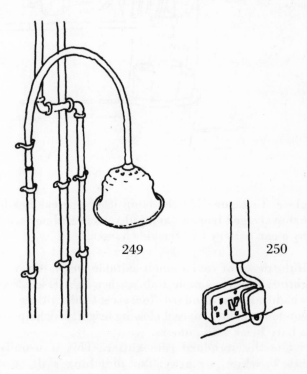

249

250

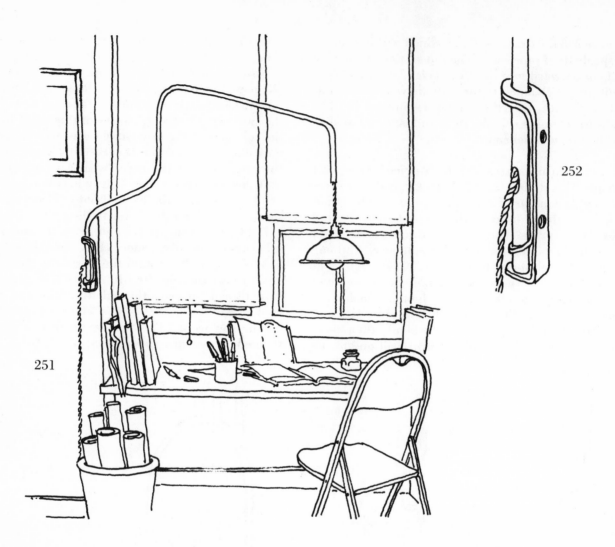

251

252

place. In Figure 251 the lamp itself is a car headlight salvaged from a damaged vehicle and powered by a car battery and trickle charger.

If the decor of your room is suitable for plastic rain gutter, try this simple wall washer light (Fig. 253) which takes a standard fluorescent tube fitting. It can look slightly surreal glowing brightly high up on a bare brick wall indoors.

Use the standard rain gutter. This is usually black, white, or gray. No plumbing skills are required for assembly. Just cut the gutter to the length you need with a hacksaw and fit it with push-on or glue-on end caps. Support it on a pair of standard brackets sold for the job. Avoid the high cost of buying new plumbing fittings by salvaging what you need from a demolition site.

Paint the inside of the gutter silver or line it with kitchen foil to reflect heat and light. Merely lay the complete fluorescent fitting along the foil (Fig. 254). The wire runs through a hole drilled in one of the end caps—make sure all sharp plastic edges are

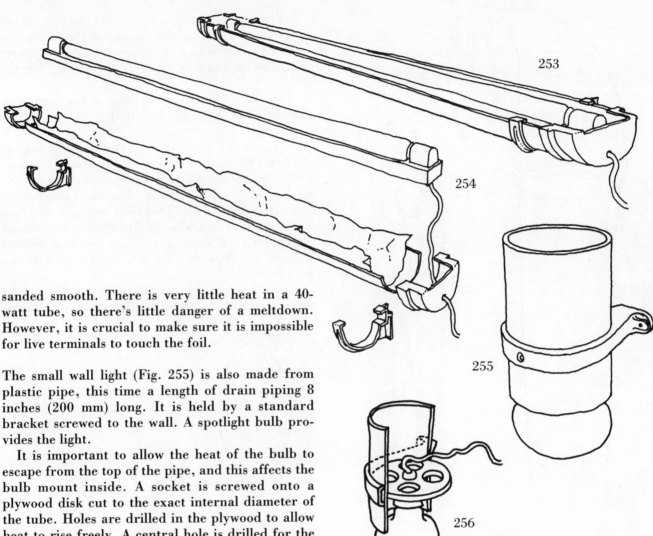

253

254

255

256

sanded smooth. There is very little heat in a 40-watt tube, so there's little danger of a meltdown. However, it is crucial to make sure it is impossible for live terminals to touch the foil.

The small wall light (Fig. 255) is also made from plastic pipe, this time a length of drain piping 8 inches (200 mm) long. It is held by a standard bracket screwed to the wall. A spotlight bulb provides the light.

It is important to allow the heat of the bulb to escape from the top of the pipe, and this affects the bulb mount inside. A socket is screwed onto a plywood disk cut to the exact internal diameter of the tube. Holes are drilled in the plywood to allow heat to rise freely. A central hole is drilled for the wire.

The disk is held in place by glue or pinned through the pipe—the pins will be hidden by the bracket. The bulb must not touch the fitting. Position the disk so that the bulb will be in the right position before gluing or pinning it (Fig. 256).

A drainage section with a glazed clay finish makes a rugged floor lamp (Fig. 257). The tall light uses one straight pipe and one bend, with the joint left "dry."

For the base cut a disk of plywood or lumbercore ½ inch (12 mm) thick to fit tightly inside the swelled end. Cut a second disk slightly larger than the external diameter of the swell and join the two disks with glue and screws. The pipe should sit squarely over this base. Drill it through to take the wire without squashing it and screw a hefty hook in the center (see Fig. 258).

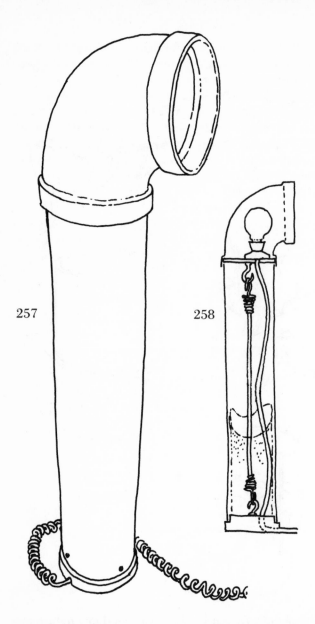

257 258

Screw a hook to the underside of the disk, keeping well clear of the wire. Hook an elastic luggage strap to both hooks to hold the assembly together. A ballast of sand or pebbles helps stabilize the lamp.

A small shelf-mounted version of the lamp uses just the bend (Figs. 259 and 260).

The standard lamp (Fig. 261) can swivel thanks to the loose-fit junction fitting near the top. However, a rigid version could be made needing no joint fittings where the pipe changes direction. One continuous straight 90 inch (2200 mm) length of pvc pipe is sufficient. The key to construction is the extreme bendability of warm pvc. Pipe bending doesn't demand huge muscles, but it is easier work with two people.

Never try to heat pvc with a naked flame—the fumes can kill. A safe and simple way of softening

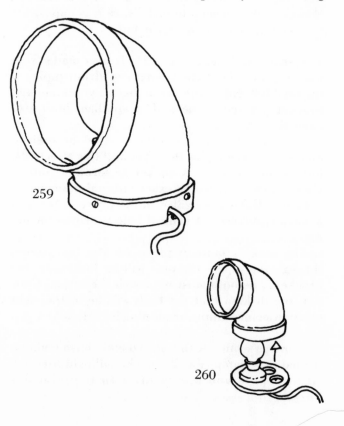

259

260

Cut another disk to form a tight fit inside the swell of the top bend (Fig. 258). Drill a hole near the edge of this disk, pass the wire through it, and wire it to a batten socket which is then screwed to the disk in the position shown (Fig. 258). Use a bulb small enough to fit in the confined space.

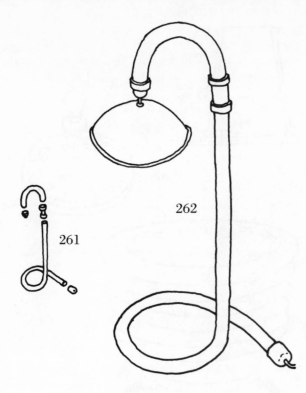

261

262

Look skyward and see the light—it could be sitting on top of the chimney stack. Flue caps and chimney pots can make fine indoor lights.

Traditional clay chimney pots are not commonly available in this country, but with diligent looking you may come across one. There is one manufacturer of clay chimney pots in the United States: Superior Clay Corp., P.O. Box 352, Uhrichsville, Ohio 44683. They will send a brochure on request.

Some of the pots can be capped with a shade, while those with vented sides may be used unadorned to produce a diffuse background light (Figs. 263 and 264).

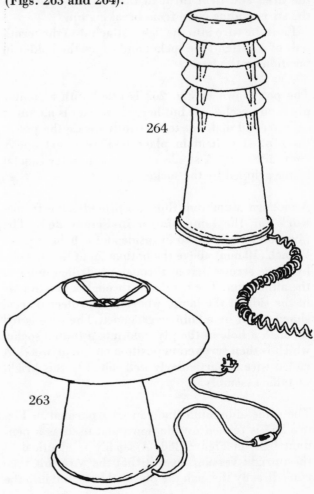

264

263

the pipe is to fill it with warm sand heated in an old saucepan. You can check whether the sand is warm enough by dipping a piece of pipe in the pan. When the pipe goes rubbery, the sand is warm enough to be poured in. A cap on one end stops the sand falling out of the pipe. Wear thick gloves to protect your hands.

Form regular curves by bending the pipe around a bucket. When you are satisfied with the shape, don't relax your grip on the pipe, as it will tend to spring back to its original shape. A second person should remove the cap and let the sand run out. Then harden the pipe by cooling it under water.

Before wiring the lamp, drill a hole in the bottom cap to take the wire. A hole is also drilled in a cap to cover the top end, the diameter depending on the type of lamp fitting you find. Pass the wire through the pipe and caps, wire it to the lamp holder, fit the holder to the top cap, and glue the cap in place. Finally, fit a shade (Fig. 262).

To make the base trace the shape of the chimney pot onto a piece of ½ inch (12 mm) plywood or lumbercore and cut out this disk with a jigsaw for the pot to sit on. To this disk glue and screw three small wood blocks so that the disk is gripped inside the pot (see Fig. 266).

Drill a hole through the center of the base for the wire and chisel out a channel in the underside to prevent the wire from being squashed (Fig. 265). Attempts to drill through the clay pot itself too often end in breakages. Drilling is simpler with unglazed pots, though possible with glazed ones. When drilling glazed pots, stick masking tape over the area and drill through this—it helps prevent the surrounding glaze from breaking up.

Feed the wire into the light, attach it to the terminals of a batten-type socket and screw the holder in position on the base.

The pot shown in Fig. 263 is fitted with a similar plywood baseboard, but here the socket is mounted on a second disk cut to fit tightly inside the pot at the top. It is held in place with two-part epoxy resin adhesive. A shade rests on a standard metal frame gripped by the socket.

A modern aluminum flue cap provides the framework for the lamp shown in Figure 267. The plywood base is cut to fit inside and is held in place ½ inch (10 mm) above the bottom lip of the flue cap by three screws driven through predrilled holes in the aluminum. The wire runs through a fourth hole in the side of the lamp, where it is protected from sharp metal by a rubber grommet. The wire is fed through a hole in the plywood into a batten socket which is then screwed in position on the plywood. A coiled wire is particularly well suited to this bright metallic assembly.

The same aluminum flue cap incorporated in Figure 267 is turned upside down and used as a pendant light in Figure 268. Assembly is identical to the upright version, except that the wire this time runs directly through the plywood base and into the

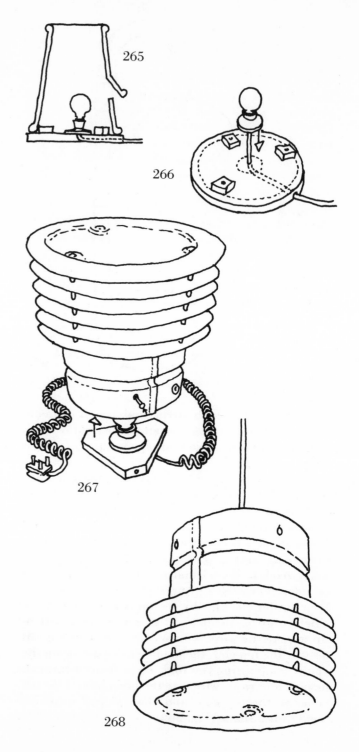

265

266

267

268

socket. The triangular mounting (seen in Figs. 267 and 269) ensures the ventilation which is essential to stop overheating.

Figures 269 and 270 show two other finds in the flue fitter's catalogue converted into lamps. The pendant light in Figure 269 washes the ceiling with light, while the standard lamp (Fig. 270) casts patterns of light around the room.

Although old aluminum fittings may be picked up free from abandoned buildings, new ones look much better and brighter. These can be bought from plumbers' and builders' suppliers or from specialist suppliers of central-heating components. Most shop-bought caps are scratched and dented, so take care to specify undamaged ones. For a particularly glamorous effect spray the aluminum with a bright metallic color or a matt black finish, bearing in mind that black will tend to hold the light. Best of all, have the metal anodized.

Familiar objects can be converted into effective lamp bases and shades. The use of fine wine or whiskey bottles as lamp bases is well known. Rather less commonplace is a pair of humble cooking molds (Figs. 271 and 272) fitted to a regular wall-mounted lamp holder. Kitchen shops are full of similar metal molds in various shapes and sizes. With their typically bright tinned finish they make good reflectors, particularly when fitted with a crown silvered bulb which throws light back into the reflector and then out into the room.

Use a normal batten-type socket, one which can be screwed straight to the wall or ceiling without a hanging wire. With the electricity supply switched off, connect the socket to the power supply from the light switch and screw it to the wall. Take off the ring which will hold the shade in place and measure its internal diameter carefully. Now cut a circular hole in the base of the mold to the same diameter. This must be a good enough fit for the shade ring to hold it securely when screwed up again. The simplest way to cut the hole would be to drill a series of holes close together around the marked-out circle

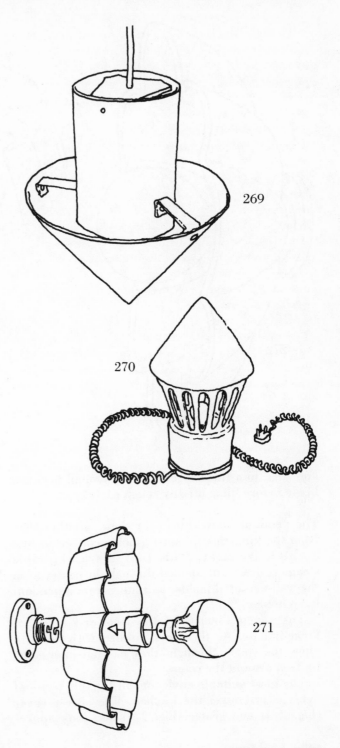

269

270

271

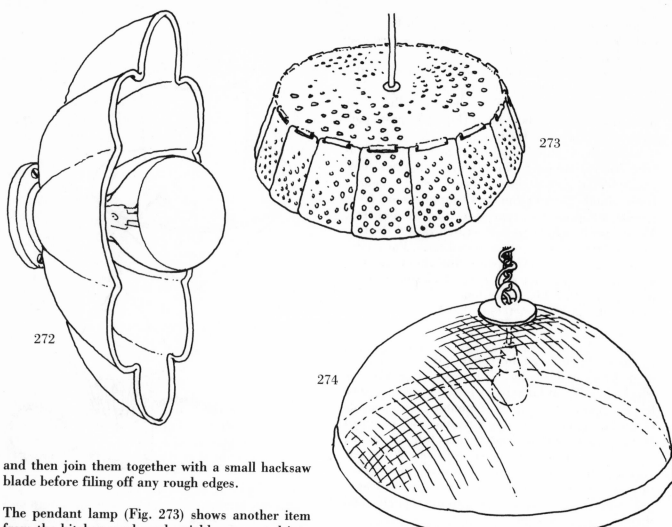

272

273

274

and then join them together with a small hacksaw blade before filing off any rough edges.

The pendant lamp (Fig. 273) shows another item from the kitchen cupboard quickly converted into an effective light. This time it's a vegetable steamer, dried out, drilled through the center as in the wall-mounted molds, and hung from a pendant lamp holder.

The rim is formed by the steamer's series of hinged flaps. As these are riddled with holes to allow the steam through, they cast an interesting pattern around the room.

The most suitable environment for this series of lights is of course the kitchen. The cheese cover (Fig. 274) and grater (Fig. 277) also look appro-

priate dangling from the kitchen ceiling. Choose other objects to make suitable reflectors in other areas—a small steel sink in the bathroom for example, or a car headlight in the garage.

With care it is possible to make surprisingly handsome wall reflectors from free materials. The devotional sconces which reflected the candlelight in New Mexican domestic shrines in the nineteenth century are well known; they were constructed from can lids, bottle tops, and opened-out cans.

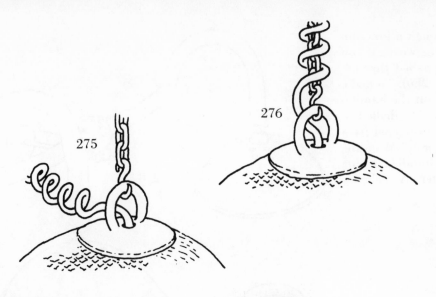

275

276

277

The effect could at times stand comparison with a Bugatti chair.

The inexpensive traditional French cheese cover is simple to adapt for lighting. Drill a hole through the top from the inside wide enough to take the wire. It is important to protect the raw metal edge with a rubber ring. The cover is suspended by a small butcher's hook from a thin chain which hangs from a hook in the ceiling (Fig. 275). This prevents any weight from being placed on the light. A coiled wire can be wound around the chain (Fig. 276) for a neat finish.

The cheese grater (Fig. 277) generates interesting lighting effects. It gives enough down light for use over a kitchen working surface, and it also washes the walls with a decorative pattern through the graters.

The grater is adapted in the same way as the cheese cover, by drilling a hole through the top to take the wire. The hole should be drilled precisely at the grater's balancing point; otherwise it will not hang straight. A rubber ring is again fitted to the metal edge after it has been filed smooth to protect the wire from sharp edges as it passes through the hole.

Most graters have a confined space inside, too small to take the standard domestic light bulb. Small bulbs are easy to buy from electrical stores. Take your grater along to check that the bulb fits, bearing in mind that room is also needed for the socket.

The height at which the light hangs inside the grater can be adjusted by moving the grater up and down on the wire. If the rubber ring will not grip the wire tightly enough, tape the wire in position.

The bicycle is the low-technologist's delight—it is simple to use, understand, and maintain; it is economical and very versatile. Pedal power is used to grind corn in Africa and mix cement in Brazil. In Figure 278 the handlebars and stem are mounted on the wall like a Picasso hunting trophy, wired up and fitted with lights.

The stem supporting the double light in Figure 278 is simply set in the wall between two wires connected to the same light switch through a junction box in the wall. Don't tamper with the wiring if you are in any doubt. The wires are pushed through holes drilled in the handlebars (Fig. 280). To make certain these holes will be hidden, put the handlebars in position and mark the spots to be drilled.

The edge of each hole should be protected by a rubber grommet. Where the wire emerges from the handlebars it goes through a plastic handlebar plug with a hole drilled through its center. A socket is

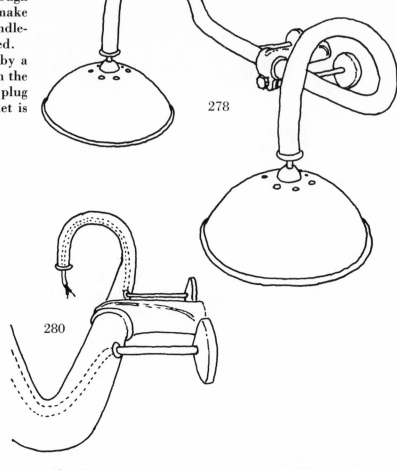

278

279

280

281

282

fitted to the end of the wire and a suitable aluminum shade fitted to the holder (Fig. 279). The longer the stem protruding from the wall, the wider the shade you can use.

The standard lamp in Figure 281 is even simpler. The stem sits in a plastic pipe clamped to the wall, leaving a small gap between pipe and wall. Two lengths of coiled wire in contrasting colors are wound up the pipe and pushed into the handlebars as in the previous design (Fig. 282). At floor level the two lights are plugged into a socket outlet.

KITCHENS & BATHROOMS

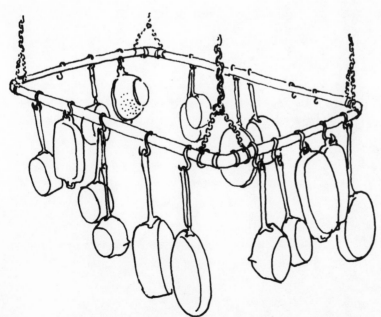

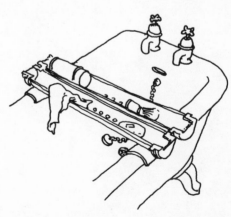

Kitchens reflect cooks' personalities. The heavyweight structure shown in Figure 283 also reflects a desire to avoid expensive fitted kitchen units and a sudden availability of cheap secondhand bricks. Boldness can create successful designs: let a single element dominate.

Take time planning your kitchen. There are many books to help, ranging from the ergonomically exact to the fanciful. When deciding on the placing of upright piers for the brick kitchen, bear in mind the dimensions of your own appliances and those of standard kitchen units such as cupboards. Ventilation is essential for most stoves and fridges, so don't block them in with walls. You could insert a few ventilation bricks near the top and bottom of their surrounding piers to allow air to circulate. Otherwise drill ½ inch (12 mm) holes through the bricks using a masonry bit.

When selecting bricks from a demolition yard, avoid uncleaned twentieth-century bricks. Modern mortar grips brick tight and is too tough to chip off without cracking the brick. Nineteenth-century mortar is soft enough to hammer off.

Bricks must be laid level, and you need to be sure your floor can stand the load. The floor should be solid, which usually confines the scheme to the ground floor. A qualified contractor could be called for a consultation to clear any doubts. Bear in mind the position of existing electrical cables/outlets and water pipes—running new pipes in concrete floors is a nightmare.

Tall brick piers should be properly laid in mortar to prevent collapse. Bricklaying can be therapeutic, but many people dislike or fear it. The nervous and wealthy can avoid the problem by employing a bricklayer. Otherwise you can build a wooden framework above worktop level and simply clad this in a bricklike facing. If dusty mortar proves problematic, point the bricks with waterproof acrylic-based mortar.

Wall cupboards could be complete shop-bought units screwed to the wall following the manufacturer's instructions. The alternative is a façade fronting the brickwork, as in Figure 286. An inner frame of 2 x 1 inch (50 x 25 mm) softwood is screwed to the rough brickwork to make a flush

front, and the outer frame of 2 x 1 inch (50 x 25 mm) wood is screwed to this. Mitered corners, as on picture frames, improve the looks of the outer frame, whereas plain butt joints are good enough for the inner frame. The louvered door bought from a furniture warehouse is hinged to the outer frame, and a two-part magnetic catch fixed inside the door and under a shelf inside holds it closed (Fig. 287). High-tech jokers may prefer to substitute a traditional metal washboard for the wooden louvered door.

Shelves serve a double purpose—besides providing storage space they brace the brick piers. At each end they rest on pegs hammered into holes drilled in the bricks. To improve the whole structure's stability, shelves are also fixed at the back to wooden battens screwed to the wall.

The shelf shown in Figure 284 runs the whole length of the kitchen wall. Where the shelf crosses a brick pier a brick-wide slot is cut out leaving a half-brick-deep solid section at the front (Fig. 285). In this way the piers are continuous but the shelf line is unbroken.

The arched fronts under shelves have a dual function—they stop the worktop from sagging and act as supporting braces between the piers. They are held to the underside of the shelf using metal brackets (see Fig. 284).

If you want to brighten up the bricks, paint them using the types of paint designed to cover outside walls.

The metallic high-tech kitchen scores on flexibility and economy. It is fast to erect, adapt, or even remove completely, which is a big virtue in temporary or rented accommodation.

The framework is constructed using industrial metal racking. The L-shaped lengths can be cut with a hacksaw and joined using the system's nuts and bolts. A range of attachments is available, from corner plates to castors. Systems are sold in gray-painted mild steel, but giving your home the industrial look doesn't necessarily mean drab gray: you can spray on bright red or yellow enamel paint,

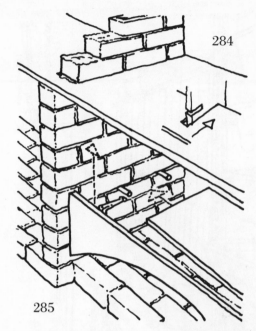

284

285

or try matt black or even a subtle pastel coat for your metal. Manufacturers supply detailed instructions on design and assembly. These are well worth studying before building begins.

Cupboards and walls are partly clad in corrugated metal. The metal sheets are too tough for a hacksaw. You will need metal-cutting shears, and

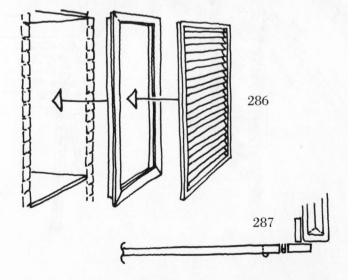

286

287

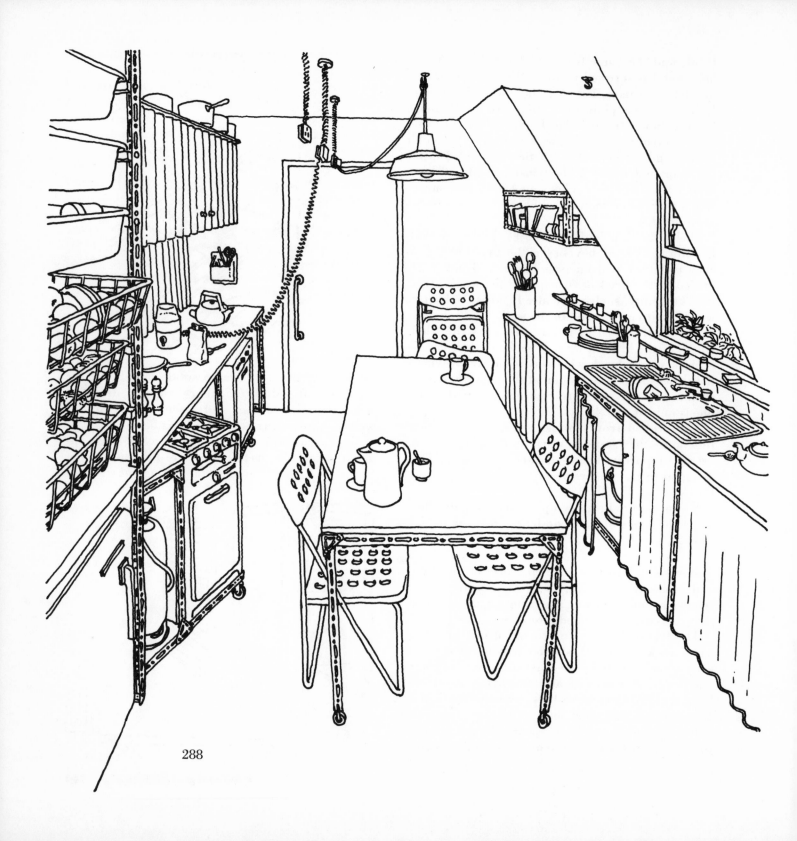

288

the going is slow. Plastic is easier to cut, drill, and attach, but less rigid and potentially dangerous in kitchen areas where there's a fire risk, such as near a stove.

Metal edges can be sharp, so cover them by pushing on a silver plastic trim; this is sold by motor accessory shops. Vicious corners can be bent over using pliers. The worktop is cut to overlap the doors by 1 inch (25 mm) to provide protection against the top edge of the doors.

Unwanted wooden cupboards could be converted by ripping off the old doors and replacing them with corrugated sheet, as in the wall cupboards in Figure 288. Behind each pair of corrugated doors under the working surface in Figure 288 is a simple twelve-sided box frame of slotted angle, reinforced at each corner with a triangular corner plate. The plates add rigidity to the construction.

Hinges are bolted to the frame uprights and through bolt-diameter holes drilled in the doors. A large bolt makes a good door handle, and with so much metal the natural closing device must be a magnet fixed to the lower shelf.

The rolling stove (Fig. 289) has several advantages: no greasy filth can gather under it; it doesn't take away working surface in a small kitchen; and it makes table-side crêpes suzette possible!

Swivel castors are mounted in each corner of the frame, which was built to house the stove and its bottled gas supply alongside. Triangular braces are used wherever upright and horizontal lengths meet. The bottle's frame finishes 1 inch (25 mm)

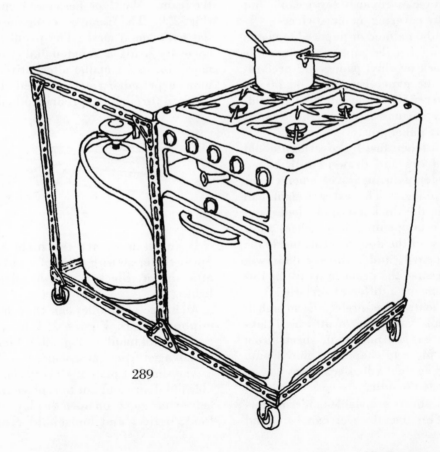

289

lower than the stove top, allowing a 1 inch (25 mm) hardwood worktop to be screwed on top. The stove sits in an open platform.

The chairs were chosen to continue the drilled metal theme. Folding chairs bring space economy; after use they are folded flat and hung from wall pegs. The table is made from slotted angle racking.

Its white laminated chipboard top is screwed from underneath through the frame.

Open wire baskets store provisions. Elaborate baskets can be found in discarded dishwashers. Baskets run on wooden rails held by screws driven through the metal frame into the wood.

A previous occupant's taste in kitchen cupboards may appall you, even though the units are in perfect condition. You can revamp serviceable but ugly kitchens fast by covering up old surfaces.

Flat surfaces can be painted or papered to match the walls, but avoid fragile paper in vulnerable positions, where cork or vinyl papers are preferable. The edges of the paper can fray and lift off unless they are covered in a frame of wooden molding, mitered at the corners like a picture frame, and held in place by panel pins.

Refresh a tired kitchen fast by covering the old cupboards' drab doors and drawers with brand new surfaces. Wooden paneling is a common choice but can cause problems. The extra weight can strain hinges, while the thickness spoils looks and can hinder doors from opening. Some hinges allow the precise thickness of the door to swing inside the cupboard when opened, and a thicker door will foul the edge. Overcome the problem by fitting different hinges or choosing a different surface.

A flexible sheet material is preferable to paneling—it is light, thin, and easy to attach. Traditional woven cane can be bought in sheets from craft shops. Cut a piece to shape and glue it onto the cupboard using contact adhesive. Edges can be covered with a wooden molding.

Metal and plastic sheets are viable modern alternatives to cane. Thin metal sheet can be found free—snip metal panels from discarded electrical appliances and screw them into place. However, plastic sheets and metal meshes are usually simpler to use. They can be bought from builders' suppliers. Green plastic sheet impressed with a reinforcing grid pattern is used on building sites. It is tough, thin, light, and smart. The plastic is held in place simply by stretching it over the door/drawer and stapling it into position. For a neat finish cover the edges with a frame of ½ x ½ inch (13 x 13 mm) half-round wooden molding, mitered at the corners and screwed into place.

A more rigid alternative to simple plastic is plastic-covered chicken wire, and beyond this are the open metal meshes. If you choose open mesh, pin it in position at 4 inch (100 mm) intervals around the edge, using U-shaped staples, before screwing on the frame. Metal meshes can be cut with wire snips (Fig. 290). The frame covering the edges will not lie flat over metal mesh. The problem is easily overcome by using a rebated half-round molding. A more unusual metallic alternative is to use aluminum carpet-edging strip mitered at the corners and screwed through the predrilled holes.

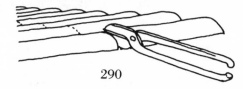

290

Open meshes leave the surface behind visible. Spray the mesh with paint of a suitable color before attaching it. Black is stylish, silver dramatic and light.

A change of handles can change the character of cupboards. In Figure 291 hospital grab bars replace dull handles (Fig. 292). Similar handles can be salvaged from bathrooms.

The simplest plan of all is to remove the undesirable old doors and not to replace them at all, but to leave your goods on open display. Manufacturers of food, drink, and household cleaning materials

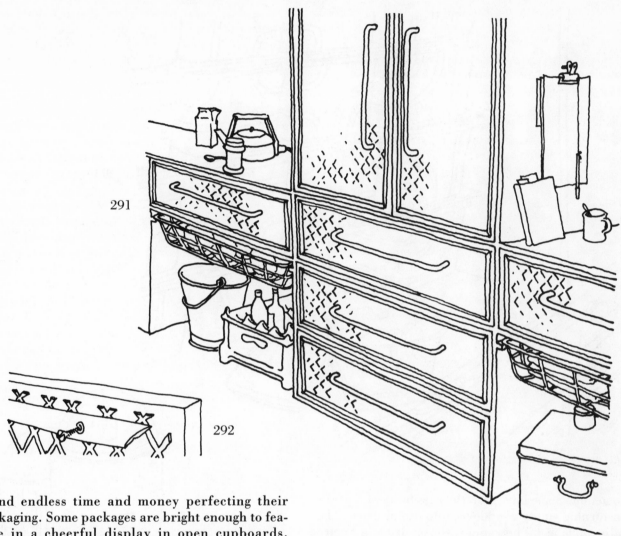

291

292

spend endless time and money perfecting their packaging. Some packages are bright enough to feature in a cheerful display in open cupboards. Inquisitive children can of course find such a colorful array of packages irresistible and wreak rapid havoc in both the kitchen and their digestive system, so make sure any open cupboard is well out of reach.

The rise of the home freezer has stimulated the reuse of food containers, as soups, stews, and homemade ice cream are packed for the big freeze.

Plastic ice cream containers are made in handy sizes for neat stacking in the freezer. Since they are also airtight and sturdy, they are worth preserving after the last ice cream has been swallowed. Decoration makes them more appealing. Work out a design running around a group of tubs (Fig. 293). Use bands of colored adhesive tape to make the pattern.

The absurdity of throwing strong and attractive containers away merely because the contents have been used has stimulated inventive manufacturers

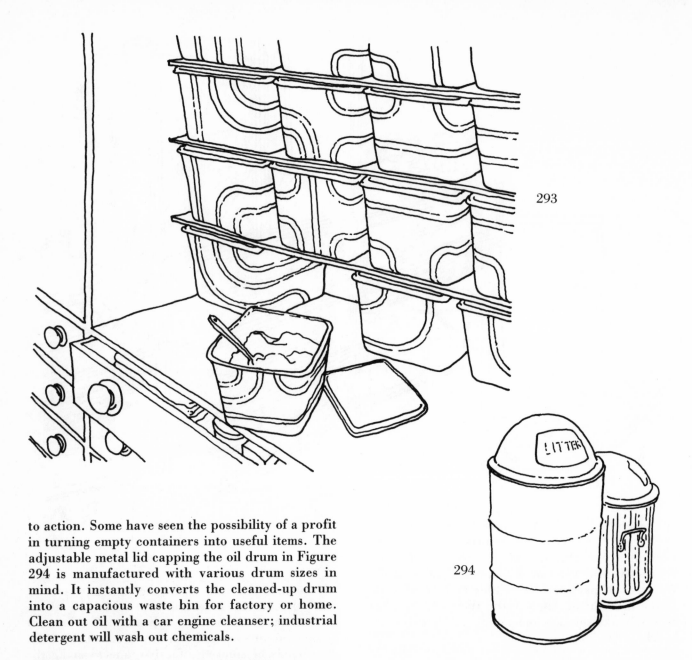

293

294

to action. Some have seen the possibility of a profit in turning empty containers into useful items. The adjustable metal lid capping the oil drum in Figure 294 is manufactured with various drum sizes in mind. It instantly converts the cleaned-up drum into a capacious waste bin for factory or home. Clean out oil with a car engine cleanser; industrial detergent will wash out chemicals.

Commercial storage systems are handy for home use. The old-style grocers' storage unit still turns up in antique shops but generally costs a lot.

An entire unit can be built from lumber to fit your kitchen (Fig. 295). The operating principle is shown in the side view (Fig. 296), with inner boxes hinged at the front to the box frame. The inner box is tilted forward to open; when the cutaway back panel touches the frame top, the box stops.

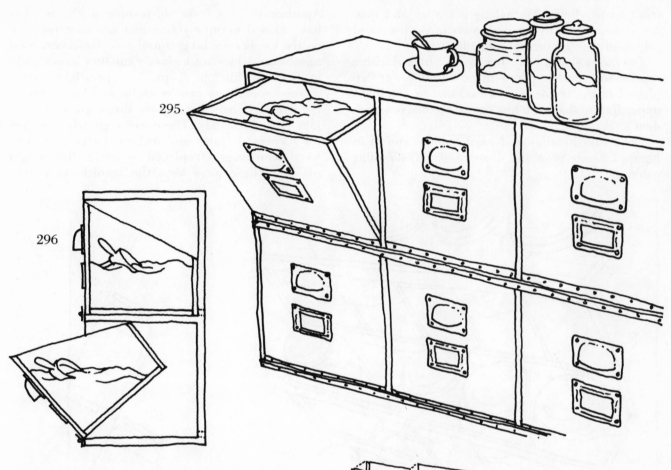

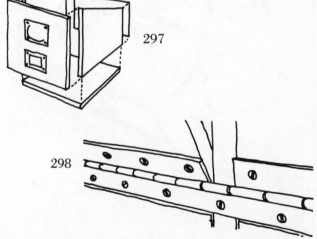

The box framework is easy to construct from 1 inch (25 mm) thick lumber or plastic-faced particle boards. Nails will hold lumber structures together, whereas special chipboard screws are needed for a secure fix in chipboard. Build up the outer frame first, pin on a Masonite back panel to improve rigidity, then add the central shelf and dividing panels.

Inner boxes can be made of ¼ inch (6 mm) plywood, with a softwood front panel to improve looks. Cut the front panel to fit neatly in its opening, then build up the boxes as in Figure 297. The box sides are angled so the box tilts forward on its hinge but cannot tip right out. The height of the back panel should be roughly two thirds that of the front panel. Begin by making it higher and then use a saw or rasp to cut away more of the back and sides and thereby increase the tilt.

The boxes shown in Figure 295 are hinged with a continuous length of piano hinge, with its lower flap pinned to the frame. Use a hacksaw to notch the upper flap so that each box can be opened independently (Fig. 298).

The brass handles and card holders shown in Figure 295 are from the drawers of a 1940s filing cabinet.

Apothecary jars from old-fashioned pharmacists have gained antique status and are therefore too costly to buy in large numbers. However, new apothecary jars and glass canisters are widely available in kitchen shops. Less prestigious commercial containers can be useful and handsome in the home kitchen. Few people throw away ceramic jam jars (Fig. 302). These are regularly recycled for homemade jams and pickles. Large glass jars have been largely replaced by clear, lightweight plastic. These have kept the traditional shape.

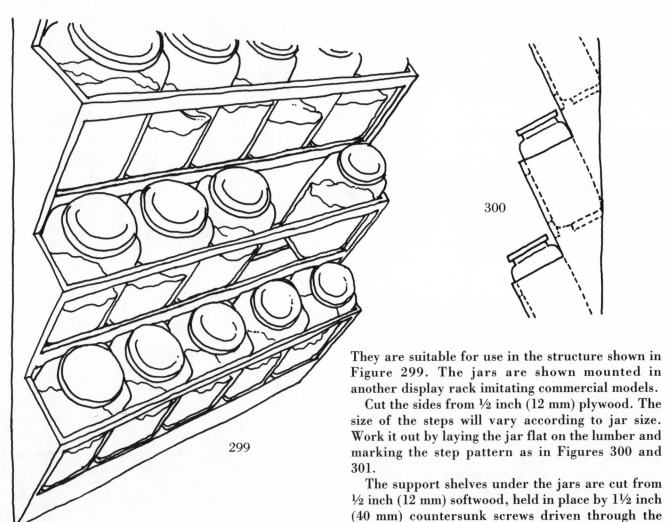

299

300

They are suitable for use in the structure shown in Figure 299. The jars are shown mounted in another display rack imitating commercial models.

Cut the sides from ½ inch (12 mm) plywood. The size of the steps will vary according to jar size. Work it out by laying the jar flat on the lumber and marking the step pattern as in Figures 300 and 301.

The support shelves under the jars are cut from ½ inch (12 mm) softwood, held in place by 1½ inch (40 mm) countersunk screws driven through the

301

302

side panels. A pair of retaining battens prevents each row of jars from toppling out of the front of the cabinet. These are lengths of 2 x 1 inch (50 x 25 mm) softwood, one fixed near the jar top, the other near the base.

Suspended storage systems are a wise way of accommodating kitchen clutter. Pots and pans can be kept conveniently close without being in the way. Air circulates freely around the hanging trays in Figure 303, which makes them particularly suitable for fresh food.

Four standard office filing trays were used in this easy-to-assemble unit. New trays can be bought from office suppliers, but cheaper ones are easy to find in secondhand shops and auctions of commercial equipment.

At each corner the trays hang from a 36 inch (1000 mm) length of steel chain bought from a picture framer. The S-shaped hooks are from the same supplier. The assembly is easily added to by hooking on additional chains and trays.

At the top the four suspension chains meet on a strong 3 inch (75 mm) screw-in hook, which is screwed into a solid ceiling joist. Locate the position of lumber joists behind the ceiling plaster by pushing a needle through the plaster.

A similar hook-and-chain arrangement is used to support the herb plantation in Figure 304. Fresh herbs will grow happily in well-lit kitchens. In Figure 304 the herbs are planted in individual pots and placed on a rimmed tray inside an uninhabited bird cage. The tray stops drips when the herbs are watered.

The hanging rack in Figure 305 is made from four plastic-coated wire grids found in a junked refrigerator. The grids which are used in cool-store display units are particularly rugged and normally covered in white plastic for durability and easy cleaning.

The four racks are joined together with simple S-hooks to form a pair of horizontal shelves and a pair of upright sides. Each side rack hangs from a pair of 3 inch (75 mm) screw-in hooks driven firmly into a batten fixed to the ceiling joists. Pots, pans, and clutter hang down from the lower shelf, with other utensils stored on the shelf above.

There is a wide choice of materials suitable to make the frame in Figure 306. Tubes are available in brass, chrome, steel, and plastic, besides solid wooden doweling. Copper plumbing pipe was chosen for the frame in the illustration.

The frame can be made from one length of tube bent at right angles at the corners using a pipe-bending spring, which can be rented. Sharp bends in the pipe will be weak: if the radius of the curve formed by the bend is less than four times the diameter of the copper tube, you may find that the metal wrinkles on the inside of the bend and is stretched thin on the outside.

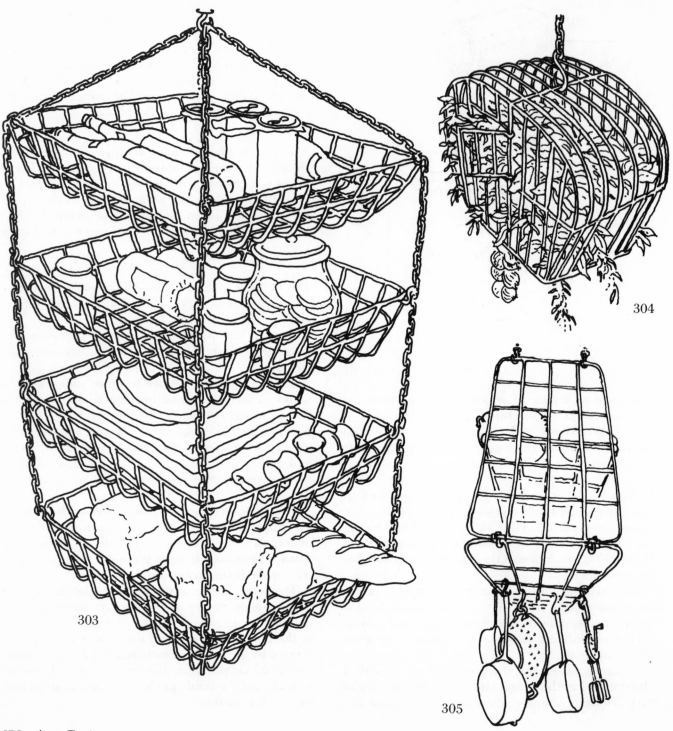

303

304

305

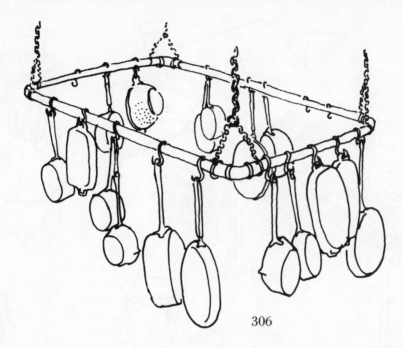

306

For a firmer framework, four lengths of pipe can be joined at the corners by normal capillary fittings, which are simply pushed onto the pipes and heated with a blowtorch until you see solder oozing out of the joint. Fittings can be bought from a plumbing supply shop. Care is needed to keep the frame rectangular, but as there's no water in the pipes you do not have to worry about watertight joints!

The frame is suspended on thin brass chain hooked through holes drilled through the copper at each side of the corner joints. The wires are suspended from the ceiling by screw hooks fixed through the ceiling plaster into the joists behind. Pans then hang from butchers' hooks.

Camping equipment is designed for speedy assembly, temporary use in confined spaces, and collapsibility—in fact it is true fast furniture. It is the perfect equipment for a small home which you don't intend to occupy for long.

In Figure 307 a combination sink and stove unit is built into a chipboard worktop supported on a scaffold base. The unit was designed for use in a trailer where space is very limited. Plumbing in the sink is simple as everything is accessible. The stove needs no plumbing at all, because it burns butane gas bought in bottles.

The same bottled gas system is used to provide lighting. This brings enviable independence from fickle outside gas and electricity supplies. The butane lamp (Fig. 309) is fed by bottled gas. Figure 308 shows the famous Tilley pressure oil lamp. It can be fitted with an effective rear reflector which makes it brighter than most household electric lights. The wick oil lamp alongside it (Fig. 310) is the equally notable hurricane lamp, which has remained virtually unchanged in design throughout the twentieth century.

The hanging canvas storage system (Fig. 311) is an old campsite favorite. It needs no wall space. When hung by S-hooks from eye hooks screwed to the ceiling it keeps food out of the reach of rodents and other low-level predators. It can be zipped up to

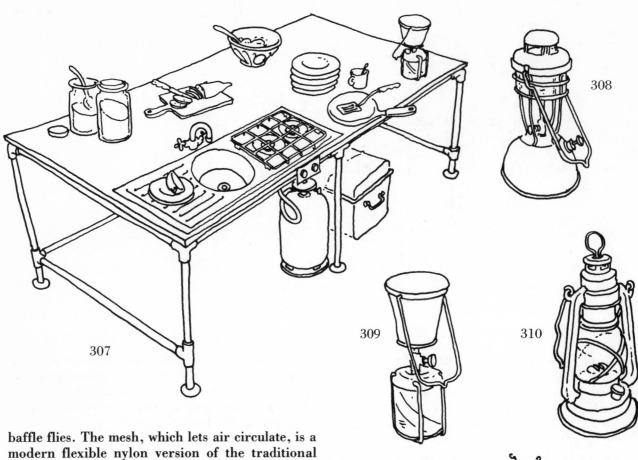

307

308

309

310

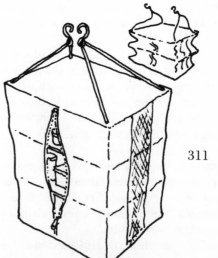

311

baffle flies. The mesh, which lets air circulate, is a modern flexible nylon version of the traditional meat safe's metal mesh. When you strike camp, the system folds flat.

A similar system can be made at home. Cut four 18 x 12 inch (450 x 300 mm) shelves from ¼ inch (6 mm) plywood. Run strong tape up each corner, and pin this to the shelves leaving a 10 inch (250 mm) gap between shelves. Finally cover it in light cotton. This job is easier when the assembly is hung up.

No zipper is necessary: tapes sewn on each side of the opening can be tied to close it. Alternatively, hook-and-loop tape (Velcro) does the job well.

The candle provides old-fashioned low-power lighting. Hazardous in crowded tents, it provides subtle light for the home. Improve the candle's performance dramatically by placing a reflecting surface behind it. A mirror is the obvious choice, and a tin can is an effective alternative. With the can's top removed, use metal snips to open out the can (Fig. 313). First snip down the side then cut three quarters of the way around the can at the base, leaving a shallow tray as in Figure 312 which will catch dripping wax. Open out as in Figure 312. Fold back sharp edges and all corners with pliers. The candle is held on an upturned nail glued to the base.

The reflector could be fixed to the wall with a nail, but a screw and wall plug would make a more secure fitting.

314

315

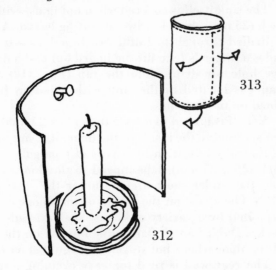

313

312

In Figure 314 an efficient stove for camping is made from two empty cans. The large upturned can stands some 12 inches (300 mm) tall over a low fish can in which sits a roll of cardboard soaked in paraffin wax. When this is lit, the heat intensity is regulated by covering more or less of the cardboard with a lid, which is made with the top of the fish can. Two holes are pierced about 1 inch (25 mm) apart near the edge of the lid, and the handle is inserted in these. The handle is merely a bent metal coat hanger, a useful tool for the low technologist (Fig. 315). The food cooks on top of the upturned can.

An insulated box (Fig. 316) can be used to make a simple slow-cooking system, particularly effective for cooking cheap meat. There are several methods of construction. Any box—even cardboard—will do to make the outer frame; crates are usually excellent, and insulated Styrofoam as in Figure 316 is highly efficient at conserving heat. A stylish wooden box could be built for the purpose. Whatever type of box you use, it should be about 4 inches (100 mm) larger all around than your casserole. The casserole lid should fit tightly; heavy cast iron is suitable.

Line the outer box with aluminum foil to reflect heat back inside. Pack it tightly with the insulating chips to within 4 inches (100 mm) of the top, and dig out a space for your casserole. The traditional insulator was hay. Insulating chips are a modern alternative. Cut a slab of Styrofoam to cover the lid, or pack insulating chips into a fireproofed fabric cushion to close in the top space.

Simmer the food on a stove for a few minutes, then remove it and put it straight into the box. Put the cushion in place. Close it in all day or all night and warm the food up when you want to eat it.

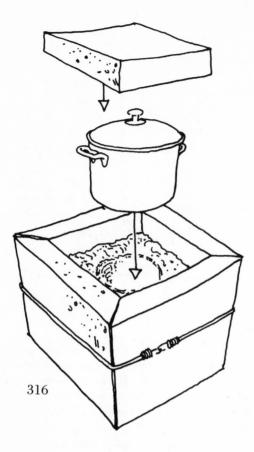

316

When the meal is over, Figure 317 is just a large cupboard with plain doors, but at dinner time it opens to reveal a complete minikitchen. The design is ideal for one-room living, where you don't want to feel that you live and sleep in a restaurant. Construction is simplified if the system is built into a deep recess, where side walls do not have to be built. The kitchen is fronted with two doors made from unframed lumbercore sheets 1 inch (25 mm) thick, fitted with high-level ventilation louvers. These vents are sold by builders' suppliers. Each door is held by two strong 2 inch (50 mm) hinges to a frame built just in front of the appliances (in this case stove and sink) and made from 2 x 2 inch (50 x 50 mm) softwood screwed securely to walls and ceiling joists. Make sure the top piece is fixed to joists and not just to plaster, and be sure all drawers and

cupboard doors have room to open when the frame and doors are attached! The doors are held closed by a standard bolt.

The exact kitchen layout is variable, depending on what appliances you want to build in. The water supply, electricity, and drainage possibilities will all influence your decisions.

Space has been economized in various ways. The "drawer" space immediately under a sink is unusable, but here the front panel—made of ¾ inch (20 mm) thick lumbercore—is hinged at the top; the flap can then be raised and held up by two stays screwed to the inside surface to provide an extra working surface.

The sink itself is covered when not in use with a 1 inch (25 mm) thick hardwood cutting board. A hole is drilled through to fulfill two functions—it provides a finger hole to lift the board out and a drainage hole for drips from the tap (Fig. 318). The panel is located in the sink with a batten frame glued on the bottom.

A shelf is hinged to a 1 x 1 inch (25 x 25 mm) batten screwed to the inside of the door; it is supported in the raised position by a pair of triangular 1 x 1 inch (25 x 25 mm) flaps hinged to the door. These fold flat under the batten to lower the shelf (Fig. 319). The space on the inside of the doors is fully exploited by a variety of hooks, shelves, rails, and racks. Don't hang inflammable objects on the side of the door where hot stove rings could start fires.

The rear wall is tiled for easy cleaning—smells lurk in an enclosed space. The top of the stove comes down to cover the rings when the cooking is over.

The hideaway principle can be employed to economize space in a restricted bathroom area (Figs. 320 and 321). The addition of a removable platform on top of the bathtub allows the basin to be positioned above the tub. The plan saves both floor space and plumbing time. As all the water supply and waste fixtures are close together, plumbing is simplified.

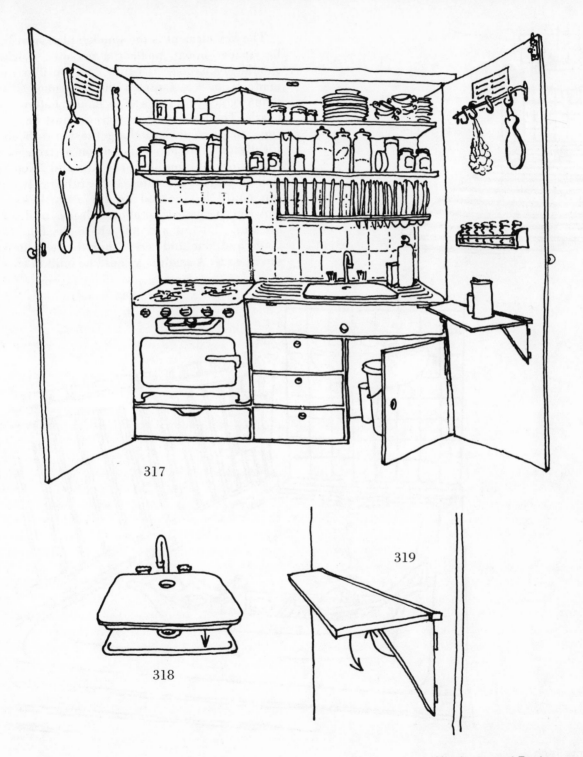

317

318

319

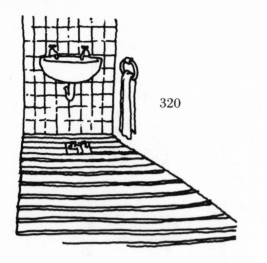

320

The key element is the wooden platform. It must be strong enough to bear a person's weight and should not damage the tub. The top illustrated is made from 4 x 1 inch (100 x 25 mm) softwood planks glued and screwed to similar battens underneath. The lower battens' screws must be countersunk to prevent scratching the bathtub enamel. Ideally the battens should sit on a strong wooden framework surrounding the tub and fixed to the wall on at least two sides. If the tub is cast iron the top could be located on the rim. Leave gaps between the boards to allow splashes to drain into the tub. Cut out a notch where the faucets protrude and glue and screw short battens under the sawed ends. A small box could be built to cover the

321

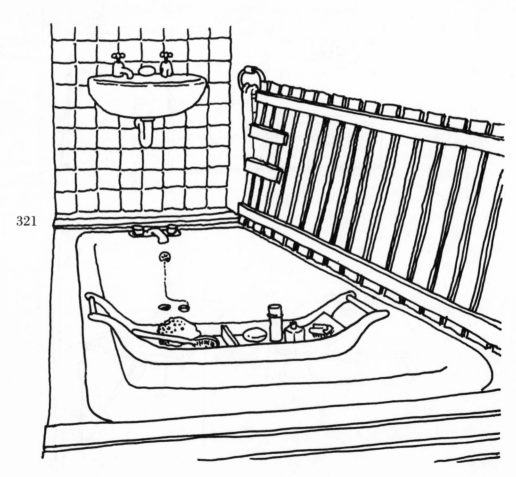

faucets and avoid painful toe-stubbing episodes in the morning.

The bathtub top now becomes the floor level for the hand basin. Position the basin at a convenient height above, using the tub's water supply and drainage pipes. One final feature—you will need a step to take you up to bath-top level.

A simple conversion often improves cheap old furniture's looks and usefulness in a new role. The cupboard base in Figure 322 was rescued from the dump and moved into the kitchen. Damp rising from the floor had rotted away its wooden feet until it wobbled alarmingly. Years of use had left the top stained, chipped, charred, and cracked. It looked awful, but the central cupboard section was sound and quite free of woodworm.

The old top was removed and replaced with a heavy 2 inch (50 mm) hardwood plank sawed to size. This makes an excellent chopping block and general work surface in the kitchen. A marble slab is a colder and flatter alternative. The butcher's block shown (Fig. 322) makes a very handsome work surface.

When the rotten feet were replaced with hefty castors the whole unit became mobile. As the back was now visible the old plywood back panel was covered in tongue-and-groove paneling.

Free-standing kitchen units from the 1950s and 1960s are slow sellers on the junk market, easily bought for next to nothing. The main doors of the typical example used for the project in Figure 323 were unscrewed and replaced by a ¾ inch (20 mm) lumbercore panel hinged at the bottom and held closed by a heavy-duty catch.

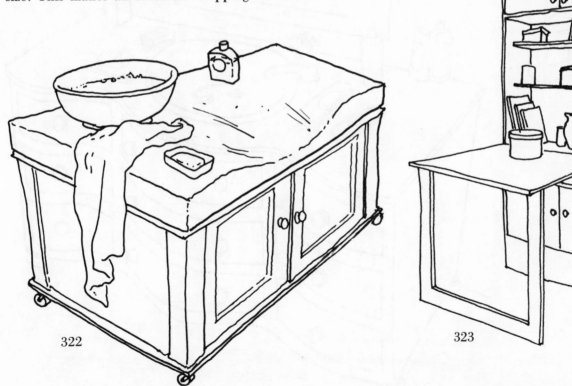

322

323

For the legs a U-shaped piece of ¾ inch (20 mm) plywood is cut out with a jigsaw to make a seamless three-sided frame, 3 inches (75 mm) wide. Don't skimp on this step; the design depends on the support you get from the continuous piece of wood. It is hinged to the foldaway panel so that the table is perfectly horizontal when in the open position (Fig. 324). The cupboard now opens out to provide a useful table/working surface which is rapidly folded away when not needed.

The working surface can be covered in a scrap of plastic laminate glued in place using contact adhesive. The outside of the entire cupboard is repainted in sky-blue gloss paint.

Old pieces of furniture can make fine housings for washbasins, particularly if you want to give your bathroom a period look. The chest of drawers in Figure 325 provides a spacious basin surround at the right height. Height can be reduced very easily by removing the chest's four feet.

Some useful drawer space has to be lost to make room for the basin and its waste fixtures underneath. The central top two drawers were quickly adapted by removing the sides, back, and base (Fig. 326). The fronts were then fixed back in position. Although glue is fast and firm, spring clips are preferable as they allow the fronts to be removed at any time to give instant access to the

324

325

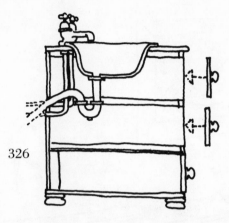

326

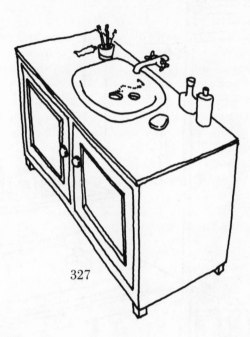

327

pipework. If spring clips or magnetic catches are used to hold the fronts, the lower drawer's base can be nailed to its runners to become a convenient shelf for bathroom cleaning materials, accessible merely by removing the front.

The oval hole for the basin was cut in the wooden top using a jigsaw, and two holes were drilled for the hot and cold water supply pipes. If you are reluctant to spoil a worthwhile piece in this way, remove the original top and replace it with another salvaged from a less desirable piece or with new synthetic marble which can be easily cut to shape.

Two coats of polyurethane varnish will protect a wooden top against damp. To stop water from seeping around the basin and taps squeeze a silicone sealant around the edges where they meet the top.

Figure 327 shows a simpler scheme based on a door-fronted cupboard. This involves no adaptation of drawers and only minimal pipework, as the water supply is carried inside the wall.

Cash-flow problems can halt major home-improvement plans. When money runs short the easy scheme shown in Figure 328 vastly improves an ugly bathroom without involving expenditure on new fittings. The plan relies heavily on shelves running round the room at two levels. This makes the room look larger and brings an integrated look to a chaotic layout.

Cheap seasoned pine floorboards are easy to buy from demolition yards. They can be cleaned with a rented electric belt sander. Three 7 inch (175 mm) boards are splined and glued together with woodworking adhesive to form a shelf. Clamp the boards tightly until the adhesive is dry. Screw the shelf to 2 x 1 inch (50 x 25 mm) softwood wall battens at 12 inch (300 mm) intervals. To strengthen the shelf at stress points such as alongside the basin and bath, glue and screw cross battens of 2 x 1 inch (50 x 25 mm) hardwood underneath and at right angles to the boards.

A lipping of 2 x 1 inch (50 x 25 mm) softwood is smeared with glue and screwed on the front of the shelves for strength and a tidy finish.

Gaps where shelves meet walls can be covered by wooden quadrant molding. All gaps are sealed with waterproof bath caulk, and boards are given three coats of polyurethane varnish to protect them from damp. Painting the pipework and the outside of the bath with high gloss paint will brighten the whole scheme.

A simpler variation of the idea is to build open slatted shelves with, say, ¾ inch (20 mm) gaps

between the shelf's three boards. Cross battens of 2 x 1 inch (50 x 25 mm) softwood glued and screwed under the boards at 12 inch (300 mm) intervals will hold the shelves together.

In Figure 330 ½ inch (12 mm) diameter dowels are glued between the shelves into ¼ inch (6 mm) deep locating holes of the same diameter. Large metal brackets from a demolished high-level toilet tank support the lower shelf.

A large woodworking project such as this always generates scraps of lumber. Eight 14 inch (350 mm) long scraps of 7 x 1 inch (175 x 25 mm) floorboards were screwed together to make the storage box/seat in Figure 329. A 16 inch (400 mm) square piece of ¾ inch (20 mm) thick plywood is nailed onto the base, with a similar piece sitting on the top. Triangular blocks of wood are glued 1 inch (25 mm) in from each corner to locate the top. Four furniture castors make the box mobile.

Showers save money by economizing on hot water. However, they may spray it all around the room, particularly with the free-standing bathtub in Figure 331. Waterproof window shades help keep the water in, while the slatted seat lets you sit down to enjoy a long shower.

329

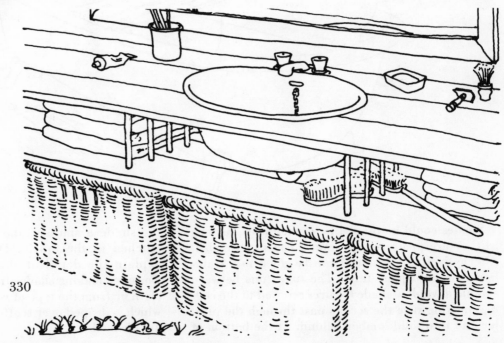

330

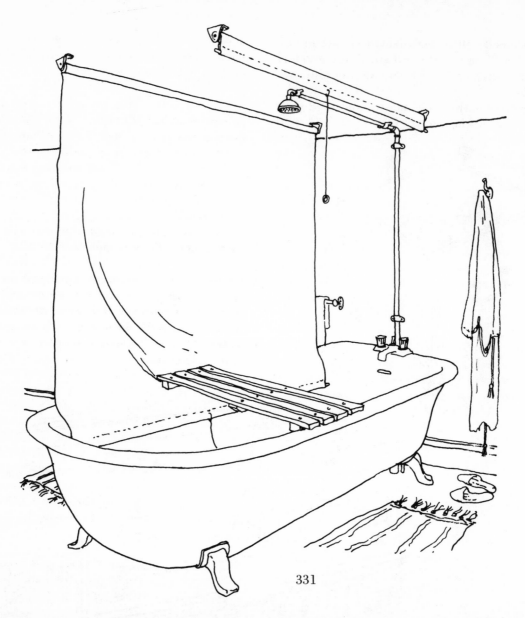

331

Shades could be pinned to wooden rods, as long as they are protected by several coats of varnish. Alternatively the material can be glued to a stainless steel or copper tube. The tube runs between standard window shade fixtures screwed to the ceiling, making sure the screws pass through the plaster and into solid lumber behind. At the bottom of the shade a similar tube is pushed into a sleeve stitched in the fabric. Do-it-yourself shade kits explain the detail of shade-making techniques. Consider making shades from brightly colored sailcloth or from the type of reinforced plastic sheeting which is draped over scaffolding when old buildings are cleaned.

The open slatted seat is made from four pieces of 3 x 1 inch (75 x 25 mm) softwood just long enough to span the tub and spaced with ½ inch (10 mm) gaps between. They are screwed onto three battens of 2 x 1 inch (50 x 25 mm) hardwood. The two outer battens sit just inside the rim of the tub and keep the seat from moving. Round off all ends with sandpaper to prevent the seat from tearing the shade.

If the shower head is fixed to a wall, the slatted seat can be screwed onto a pair of wall-mounted nonrust brackets under the shower.

The neat sponge rack in Figure 332 is made from scraps of plastic guttering, which are admirably adapted to life in a wet environment and easy to cut to length with a hacksaw. Two pieces are cut long enough to span the tub. Standard end stops are pushed onto each end of the guttering. Styrene cement glues the two trays to a pair of inverted lengths of the same guttering, positioned to sit on the rim of the tub. Four drainage holes ½ inch (10 mm) in diameter are drilled in each tray and the rough edges sanded smooth.

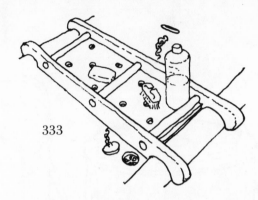

333

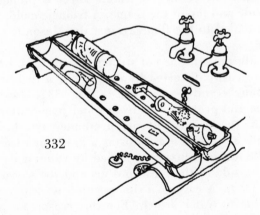

332

The rungs of a bathtub-width section of a broken ladder are shaped with a rasp or jigsaw to sit on the tub rim in Figure 333. A drilled sheet of ½ inch (12 mm) thick lumber is screwed to the ladder and the entire assembly varnished with polyurethane.

Figure 334 is the lowest of the low tech—a garbage can brings the joy of the pack-away shower to homes with no drainage. You turn on, climb in, and clean up. The water accumulates in the can, to be carried out and poured away when the washing's done. The whole shower packs away tidily (Fig. 336).

A standard push-on shower mixer attachment is extended by adding a long section of plastic hose in between its two elements. At the shower end the hose passes through a hole drilled in the can's rubber lid. A plastic shower curtain 1½ times the circumference of the lid is loosely stitched inside the rim of the lid. The lid is suspended from a 3 inch (75 mm) ceiling hook by a four-way elastic cable, or "spider," bought from a motorcycle dealer. The cable's four arms run through 4 inch (100 mm) diameter ventilation holes cut in the lid (Fig. 335) using a sharp knife.

Hiding plain, inexpensive, or unattractive materials behind a luxurious façade is an age-old commercial practice. In Figure 337 the principle is employed to great effect in a bathroom design which gives a dull bathtub a fast touch of glamor with the bonus of a warmer bath.

The space around the tub was packed with Styrofoam blocks used for hi-fi packaging and readily found outside city shops at night. The material's high insulation value keeps the bath water warm and so saves energy. Styrofoam pellets—again sal-

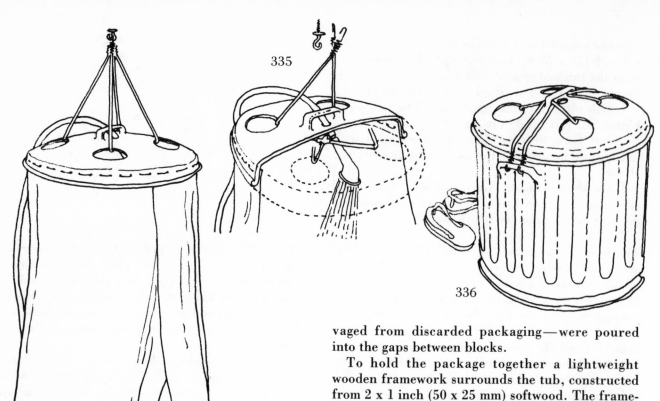

335

336

334

vaged from discarded packaging—were poured into the gaps between blocks.

To hold the package together a lightweight wooden framework surrounds the tub, constructed from 2 x 1 inch (50 x 25 mm) softwood. The framework is nailed together and attached to the walls and floor by screws. Masonite sheet is pinned to the side and top of the frame. A triangle molding is then nailed to the floor against the Masonite (Fig. 338).

A Masonite top is not strong enough to sit on. It is also easily distorted by damp. For a firmer top lay tongue-and-groove boards (Fig. 337) over the frame and protect them from water penetration by sealing the boards with polyurethane varnish. The boards are easily shaped using a jigsaw or rasp.

The touch of luxury is added by running carpet up the side of the bath and around the surround (Fig. 339). A carpet in this position is clearly vulnerable to water attack. For this reason we used plastic artificial grass bought cheaply at the end of an exhibition where it had been used on one of the stands.

The carpeted framework can of course be used without any inside insulation. It is a neat method of reducing the visual impact of an ugly bathtub.

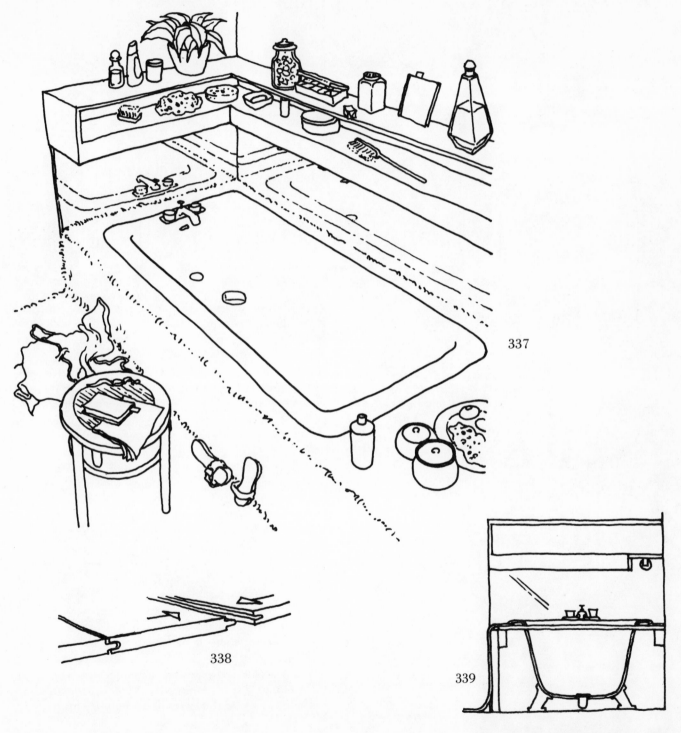

337

338

339

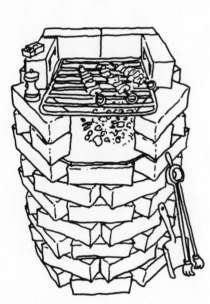

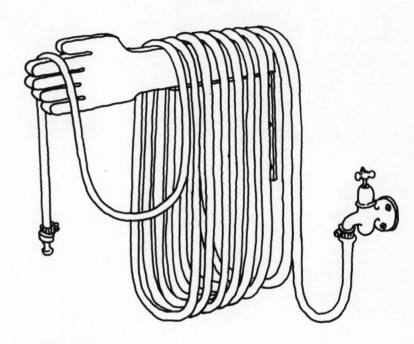

There are several construction elements admirably suited to making outdoor planters. Round sewer pipes, clay flue liners for chimneys which come in round or square shapes, lowly gray cement building blocks, and even chimney pots, when you can find them, look striking grouped together (Fig. 340).

You will find these elements at salvage yards, and they are inexpensive to buy new at building supply stores.

Pipes, liners, or blocks can be sunk directly into the ground, filled with soil, and planted. Or if you want to use them on a patio or indoors, some modification will be necessary to create a bottom. Two holes can be drilled with a masonry bit into the side of the pipe or liner, and chicken wire lined with sphagnum moss can then be wired in place. Or, fiberglass-reinforced plastic can be cut to fit the bottom of your newly created container and glued in place with epoxy glue. Holes must be drilled in the plastic for drainage; to further help drainage, put some gravel or broken pots in the bottom before filling with earth.

Round pipes may hold a flower pot without modification. If they need support to keep them from dropping through, a wire frame can be formed by bending two coat hangers as shown in Figures 341 and 342.

Chimney pots or flue liners are admirably suited to growing herbs. Use the herbs you have grown to flavor the meat cooking on this homemade, loose-laid, brick-built barbecue (Fig. 343). It can be assembled in half an hour, and dismantled even faster when the party's over.

Build the barbecue from new or old bricks. Be sure to choose reasonably regular bricks, otherwise they won't stack neatly. For easy mortar-free laying the best type of brick has only a small frog (indentation) on top, well clear of the edge. Modern mortars are almost impossible to remove from bricks, so choose either clean bricks or old ones. The construction stands on a level slab at least 24 inches (600 mm) square.

The low-level barbecue shown (Fig. 343) stands some 24 inches (600 mm) tall. Each additional brick course adds about 2½ inches (65 mm) to the

340

341

342

height and uses another six bricks. Fifty-eight bricks are needed to build the design shown. Buy a few extras to replace uneven or broken bricks.

Note the pair of half bricks on each side of the hearth opening in the second course from the top, and the four bricks placed on end as a windbreak around the grill. The grill itself is taken from a normal domestic stove. The charcoal burns on a metal sheet cut to shape with metal snips. It is simply placed between two courses of brick as shown.

Once the charcoal is burning, the draft can be controlled by putting a brick in the hearth opening.

Outdoor meals can be eaten on the aromatic table shown in Figure 344. Two bulbous herb-planted pots are placed 36 inches (1 m) apart and covered with a marine plywood top (Fig. 345). The top

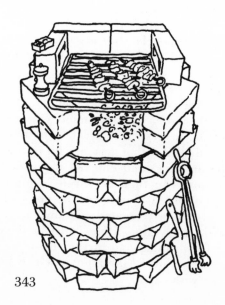

343

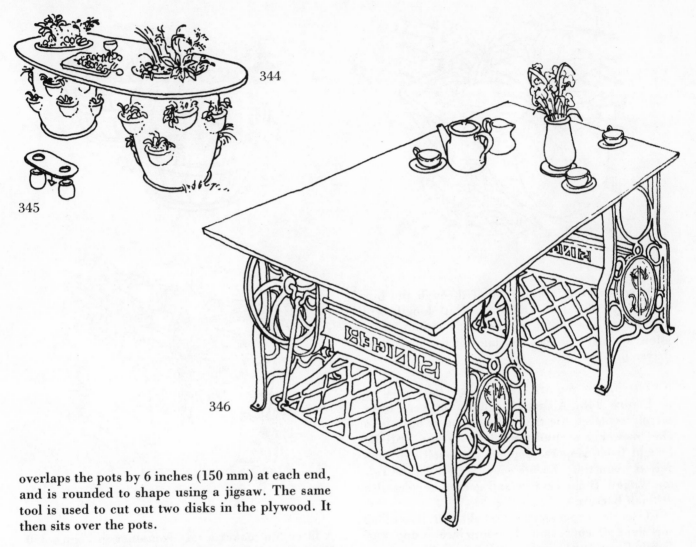

344

345

346

overlaps the pots by 6 inches (150 mm) at each end, and is rounded to shape using a jigsaw. The same tool is used to cut out two disks in the plywood. It then sits over the pots.

An instant table for outdoor eating is seen in Figure 346. The twin trestles are sewing machine bases, which are of course made to give the ideal height to sit at.

The top in the table illustrated is the marble top taken from a worm-eaten wooden washstand. This gives a suitably waterproof surface, and remains stable on the table without any fastening. A wooden top will need a protective coat of preservative before being exposed to winter's wind and rains.

Planters sold by garden centers can be very expensive. Such high costs force low technologists to act. All over the western world clever gardeners have found cheaper alternatives to do the job.

The wall-hung container in Figure 347 is the grass box off a lawnmower. A small ¼ inch (6 mm) diameter drainage hole is drilled halfway up each side. This prevents the box from becoming waterlogged but allows water to collect in the bottom ready to rise and feed the plants during dry spells.

347

348

349

Drive a strong masonry nail through the box mountings and into the wall. Nail length will depend on the design of the box's mountings—allow at least 2 inches (50 mm) of the nail to be driven into the wall.

No fastening is required for the beer barrel halves in Figure 348. Although aluminum kegs have largely replaced the traditional wooden barrels in the brewery, secondhand barrels can still be bought from coopers. Coopers often sell half barrels as plant tubs. Locate coopers through the *Yellow Pages*. Home centers and garden centers also sell half barrels.

Check the iron hoops around old barrels, looking for signs of corrosion. If hoops are sound and tightly fixed, the barrel is probably usable.

Plants grow in wall-mounted paint cans in Figure 349. One hangs on a metal wall bracket, the other is held by a masonry nail driven through the can and into the wall. Three drainage holes are drilled 3 inches (75 mm) from the base.

The paint manufacturer's trademarks may seem unsightly on your garden wall. The solution lies in the can—paint. An array of brightly colored cans makes a cheerful display.

A litter bin makes a tidy container in Figure 350. Bins can be bought from industrial equipment suppliers. Designs vary, but they are typically hooked onto two bolts driven into the wall and left protruding ½ inch (10 mm).

The various links in a domestic drainage system, from sink to sewage pipes, can be used in the garden. Secondhand sewage pipes are undesirable; new ones may be available when drains are being laid. Broken drainage sections are no use on site, and the foreman may sell you some cheap.

The large pipes are concrete and astoundingly heavy—muscular friends and a van will be needed to get them home (Fig. 351). Pipes are designed for interlocking, and you can raise the height by stacking the sections.

A coat of paint improves the appearance of concrete. Use exterior grade emulsion paint or masonry paint. The narrowed end can be painted in a contrasting color to the rest of the tub.

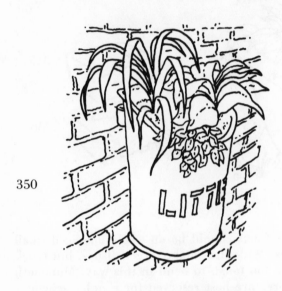

350

351

Cast iron tubs are often smashed and sold for scrap during demolition or renovation jobs. If you want to salvage a tub, ask the foreman before work begins and the tub is endangered. Take into account the cost and problems of transporting a very heavy cast iron tub.

The plughole provides a ready-made drainage system. Put a few broken crocks around it to stop soil blockages (Fig. 353).

The humble toilet bowl in Figure 352 might benefit from the disguise which gives the sink in Figure 354 its ancient stone trough look. First coat the sink with industrial glue (Fig. 355). When this is tacky slap on a mixture made of equal parts of sand, cement, and peat (Fig. 356). One bag of cement would more than coat a sink. Ask your builders' supplier for a broken bag—it's cheaper.

Every year hundreds of millions of tires wear out on the world's roads and are thrown away. This heap of discarded rubber has become a valuable resource to the world's low technologists. Moroccan shoemakers shape them into soles for sandals. African craftsmen sew strips of tires together to make water-carrying vessels. French winegrowers burn them in Burgundian vineyards to ward off frost. And now modern technology is building old tires into the roads they once rode. The tires are ground into "crumb" and incorporated into the road surface.

352

353

354

355

356

Tire dealers may give you a few from their discard pile; you could buy them cheap from wreckers' yards when they are too worn to reuse on the road. Signs of wear are bulging carcasses, cracked rubber, irregular tread wear, and scuffed sidewalls.

The whole wheel was salvaged from a scrap car for Figure 357, with the tire still on the rim. The tire is sliced into two around its circumference using a fine-toothed woodworking saw. A simple cutting knife cuts through thin, bald tires, whereas a hacksaw will be needed to cope with steel-braced tires. The two rubber flaps are then folded outward (Fig. 358). They will naturally hold the cupped shape shown, though a certain amount of trial and error may be needed to get a satisfactory shape.

First efforts should be on easily managed small car tires. Wide tires make larger dishes, but truck tires are too tough to bend in this way. Mammoth truck tires are best reserved for simpler schemes, such as the instant sandbox in Figure 363.

The tire need not be cut centrally. In Figure 359 the cut is made near one edge, so that the top section forms a large dish, the lower one a small plinth.

The bolt holes in the rim provide drainage. Place a few broken pots around them and fill the planter with earth. An avenue of these planters could look appropriate along a driveway.

Dull black tires can be livened up with paint. Rubber-based paint for tire wall decoration is sold by automobile accessory stores. Silver spray can look dramatically handsome.

A steel wheel rim, without its tire, is mounted on the wall near the garden tap and becomes a hose reel in Figure 360. Screws can be driven into the wall through the existing bolt holes, but this system keeps the wheel from turning. On the other hand the wheel will still spin if it rests on a metal pipe cemented into the wall to act as a spindle. The flange shown on the spindle (Fig. 360) stops the wheel from falling off—it will also stop it from going on, so don't attach it before the wheel is in place.

A pile of tires can simply be filled with earth and plants (Fig. 361). For extra stability push metal rods down through holes drilled in three places through all the tires. Drill holes before you pack the earth in.

Tires can be stacked to build a cheap, quick, durable, effective, and mortar-free wall which can be dismantled at will. Tire walls form effective barriers against noise or drifting sand. The principle of construction is to lay tires several wide at the base, reducing the number toward the top.

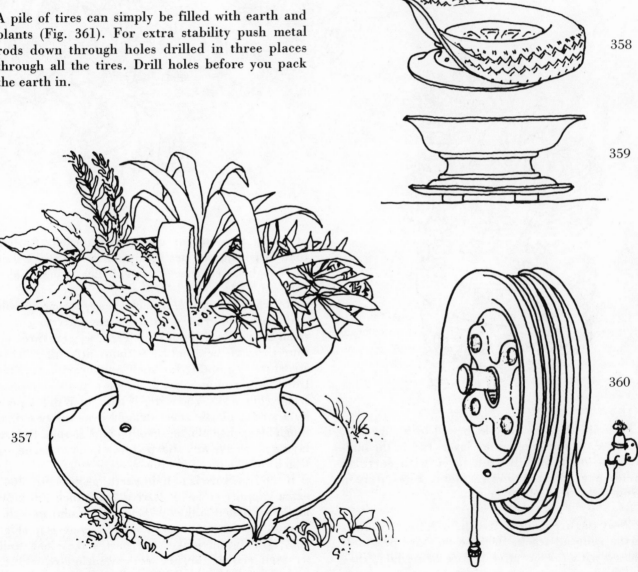

358

359

357

360

362

361

To build the three-tire-high wall in Figure 362, lay three tires on the bottom layer, two in the middle, one on top. Fill each layer with earth to encourage plant growth. Metal bars driven through the tires add strength.

Railway ties are made to last through harsh winters on the railroad track. Because they are pressure-treated with preservative before being laid, they are ideal for outdoor use in the garden. Rather than disguising the ties with paint or plane, exploit the rough-sawed rugged appeal. Leave both holes exposed.

Railroad ties are extremely heavy, and you will need suitable transport arrangements to carry them home. Because of their great weight, three or four ties can be stacked without attaching. This structure is suitable for such temporary constructions as a summer sandbox or a paddling pool frame (Fig. 371). The water is contained in the pool by a strong plastic sheet draped over the ties. Use tough 500 gauge plastic sheeting laid double. Before laying it remove any sharp stones from underneath which could cause punctures.

If the structure is to hold earth, as in Figure 364, extra support is useful. Drive 2 x 2 inch (50 x 50 mm) sharpened stakes 9 inches (250 mm) into the ground at each corner and where ties overlap (Fig. 365). Hardwood makes the best stakes: oak and western red cedar are very weather-resistant.

Wood should be soaked with preservative. Three-inch (75 mm) nails fix the stakes to the ties (Fig. 366).

Railroad ties need no foundations—lay them straight on earth. No stakes are needed if ties are tilted back (Figs. 367 and 368).

Railroad ties stand in a row (Fig. 369) to keep earth from slipping over the patio. A 6 inch (150 mm) thick layer of hardcore (broken bricks or clean rubble) is packed between the ties and the earth behind (see Fig. 370). Hardcore also packs the bottom 4 inches (100 mm) of a trench 18 inches (500 mm) deep and is built up 8 inches (200 mm) around the tie. A concrete mix of one part cement, four parts broken bricks or stones, and three parts sand is poured in and packed down hard. You will need about six bags of cement to fill 36 cubic feet (1 m^3).

Vary railroad tie heights at the top to add interest. But remember that sawing ties is tough work. A rented chainsaw makes it easier. The wooden tie

363

364

365

366

surface can also be used to hang flower baskets or pots of herbs.

Ties are slotted between H-section rolled steel joists to make the solid yet simple fence in Figure 372.

Measure your ties' length to establish the gap you need between uprights. These are rolled steel joists, another demolition-site buy. They sit in 18

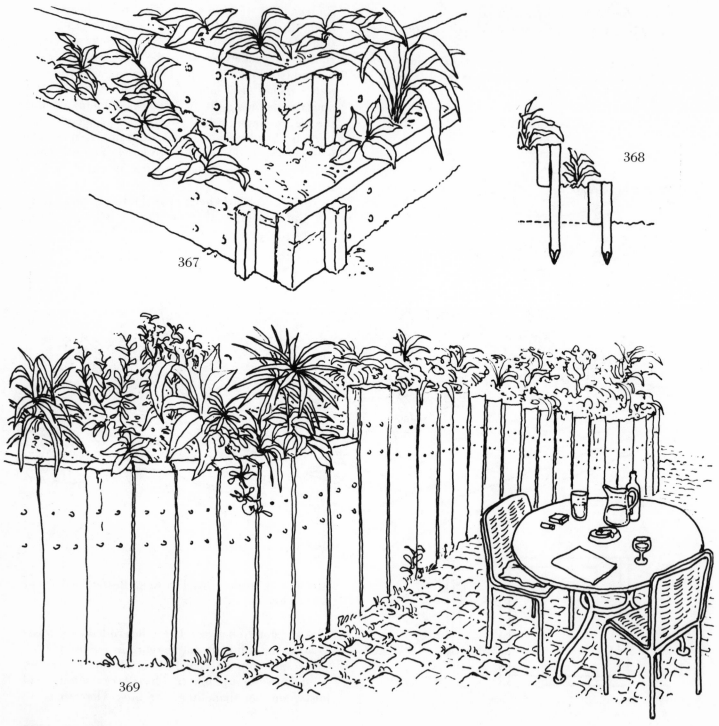

367

368

369

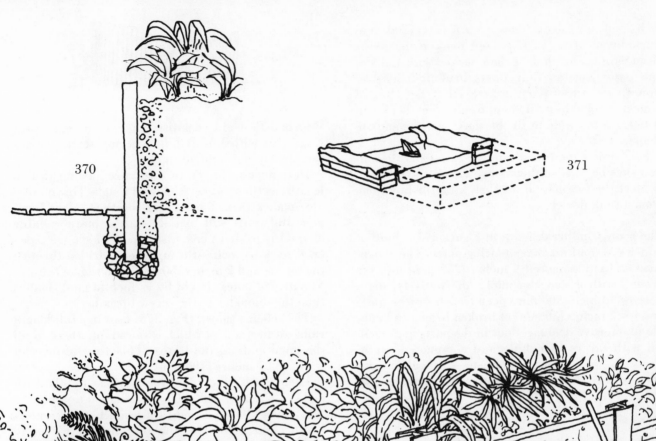

370

371

372

inch (500 mm) deep holes on a 4 inch (100 mm) thick layer of well-compacted broken bricks or clean rubble. The hole is then packed with a mix of one part cement, four parts broken bricks or stones, and three parts coarse sand. One bag of cement is enough to fill about 6 cubic feet (0.15 m³). If ties are too wide to fit the slots, saw the ends to shape.

Steel joists tend to disappear fast from demolition sites because of their scrap value. Buyers need to alert the foreman at an early stage or buy them from a junk dealer.

The wavy windbreak/fence in Figure 373 is built of 3 inch (75 mm) diameter fencing posts. The sharpened end is hammered 9 inches (250 mm) into the ground with a sledgehammer. Alternatively, dig a narrow 12 inch (300 mm) deep trench for the posts and lay 2 inches (50 mm) of broken bricks and rubble to improve drainage, put in the posts and backfill with layers of rubble and compacted earth. Posts are too expensive to waste—treat them with preservative before banging them in. Post heights can be varied as in Figure 374.

374

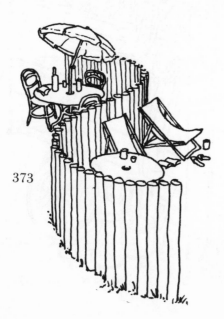

373

Railroad ties laid edgewise make a low patio seat (Fig. 375) with lift-off lids covering storage space for garden tools and clutter.

Design your boxes to minimize sawing ties to length, as the ties are thick and tough. This quality also makes them hard to fix together. Mere hammer and nails will usually fail; a more reliable method is to drive coach screws—which are tightened by a wrench—through holes drilled through the top tie and 2 inches (50 mm) into the tie behind. The drilled holes should be ⅛ inch (3 mm) smaller than the diameter of the screw thread.

The scheme shown (Fig. 375) uses five full-length railroad ties, one of which is sawed into three to fill the open ends of the boxes. This gives an overall width of 27 inches (700 mm).

Each top is made of three railroad-tie planks 9 inches (225 mm) wide. They are nailed to a pair of 4 x 1 inch (100 x 25 mm) softwood battens underneath (Fig. 376). Cut the battens to fit exactly between the ties, so that the tops are held in position (Fig. 377).

All the wood in the tops was given three protective coats of polyurethane varnish. To prevent rot from setting in, exposed end grain and points where nails were driven in were filled with plastic wood before varnishing.

When the handle snaps off a fork or spade, prolong its useful life in the garden by converting it into a handy mobile organizer for tools, string, gloves, and other small oddments (Fig. 378). The tip is sharpened so it will stand upright in the ground—it can also double as a dibble for making holes for bulbs at planting time.

Two empty coffee cans are attached to the handle by a screw driven through a hole drilled near the can's top rim. A rubber band around the middle

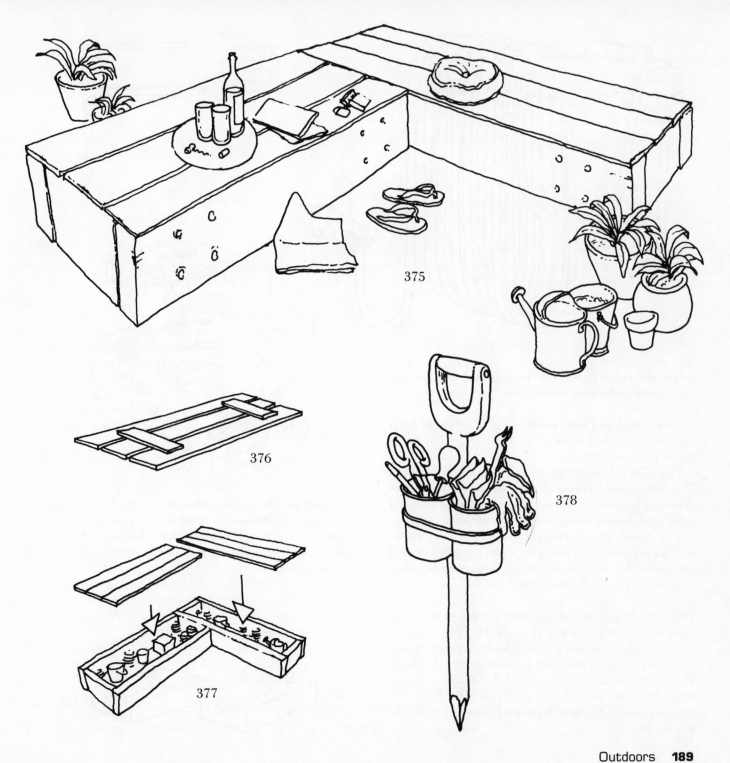

375

376

377

378

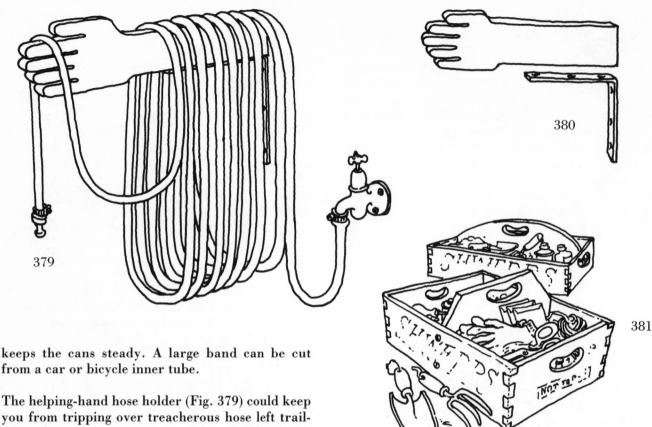

379

380

381

keeps the cans steady. A large band can be cut from a car or bicycle inner tube.

The helping-hand hose holder (Fig. 379) could keep you from tripping over treacherous hose left trailing in the grass.

The hand is screwed to a rigid metal bracket (Fig. 380) fixed to the wall near the water supply. A cast iron bracket salvaged from underneath an old toilet tank would be both strong and decorative.

The hand is cut from 1 inch (25 mm) thick marine plywood, shaped with a powered jigsaw and painted with wood primer and a decorative top coat to protect it from the weather.

Tools can be carried around the garden in an easily adapted wooden crate (Fig. 381). The central divider/handle is cut from 1 inch (25 mm) thick softwood to span the gap between the box sides. The carrying hole can be chiseled out, but a jigsaw simplifies the job. The same saw will form the rounded top of the insert shown in the upper box of Figure 381.

Smear woodworking adhesive on the bottom and side edges of the insert, drop it into position in the center of the box (Figs. 382 and 383) and hold it with three 1½ inch (40 mm) nails driven through the box sides.

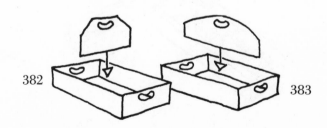

382

383

When the seedlings are planted out, the gardener can relax over a game of checkers played on the patio with the empty pots as pieces (Fig. 384).

Large-scale chess games played with giant chessmen are common in Europe's public parks and town squares. Checkers or draughts pieces are easier to improvise; the only essential is that each player's twelve identical pieces must be a different color from the opponent's. Paint clay pots with external grade emulsion paint.

Chessboards are normally black and white, but other color combinations are acceptable and better suited to most gardens. Alternatives are cream and brown squares or white and green ones. Checkers can be played on a dark green and buff board.

The square board contains sixty-four 12 inch (300 mm) square concrete slabs, laid with eight on each side. Slabs can be bought from garden centers in various colors, and they are not expensive. However, they are even cheaper to make at home, and casting the slabs in a homemade mold is simple. The technique is explained on pages 215–216.

To color the concrete, special concrete dye is stirred into the mix before it dries. If you choose the white and green combination, you could save on casting time by allowing grass to grow in the thirty-two green squares.

For a durable playing area, lay the slabs on a 2 inch (50 mm) bed of sand spread over a 3 inch (75 mm) base of hardcore. This is not crucial. Soil can be swept between the slabs to encourage plants to grow.

Concrete slabs left over from the checkerboard can be stacked to make a low table for the patio. The table shown (Fig. 385) uses sixteen square slabs, simply loose-laid in four piles four high. Height can be changed instantly by adding slabs. Modernists may like one corner stacked higher than the others and may even find the table's stark looks fit for indoor use.

Concrete is hard and rough to touch; the table-top can be covered by a more friendly surface such as wood.

Despite legislation to ban disposable bottles, unwanted empties are still a worldwide problem. Throwaway bottles can be incorporated into walls.

If you don't generate enough disposable empties at home ask a local restaurant for supplies. Dispos-

385

384

ing of wine bottles is a problem most are happy to solve so simply.

Whole bottles laid flat in a concrete wall (Fig. 386) economize on concrete. This is the low-tech version of the glass cube walls fashionable in the 1930s.

A weak concrete mix is suitable to bind the bottles, with one part cement, six parts sand, and three parts stone aggregate. Each bag of cement should fill 12 cubic feet (0.3 m^3). Upturned bottles add a decorative touch on top, and plants can be grown inside them. These are a mixture of green

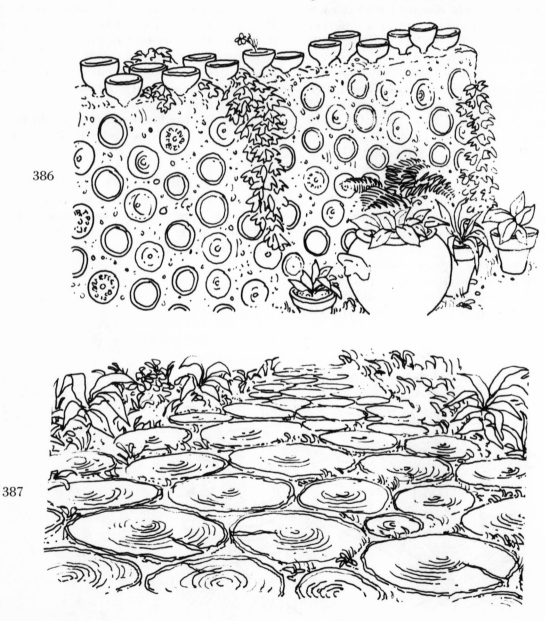

386

387

and clear glass wine bottles with the bottom half removed neatly with a patent bottle-cutting tool (see p. 210). Cutting the necks off the horizontal bottles maximizes the light passing through the wall.

Wear leather gloves when you are working with cut bottles.

Environmental groups opposing the disposable bottle have also campaigned against the wanton destruction of woodland. When an old garden tree becomes dangerous and must be felled, it can remain an integral part of the garden. In Figure 387 sections of a tree trunk 2 inches (50 mm) thick are bedded in a layer of well-compacted coarse sand to make a rustic path. Moss looks good growing between the slices, but beware—wet weather makes wood very slippery.

People who maintain or remove trees will usually slice a tree for you, but carrying even a 36 inch (1000 mm) length of the trunk from a fully grown hardwood tree can be extremely heavy work. You must arrange adequate transport and help. Otherwise cut the slices on the spot yourself with a hired cordless chainsaw. Try to cut some small disks to fill in gaps between the large slices.

LOW TECH TECHNIQUES

Moldings

Accurate sawing and attaching demands the skill and care of the craftsman, which few fast furnishers have. Ragged edges and poor joins in woodwork are often easy to disguise by pinning on a standard wooden molding. Lumberyards stock a wide range for all purposes, some of which are shown in Figures 388–401.

Moldings are normally nailed with finishing nails and glued in place. Use white woodworking adhesive on lumber. Water-resistant impact adhesive can be used in damp conditions. For a neat finish push panel pins below the wood surface and cover with wood filler.

Aluminum edging strips and moldings, such as those widely used by furniture manufacturers, are also on sale to the amateur.

Quadrant (Fig. 388)—covers gaps on joints, for example where baseboard and floor meet.

Cove (Fig. 389)—a decorative alternative to quadrant molding.

Triangle (Fig. 390)—use as quadrant.

Half-round (Fig. 391)—hides gaps between butted panels.

Twice rounded (Fig. 392)—use as half-round.

Reeds (Fig. 393)—decorative joint cover.

Astragal (Fig. 394)—shouldered half-round.

Birdsmouth (Fig. 395)—decorative and protective cover for outside corners.

Flat corner (Fig. 396)—a plain alternative to birdsmouth.

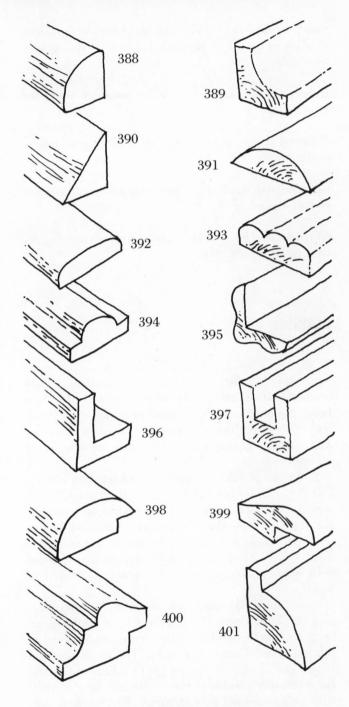

Single groove (Fig. 397)—channel for sliding doors of glass or wood. A double-grooved version is also available.

Rebated half-round (Fig. 398)—popular cover for panel edges.

Rebated utility (Fig. 399)—does the same job as half-round.

Rebated astragal (Fig. 400)—another alternative to half-round.

Glass bead (Fig. 401)—holds glass in its frame, with or without putty.

Lumber

Traditional lumber is lovely to look at but very expensive to buy. Buying it secondhand cuts lumber costs considerably. If you are forced to buy new, choose softwood (lumber from evergreen trees) rather than the costlier hardwood (from deciduous trees such as oak, beech, and mahogany).

Softwood planks are easy to find from ½ inch to 2 inches (12–50 mm) thick and 1–9 inches (25–225 mm) wide, with larger sizes available on demand. But be careful—these sizes are measured before the wood is planed smooth, so the actual measurement will be some $3/16$ inch (5 mm) smaller. Avoid split lumber, damp wood, and lengths covered in knots.

Sheet materials such as plywood, lumbercore, and chipboard provide a rapid way of building up large flat surfaces without the problems involved in joining several narrow planks. The most common board size is 96 x 48 inches (2440 x 1220 mm), and for economy's sake projects should be designed with this standard size in mind. For smaller sizes look for scraps in the lumberyard.

Plywood (Fig. 402) is made by gluing together several thin layers of wood, generally with a decorative veneer on the outside such as birch or pine. Mask cut edges with adhesive veneer tape or wooden molding. Normal thicknesses are from ⅛ to 1 inch (3–25 mm). The price rises with thickness. Plywood is equally strong in all directions, so it can be cut in odd curves without risk of snapping along the grain.

Lumbercore (Fig. 403) looks the same as plywood on the surface, but inside are blocks of wood glued alongside each other. It is easy to work and handsome enough for use in furniture and shelving.

Chipboard (Fig. 404) is cheaper than plywood or lumbercore, but it is not as strong. It consists of wood chips covered in resin glue and compressed into sheets. It is fairly brittle along the edges. Chipboard cannot get a firm grip on nails or screws driven into the edges without using one of the special chipboard connectors shown in Figure 405. Planks of veneered chipboard are also available in widths from 6 to 48 inches (150–1220 mm). Iron-on edging strip can be bought in rolls to cover up raw

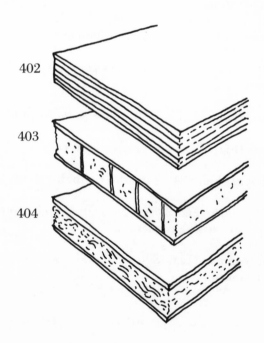

402

403

404

edges. Edges can also be protected decoratively by hardwood lipping.

The veneer on chipboard is easily chipped if you use a coarse saw. Prevent damage when sawing along a board by supporting both sides of the cut so the last few inches of uncut board cannot snap off.

Masonite is made of processed fibers pressed together into flexible boards. Most are ⅛ inch or ¼ inch (3 mm or 6 mm) thick, with 96 x 48 inch (2440 x 1220 mm) the most common board size. Masonite is widely used on the back of furniture and can be nailed down as a cheap flooring material over uneven and drafty floorboards. Ideally sheets should be sprinkled with water and stacked for a couple of days to acclimatize in the room before being used. Pierced Masonite panels can be used for decorative effect. Some patterns are shown in Figure 406.

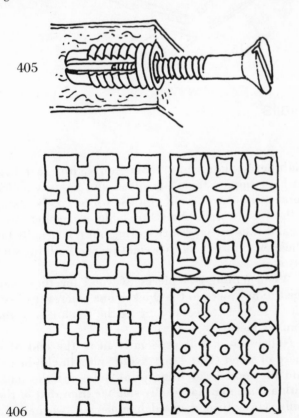

405

406

Sawing

If you find sawing by hand exhausting, your saw may be blunt. Have it resharpened and set through your local tool supplier: the cost is low and the improvement immediately obvious.

Sawing can damage lumber. Wood tends to split where the teeth emerge. If this matters, always put what will be the top side of the wood face up when cutting with a handsaw, the other side up for a jigsaw or circular saw. Support both ends of the piece to prevent snapping when the cut is nearly through.

Joints

The fast furnisher makes firm joints without resorting to the tricky precision work beloved of cabinet makers.

The *butt joint* (Fig. 407) is the simplest. The two pieces are simply laid alongside each other. For a neat joining the ends of each piece should be square. Glue both with white woodworking adhesive and fix them together with nails or screws.

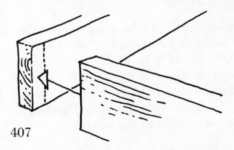

407

A *dowel joint* (Fig. 408) is a butt joint held with glued wooden dowels rather than screws or nails. With the two pieces in position drill a hole of dowel diameter through one and into the other. Smear glue on the dowels and the surfaces to be joined and hammer the dowels home.

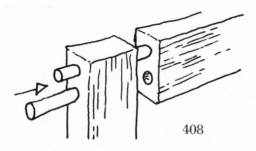

408

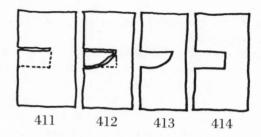

411   412   413   414

A *spline joint* (Fig. 409) is a fine way of joining two long boards together, for example, when making a tabletop from planks. The job is too hard without an electric router; with one it's very simple. You rout out a ¾ inch (20 mm) deep and ¼ inch (7 mm) wide channel in each adjoining piece. A 1¼ x ¼ inch (32 x 7 mm) spline—which is simply a strip of hardwood—is then smeared in white woodworking adhesive and pushed into one of the grooves. The second board is pushed over this. Clamp the work and hold it flat until the adhesive dries.

A *half-lap joint* (Fig. 415) is a method of interlocking two battens. Matching grooves are cut out of the two pieces, as wide as the battens and half as deep. First mark out carefully, then use a fine-toothed saw to cut down to the halfway point at each side of the joint. Chisel out the waste.

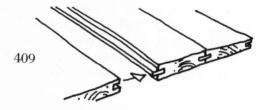

409

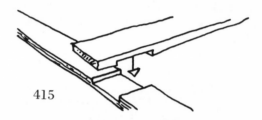

415

The router can also be used to cut slots to the halfway point in two pieces of wood which are to interlock (Fig. 410) to make a very simple and strong joint. A jigsaw is a readily available alternative to the router and gives excellent results. Four cuts are involved, illustrated in Figures 411–414. The slots are as wide as the boards.

Nails

Cabinet makers may scorn nails, but fast furnishers employ them for speed and ease. A nailed joint will be stronger if you use white woodworking adhesive as well. Nails are sold in packets and small boxes by hardware stores, but it is usually far cheaper to buy them by weight from a building supply store.

When nailing two pieces of wood together, nail the thinner piece to the thicker one wherever possible. Use nails twice as long as the thickness of the thinner piece.

Nails split wood, especially near the end of a piece of wood (Fig. 416). Avoid splits in chipboard and plywood by drilling pilot holes for the nails with a diameter marginally smaller than that of the nails. On softwood avoid hammering two nails in

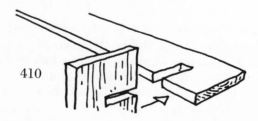

410

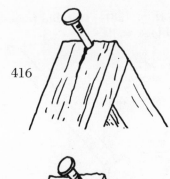

416

417

on the same line of grain (Fig. 417). For maximum security blunt the point of the nail.

Drive nails into wood at an angle to increase the strength of the joint. The strongest nail fastening comes from one nail driven in at an angle of 45° one way and a second at 45° the other (Fig. 418).

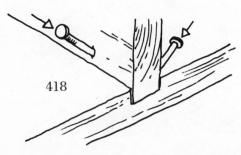

418

Clench nailing makes a really strong joint. Hammer a pair of nails through both pieces of lumber from opposite sides and about ½ inch (10 mm) apart. The nails should be long enough to stick out at least 1 inch (25 mm) as in Figure 419. Hammer the projecting ends flat (Fig. 420). Round wire nails are good for this purpose.

For "secret" nailing in tongue-and-groove board hammer nails into the tongue at a 45° angle, so they

emerge through the full board. The groove in the next board now covers the joining (Fig. 420).

419   420

Box nails (Fig. 421)—well suited for general joinery. Avoid split wood by hammering them in with the nail's long side parallel to the wood grain.

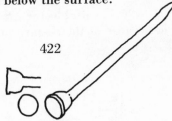

421

Casing nails (Fig. 422)—stronger than ovals and easily punched below the surface.

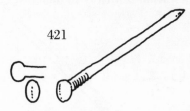

422

Common nails (Fig. 423)—strong nails for rough carpentry. They tend to split wood.

423

Cut floor nail (Fig. 424)—used for attaching floorboards. Rectangular in section, with rectangular head.

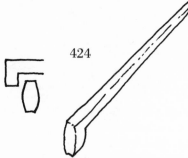

424

Finishing nail (Fig. 425)—light nails used for attaching moldings. Grooves on the nails keep paneling such as Masonite firmly in place.

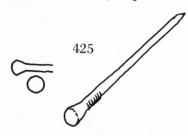

425

Tacks (Fig. 426)—suitable for attaching carpets and fabric because of their sharp points and large flat heads.

426

Staples (Fig. 427)—U-shaped nails which grip wire. Available with insulated lining for electric cable.

427

Masonry nail (Fig. 428)—suitable for use in brick and concrete block walls.

428

Braces and Corner Joints

Wood joints can be reinforced with inexpensive metal repair plates, which are made in a variety of shapes and sizes (Fig. 429) to cope with specific jobs.

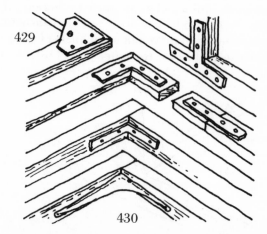

429

430

The traditional metal corner bracket (Fig. 430) will join two pieces of wood to each other at right angles. Two-part plastic assembly joints (Fig. 431) are growing in popularity as an easy way of doing the same job. They are also known as "corner joints" or "KD fittings" from their widespread use by manufacturers of knock-down (KD) furniture. They are particularly handy when joining veneered chipboard, lumbercore, or plywood, which are

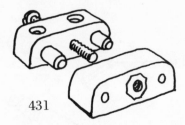
431

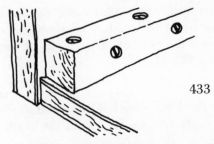
433

hard to joint using the traditional cabinet maker's techniques. The modern joint makes it possible to join wood quickly and securely, making the slow dovetail redundant in fast furnishing.

Screws

Screws pull joints tightly together; they hold joints better than nails can and they are easier to withdraw than nails when you want to dismantle furniture.

To join two pieces of wood, screw the thinner one to the thicker. First mark and drill a clearance hole in the top (thinner) piece with the same diameter as the screw's shank (the part just below the head). Holding the two pieces together, mark the lower piece where the screw will enter and make a pilot hole for the screw with a bradawl or drill. The pilot hole is particularly important with hardwood, which splits easily.

A screwed butt joint will join sheet materials. Make the joint stronger by pushing a masonry plug into a hole drilled in the horizontal board where the screw will enter (Fig. 432). For a stronger though sometimes more obtrusive joint, screw a batten inside the angle (Fig. 433).

If you want extra strength and don't expect ever to need to dismantle the furniture, you can add glue to the joint. The technique is known as "glue and screw." Smear the surfaces with white woodworking adhesive before screwing them together.

Do not screw into end grain of lumber if you can avoid it; it is a weak joint which may split the wood. Strengthening such joints is time consuming—it involves inserting wooden dowel in a hole drilled across the grain in the screw's path (Fig. 434). A plastic assembly joint (Fig. 431) is often a simpler alternative.

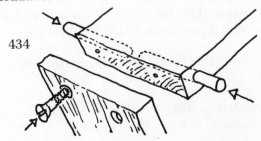
434

You can reduce both expense and effort when joining two thick planks by deep countersinking (Fig. 435). Drill a hole marginally wider than the screw head in the top piece to within 1 inch (25 mm) of the lower piece. At this point the pilot hole is reduced to shank width.

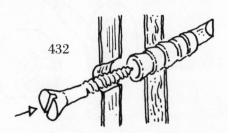
432

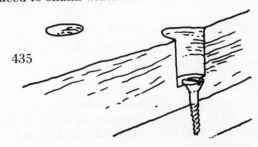
435

Countersunk (Fig. 436)—the normal screw for joining wood to wood. Use a countersink bit in your drill if you want the screw to sit flush with the work surface.

Roundhead (Fig. 437)—suitable—because of the head's flat base—for holding metal sheets on wood. Use a protective washer under the head.

Raised head (Fig. 438)—decorative screws which can be countersunk to the rim.

Rosette (Fig. 439)—the mirror screw, with a threaded hole in the top to take a decorative cap.

Lag screw (Fig. 440)—for heavy-duty work. The bolt-shaped head is tightened with a wrench.

Chipboard (Fig. 441)—threaded right up to the head to give a strong grip in chipboard.

Self-tapping (Fig. 442)—cuts its own thread when driven into a pilot hole. Made for sheet metal.

Screw hook (Fig. 443)—versatile basic hook with a sharp point to bite in wood.

Cup hook (Fig. 444)—similar to the common screw hook but with a depth-stop shoulder.

Eye screw (Fig. 445)—useful where objects are hung semipermanently and the risk of falling must be minimized.

Screw cups (Fig. 446)—decorative screw finishes. Brass cup washers are one of several varieties.

Screws are made in different widths, each one needing clearance holes and pilot holes of a suitable diameter. See table for guidance.

Screw gauge	Clearance hole	Pilot in softwood/hardwood
No. 4	1/8 in. (3 mm)	use bradawl—1/16 in. (2 mm)
No. 6	5/32 in. (4 mm)	use bradawl—1/16 in. (2 mm)

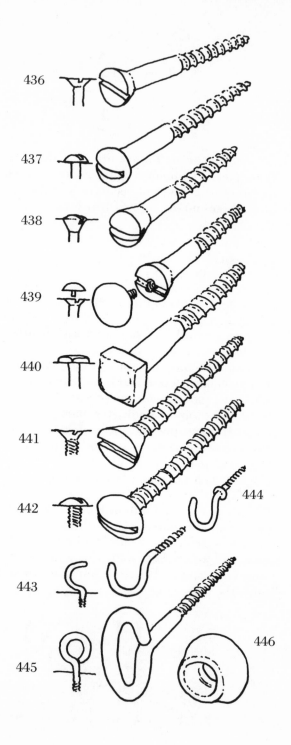

436
437
438
439
440
441
442
443
444
445
446

No. 8	3/16 in. (5 mm)	1/16 in. (2 mm)—1/8 in. (3 mm)
No. 10	3/16 in. (5 mm)	1/16 in. (2 mm)—1/8 in. (3 mm)
No. 12	1/4 in. (6 mm)	1/8 in. (3 mm)—5/32 in. (4 mm)
No. 14	1/4 in. (6 mm)	5/32 in. (4 mm)—3/16 in. (5 mm)

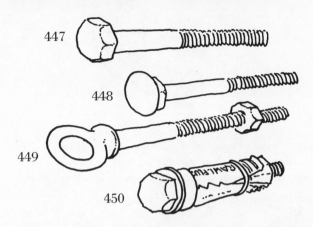

Bolts

Bolts make extremely strong joints. They are also useful in temporary assemblies as they are easily undone. Wherever possible the load is spread, and the work surface therefore protected, by inserting a washer under both bolt head and nut. Some types are tightened with a screwdriver, others with a wrench. Four types in widespread use are illustrated in Figures 447–450.

Machine bolts (Fig. 447)—available in almost any length, with diameters from ¼ inch to 3 inches (6–75 mm). Head pattern may be hexagonal or square, rounded or countersunk. To fit, drill a hole through the work of the same diameter as the bolt.

Coach bolts (Fig. 448)—used mainly for joining wood to wood. Thanks to the shape just below the head, the bolt grips work while the nut is turned. Use a washer between the nut and the wood.

Eye bolts (Fig. 449)—useful when objects must be hung from the bolt.

Expanding bolts (Fig. 450)—provide a very strong hold in masonry walls. Particularly suitable for use in hot spots.

Wall Fasteners

You can't rely on a screw driven directly into brick, concrete, or plasterboard walls. In hollow wood-framed walls, drive screws into studs where possi-

ble. Locate these by pushing a needle through the plaster. Manufacturers have invented an ingenious selection of devices to make wall fastening easy in any surface. Some common designs are shown in Figures 451–456.

Fiber wall plugs (Fig. 451)—the traditional plug for brick and concrete. Use a plug as long as the screw's threaded section.

Plastic wall plugs (Fig. 452)—a more convenient modern equivalent of fiber plugs. Simply drill a hole in the wall to the plug's depth and push the plug in.

Compound filler (Fig. 453)—used to fill irregular holes in the wall. Bought as a powder and mixed with water before use.

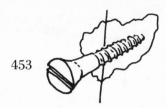

453

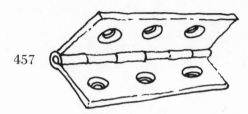

457

Toggle bolts (Figs. 454–455)—provide sound fixing in hollow walls. Not reusable, as the toggle drops down inside the wall when the screw is withdrawn.

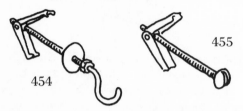

455

454

Rubber-sleeved anchors (Fig. 456)—can be used in plastic and metal sheets as well as thin cavity walls. Insert into a hole the same diameter as the rubber sleeve.

456

Surface mounted hinge (Fig. 458)—fixed to the front of both door and frame, so the whole hinge shows when the door is closed. No mortises are needed. There are many types of surface mounted hinges, including strap hinges, H, H/L, and butterfly hinges, all of which are decorative.

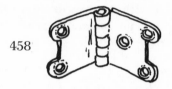

458

Concealed hinge (Fig. 459)—tidy hinges that are out of sight when closed. They are widely used by furniture manufacturers for lay-on doors in kitchen cabinets. Lay-on doors sit in front of the frame. The hinges are adjustable after they are attached. The hinges' design allows adjacent doors to swing open without obstructing each other. Available with or without spring-closing mechanism.

Hinges

The choice of hinge designs is huge. They range from the simple butt hinge to bewilderingly complex multipivoted varieties. Choosing the right one can be hard—ask your dealer for advice.

Butt hinge (Fig. 457)—traditional hinge used to hang heavy doors in the frame. The two leaves are mortised into the door and frame so that the hinge lies flat when closed.

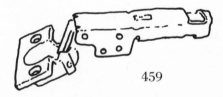

459

Piano (continuous) hinge (Fig. 460)—generally available up to 84 inches (2000 mm) long. Provides maximum resistance against warping and is widely used for hinging lids.

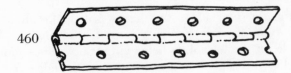

460

Pivot hinge (Fig. 461)—reliable and easy to fit to door and frame as it requires no mortises. Allows the door to open to 180°. Buy the hinges in pairs to fit to the top and bottom of lay-on doors.

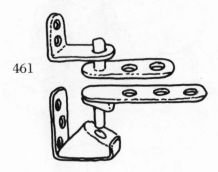

461

Screen hinge (Fig. 462)—a three-section hinge movable in both directions and therefore suitable for screens.

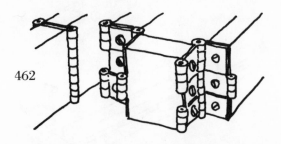

462

Card table hinge (Fig. 463)—used for desk flaps and occasional-table leaves as well as card tables.

463

Tools

Most people possess a basic tool kit, though the contents may be scattered all around the house and not in prime condition. An average collection comprises a hammer, screwdrivers, panel saw (Fig. 464) and hacksaw (Fig. 465), chisel, trimming knife (Fig. 466), and steel measuring tape (Fig. 467). We therefore assume that these tools need no introduction.

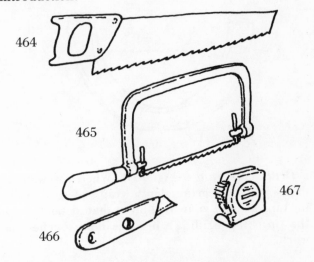

464

465

467

466

An electric drill is a sensible addition to the standard tool kit. It is a genuine saver of time and effort. An ever-growing range of attachments temporarily converts the drill into a jigsaw, circular saw, plane, sander, router, paint stripper, and polisher. When these tools are bought separately, with their own power units, they are more expensive but are often better balanced, tougher, and more efficient.

It is unwise to buy cheap tools—they normally disappoint. Good new tools can unfortunately be horribly costly, so where possible buy them second-hand or rent them whenever you need them.

Some possibly less familiar tools proved useful on occasion in the *Low Tech* projects; these are described and illustrated below. The first two were improvised, completely free, and very effective.

Pipe level (Fig. 468). Like other liquids, water always finds its own level. You can exploit this to make an accurate alternative to the professional spirit level. It will help you attach battens and shelves perfectly horizontally on the wall. Almost fill a U-shaped length of transparent plastic pipe with water, making sure that no air bubbles are left in the pipe. The water level on each side of the U shows true horizontal.

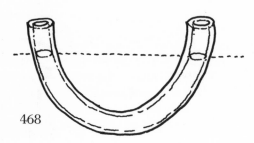

468

Drill depth gauge (Fig. 469). When you want to drill a hole to a certain depth wrap a piece of masking tape around your drill bit at that distance from the tip. Stop drilling when the tape touches the work.

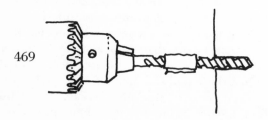

469

Belt sander (Fig. 470). A power belt sander removes wood fast. It will clean up old floorboards for reuse. Begin with a coarse grade of belt, and work up through a medium grade to fine for finishing. Always work along the wood grain, not across it. The dustbag on the sander catches the debris.

Jigsaw (Fig. 471). The jigsaw will make almost any type of cut—straight, curved, and angled. A guide on the baseplate helps cut straight lines parallel to the edge of a board and near the edge. You can clamp a straight edge on top of the board (Fig. 472) and push the saw against this to keep the cutting line straight. Wear goggles to protect your eyes. The hand-powered equivalent is the padsaw or keyhole saw (Fig. 473).

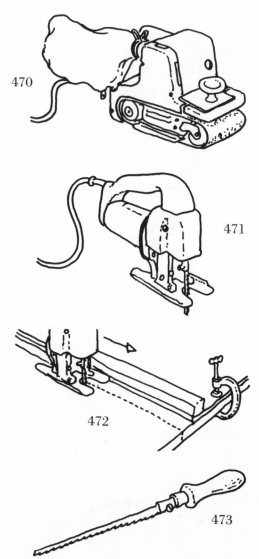

470

471

472

473

Circular saw (Fig. 474). The high-speed pur-pose-built unit is a more efficient cutter than the inexpensive drill attachment. It will cut rapidly through wood, metal, and laminates. The general-purpose blade will cut wood both along the grain and across it. Other blades can be fitted in seconds to cope with other materials. The saw can be extremely dangerous. Keep children well clear and never leave the saw lying around accessible and untended.

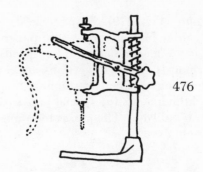

476

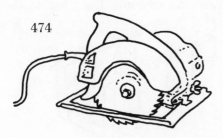

474

Chainsaw (Fig. 477). The cordless chainsaw is incomparably effective in slicing through large amounts of wood remote from a power source. However, it is also incomparably dangerous. It can maim a careless or unlucky user. Always wear pro-tective goggles and gloves and don't work alone if possible.

Router (Fig. 475). An extremely useful addition to the fast furnisher's tool kit, capable of tackling a wide range of otherwise exhausting jobs. Its main use is in cutting long grooves in lumber, which it can cut straight, V-shaped, or rounded.

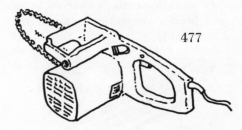

477

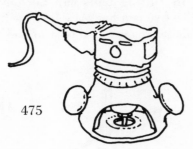

475

Eyelet fixer (Fig. 478). This riveting tool is bought from craft shops. It pushes holes through fabric and fixes a brass eyelet around the edge of the hole. This prevents fraying or tearing when the hole is laced.

Drill stand (Fig. 476). It can be very difficult to drill at the correct angle—the drill stand and jig overcomes the problem. A cheaper alternative is to use a scrap of junk which you know has been cor-rectly drilled as a guide for the new drill cut.

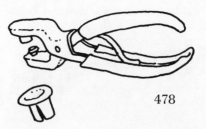

478

Staple gun (Fig. 479). Stapling is an efficient way of attaching fabric, carpet, and paper to wood and boards. A mechanical stapler speeds up the work enormously. Electric versions are now available for completely effortless stapling. Some staple guns have attachments for special jobs such as stapling cylindrical rods. The gun is too dangerous to allow near children.

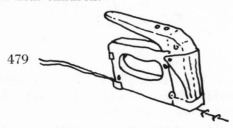

479

Shaping tool (Fig. 480). Also known as a rasp. Although lacking the precision of the traditional plane, this versatile tool will rapidly work wood and plastic to shape. Unlike the plane it can cope with wood containing nails or covered in paint. Flat and round blades are manufactured. Blades are changed in seconds.

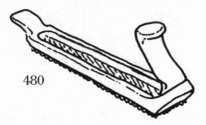

480

Sash clamp (Fig. 481). Expensive but handy for holding butcher's block tabletops and large frames together while the adhesive dries. The much cheaper G-clamp (Fig. 482) does the same job on smaller pieces. When using clamps prevent damage to the work by placing waste wood between clamp and work.

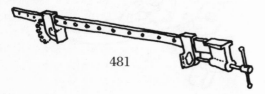

481

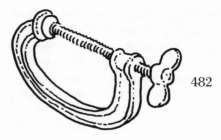

482

Miter box (Fig. 483). A great help in cutting across wood at a 45° angle, to make the corners of a picture frame, for example. Use a fine-toothed saw.

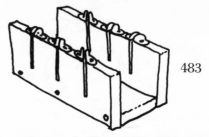

483

Bottle-cutting tool (Fig. 484). This bizarre but effective tool slices the tops off bottles to convert them instantly into ashtrays, candy dishes, and other handy articles. The technique takes time to master, so don't practice on your most treasured bottles. The cut edges have to be rubbed smooth for safety. Wear eye protection when working with glass. Bottle-cutting tools can be hard to find. Equally effective is a hacksaw fitted with a proper tungsten blade. Draw a line first to make a proper cut.

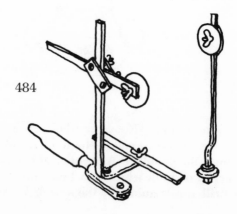

484

Pipe-bending spring (Fig. 485). Inserting the spring in copper tube stops it from splitting or distorting when you bend it. Grease the spring, push it into the tube, bend the tube to shape over your knee, and withdraw the spring. If it sticks, you may need to insert a bar in the end loop; turn this clockwise and tug it out.

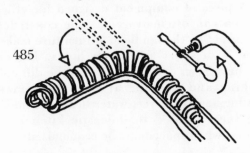

485

Metal snips (Fig. 486). Snips are made in several designs, all incorporating the scissor action which cuts through the metal. They cut curves through metal more easily than a hacksaw.

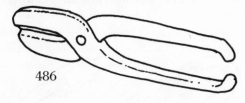

486

Pipework

Plumbing pipes need not carry water to be useful. Efficient storage and seating systems can be built up using jointed pipework. Since the joints need not be watertight, connecting the pipes is a straightforward matter.

Copper pipes can be joined cheaply and easily with capillary fittings, such as the elbow and T-fittings shown in Figure 487. To make a proper capillary joint cut the pipes to length with a hacksaw and clean out the inside of the fitting and the outside of the pipe with steel wool until they shine.

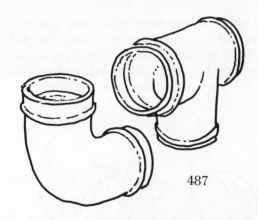

487

Steel wool can be bought in economically large packs from builders' suppliers. Flux, which is sold in small cans by building supply stores and some hardware stores, is smeared over both surfaces. Push the parts together and heat the joint with a blowtorch. A ring-shaped recess in the fitting is filled with solder during manufacture; the heat melts the solder, which then travels by capillary action—hence the name—to the end of the fitting. When a ring of solder oozes out of the end, the joint is made.

Rigid pvc tubing is normally used for domestic cold water services and rainwater drainage. The system is well suited to low-tech furniture projects. Jointing systems vary from manufacturer to manufacturer. Each one will supply detailed instructions for their particular system.

Two lengths of tubing are joined together by welding both inside a pvc socket with solvent cement. Cut the tubes to length with a fine-toothed saw—a hacksaw is ideal. Take care to cut square. File away the rough edges. Roughen the surfaces to be joined with sandpaper. Assemble the system without adhesive to check that it all fits correctly. Dismantle the joint and wipe the surfaces with the recommended cleaning fluid. Coat the clean surfaces with solvent cement, push the parts together, and hold them for about fifteen seconds. Remove surplus adhesive with a dry cloth before it dries. Don't put weight on the joint for twenty-four hours.

A number of standard fittings are illustrated in Figures 488–494. They are the elbow (Fig. 488), T-junction (Fig. 489), right-angle T-junction (Fig. 490), collar (Fig. 491), wall brackets (Figs. 492 and 493), and the end stop for guttering (Fig. 494).

Marine Equipment

The fast furnisher will find an awesome selection of wonderfully useful equipment in a marine supplies catalogue. Marine equipment has evolved over the centuries to reach a point close to perfect functionalism. A piece of equipment designed for efficient use at sea can often overcome the construction problems met by the landlocked furniture maker.

Space is in short supply on boats. Ingenious devices have been developed to ease the difficulties of cooking and washing at sea. Many marine designs for basins, stoves, water heaters, and sinks can be incorporated in domestic kitchens and bathrooms when space must be economized.

Shackles (Figs. 494–499). Strong metal links manufactured in many forms. The simplest type is shown in Figure 495. Some have springs to snap them shut safely (Fig. 498). Others incorporate a safety lock to prevent accidental opening (Fig. 499).

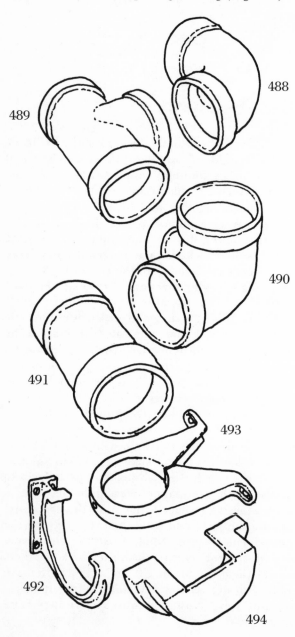

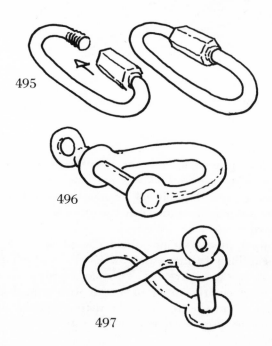

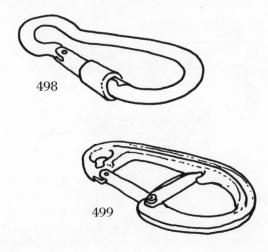

498

499

Pulleys (Figs. 503–505). Besides the straightforward pulley block (Fig. 503), other designs include the swivel pulley (Fig. 505) and the double pulley (Fig. 504).

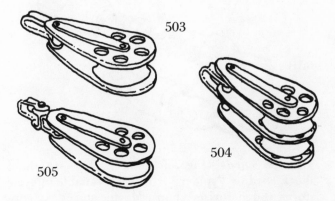

503

505

504

Cleats (Figs. 500–502). Cleats grip rope. Three types are shown here: the basic modern plastic cleat (Fig. 500); the traditional 5 inch (125 mm) mooring cleat (Fig. 501); and the heavy-duty cam cleat (Fig. 502), available in nylon or metal.

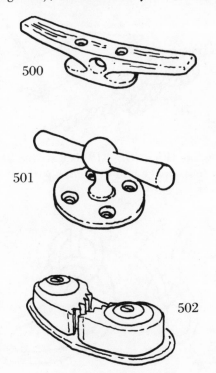

500

501

502

Turnbuckles (Figs. 506–507). Wire or rope is tied to each end and the screw tightened to increase tension. Figure 507 shows a variation—the hook-and-eye straining screw.

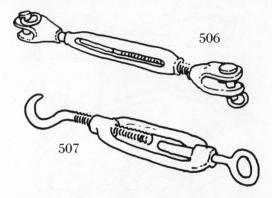

506

507

Cable terminals (Figs. 508–511). Terminating wires and cables securely is sometimes difficult. This simple assembly does the job fast. No special tools are required for fitting.

508

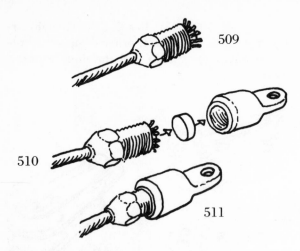

509

510

511

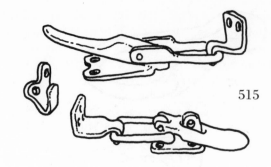

515

Rope

Shock cords (Figs. 512–514). The standard shock cord or "spider" is widely available in cycle stores and motorists' shops. Marine stores can supply a variant with snap-on safety clips (Fig. 513) or nylon hooks (Fig. 514), which allow you to make your own to whatever length you need.

Some simple nautical techniques are useful in fast furnishing. Three methods of dealing with rope are illustrated in Figures 516–525—knotting, splicing, and whipping.

The *figure eight* (Fig. 516) prevents the end of a rope from being pulled through a hole, as in Figure 517.

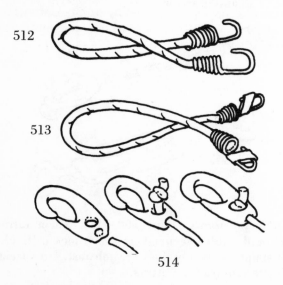

512

513

514

517

516

The *bowline* (Figs. 518–519) is a strong knot used to form a loop in the end of a rope without splicing it.

Toggle fasteners (Fig. 515). A strong fastener to hold lids securely closed.

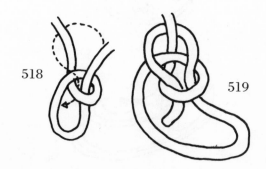

518

519

The *eye splice* (Figs. 520–522) is strong and tidy. Begin by unlaying three strands at the end of the rope long enough to make three tucks (you will need about one turn per tuck) and form the eye shape. Tuck the center strand (*a* in the drawings) under the nearest strand of the rope. Tuck strand *b* under the strand to the left of *a*. Turn the rope over and tuck strand *c* in from right to left. Pull the splice tight. Take each of the three strands over one strand and under the next on the left. Pull it tight again and repeat.

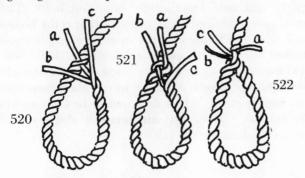

Whipping (Figs. 523–525) is a way of wrapping rope or string around a drum without any fastening at all. Begin as in Figure 523 with the top loop overlapping the top of the drum and the lower end protruding about 12 inches (300 mm) at the base. Wind the rope tightly around the drum. Push the top end through the loop and pull on the lower end until the top is well tucked in. Cut off the lower end.

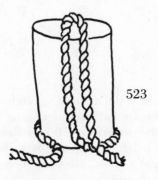

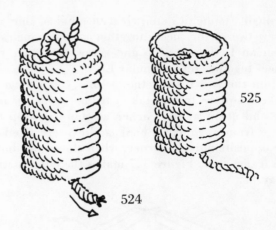

Concrete Slabs

Casting your own concrete paving slabs saves money and demands no expensive equipment or previous experience. Even an old cake pan makes a serviceable mold. The simple homemade wooden mold in Figure 526 makes casting square slabs easy. The same principles can be used to design molds for slabs of other shapes.

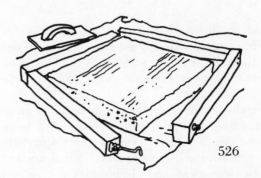

To make 12 inch (300 mm) square slabs you will need four pieces of 1½ x 1½ inch (38 x 38 mm) planed softwood 14 inches (350 mm) long. Scraps this length should not be hard to find.

Using waterproof woodworking adhesive and a pair of 3 inch (75 mm) number 10 screws driven through 3/16 inch (5 mm) clearance holes, glue and screw two of the pieces together at right angles to form an L shape. Glue and screw the other two pieces together into a similar L.

Join the two L's together with a strap hinge to make a square frame; take care not to screw into the end grain at the corner as this will stop the hinge from opening. A hook and eye are fixed on the opposite outside corner; when closed this holds the frame shut. Figure 527 makes the construction clear.

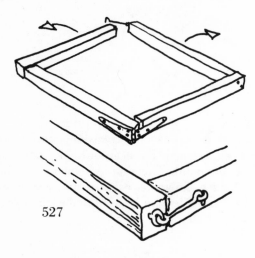

527

Sand the inside surfaces of the mold perfectly smooth, using an exterior grade wood filler if necessary. Coat the surfaces with clean car engine oil to prevent the concrete from sticking. Oil the surfaces again before each use.

To make a slab place the closed mold on an oiled plywood base and pour in the concrete. A suitable concrete mix is 2 parts sand, 3 parts aggregate, 1 part cement. Pack the concrete well down in the mold to clear away any air bubbles and smooth it off level with the top of the frame using a float. Leave the concrete to dry for several hours. Unhook the catch and release the slab.

Although the slab should be firm enough to come out of the mold in hours, it is not ready for use for at least three weeks. During the first week keep the slab covered with a plastic sheet to prevent over-rapid drying. Don't leave drying slabs outdoors when frost threatens.

While the slab is fresh from the mold, the top surface can be dampened and brushed away with a stiff brush to reveal the pebble aggregate.

Slotted Angle

Slotted angle is simple to use—the pieces are cut to length and held together by nuts and bolts. The basic unit in slotted angle construction is the boxed bay, with the flanges on the upright angles turned inward for strength and economy (Fig. 528). Several boxed units can be connected as in Figure 529 to build up longer multiple bays. Manufacturers can supply steel shelves designed to be bolted onto the system. Chipboard, lumbercore, and plywood are well suited for the job.

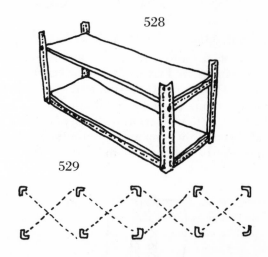

528

529

It is useful to make a simple sketch of your units before you begin cutting pieces to length. The thickness of the materials will add 3/8 inch (10 mm) to the overall length of a boxed bay. When systems must fit in tight spaces, allow 1/2 inch (12 mm) for the bolts at each end.

Cut the lengths you need using a hacksaw. Assembly will be simplified if attachment hole patterns match on all pieces, so measure from the same point in the hole pattern on all pieces. File rough edges smooth. Now bolt up the structure.

Angle is easier to handle when it is laid out flat on the floor. Begin by building side frames. First fit baseplates or push-on plastic feet to the uprights, bolt the whole side together finger-tight, square the pieces up, and tighten the bolts with a wrench. Then fit the horizontal pieces front and back, lift the structure upright, check again that it is all square, and tighten the loose bolts. Any castors are fitted last.

Angle, nuts, and bolts (Fig. 530). The basic elements in the system. Hole patterns vary from one manufacturer to another.

Baseplates (Figs. 531–532). Use baseplates to protect the floor under weighty structures. Push-on plastic feet (Figs. 533–534) are an alternative.

Castors (Figs. 535–536). Nylon castors are available in fixed or swivel versions to make racks mobile.

Cleats (Fig. 537). A scrap of angle can be used as a cleat to bolt a horizontal length onto the blind face of an upright.

Corner plates (Fig. 538). Don't count on single-bolt attachments to hold a structure rigid. Triangular plates sandwiched between horizontal and upright sections improve rigidity.

Bracing (Fig. 539). Diagonal bracing across the back of the rack improves stability. A piece of slotted angle can be sawed to length and bolted in place as a brace. The structure should be fixed to the floor if the height is over five times the distance from front to back.

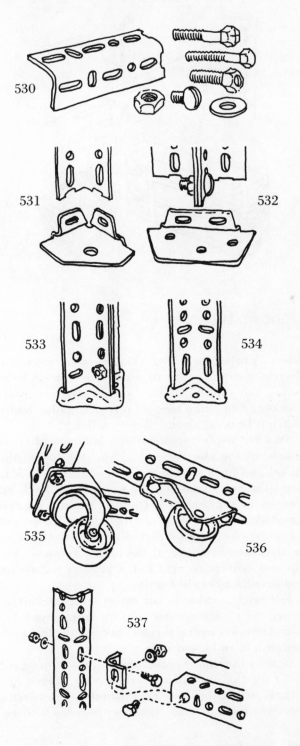

530

531 532

533 534

535 536

537

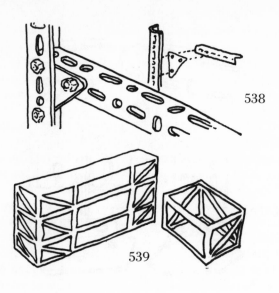

538

539

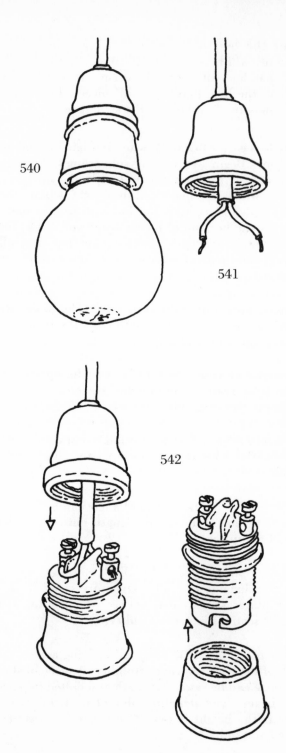

540

541

542

Light Fixtures

When a project involves making a connection to the electricity supply, your first step must always be to switch the supply off at the fuse box or circuit breaker. And make sure no one can inadvertently switch it back on again before you finish!

To wire the plain socket shown in Figure 540 first switch off the electricity. Unscrew the top of the socket and push it onto the wire as in Figure 541. Bend the two exposed ends of the wire back on themselves as in Figure 541, push them into the two terminals of the socket, and tighten up the screws using an electrician's screwdriver. Fit the wire neatly around the top of the pillar. Screw on the top and bottom covers. Put a bulb in the socket and switch on the electricity.

For safety's sake do not use cracked sockets or frayed wire. Always use sockets from reputable manufacturers with a shroud covering the live bulb contacts, as in Figure 540.

Besides the simple socket in Figure 540, designed to fit on the end of a pendant wire, there are sockets which incorporate a switch, sockets with screw connections, and sockets with batten holders.

Others are made to fit tightly in the neck of a bottle or jar to convert it into a lamp. Each type has its particular purpose. Ask an electrical goods supplier for advice on the right type for the job in hand.

Clamp-on lamps, designed for industrial use and often sold as car inspection lamps, have proved popular with high-tech furnishers. Industrial equipment suppliers can provide moisture-proof lamps for outdoor or bathroom use.

Safety

There is no point making your own furniture to save money if you lose a finger or an eye in the process. Be aware of the risks you take and reduce them.

Keep the first-aid kit well stocked with sterile finger dressings, eye pads, and cotton, as well as antiseptic cream, plasters, dressing, bandages, safety pins, scissors, and tweezers.

Always protect your eyes when anywhere near noxious liquids, a category which includes certain paint strippers and rust removers. Eye protection is also vital when you are drilling or hammering into masonry, using a power saw, sanding, grinding, or working with glass.

Industrial workers are provided with emergency eyewash stations for use if any unpleasant liquid gets in their eyes. If such accidents happen at home put your face under running water immediately, then get to a doctor or hospital fast.

Protective clothing is normally designed and sold for use in industry, and it can be remarkably hard to find on public sale. Look in the *Yellow Pages* under "Industrial Equipment and Supplies." An industrial equipment mail-order catalogue may provide the answer. You will be able to buy inexpensive safety spectacles, goggles, and face shields, as well as a wide selection of gloves, boots, and overalls. The same catalogue, incidentally, will provide many of the materials needed to make fast furniture.

Children are always in danger of poisoning themselves by swallowing dangerous liquids. Even the most economy-minded recycler in the fast-furnishing field should squash the temptation to store chemicals in empty soft drink or wine bottles. The contents of all bottles should be marked on the label, and the "Poison" warning could usefully be added.

Air is good for you. Keep rooms well ventilated where there's a risk of fumes or dust. A face mask can be worth wearing, even though it is often uncomfortable. Oddly enough, hardwood dust is a worse throat irritant than softwood. Protect your ears with inexpensive soft plastic ear plugs.

The best way to avoid slashing yourself with cutting tools is to keep the tools sharp! Blunt tools have to be forced through the material and can easily slip out of control. Always keep your hands behind the tool, so slippage will not threaten your fingers. Heavy leather gauntlets protect against minor cuts, but they can't offer much protection against a rampant electric saw.

Saws slice fingers as well as wood, and electric saws are the most menacing. Never remove the safety guard, even if it gets in your way. Always unplug the power tool before you change blades or fit saw attachments on a drill, or indeed tamper with the tool in any way.

Electricity shocks and kills. Please don't attempt electrical work unless you are really sure you know what you are doing. Always switch the main supply off before tampering with the system, and be sure this has cut off the supply where you are working.